Just Me

from Melanie.
6. April 2020

Just Me

SHEILA HANCOCK

BLOOMSBURY

First published in Great Britain 2008

Copyright © by Sheila Hancock 2008

The author has asserted her moral rights

No part of this book may be used or reproduced in any manner whatsoever
without written permission from the Publisher except in the case of
brief quotations embodied in critical articles or reviews

Every reasonable effort has been made to trace copyright holders of
material reproduced in this book, but if any have been inadvertently
overlooked the publishers would be glad to hear from them. For
legal purposes the copyright acknowledgements on p. 271
constitute an extension of the copyright page

Bloomsbury Publishing Plc
36 Soho Square
London W1D 3QY

www.bloomsbury.com

Bloomsbury Publishing, London, New York and Berlin

A CIP catalogue record for this book
is available from the British Library

Hardback ISBN 9780747588825
Trade Paperback ISBN 9780747598619

10 9 8 7 6 5 4 3 2 1

Typeset by Hewer Text UK Ltd, Edinburgh
Printed in Great Britain by Clays Ltd, St Ives plc

The paper this book is printed on is certified by the © 1996 Forest Stewardship
Council A.C. (FSC). It is ancient-forest friendly. The printer holds
FSC chain of custody SGS-COC-2061

FSC
Mixed Sources
Product group from well-managed
forests and other controlled sources

Cert no. SGS-COC-2061
www.fsc.org
© 1996 Forest Stewardship Council

With profound thanks to my editor Victoria Millar,
whose patience, diligence and friendship were invaluable.

Contents

Try to praise the mutilated world.
Remember June's long days,
and wild strawberries, drops of wine, the dew.
The nettles that methodically overgrow
the abandoned homesteads of exiles.
You must praise the mutilated world.
You watched the stylish yachts and ships;
one of them had a long trip ahead of it,
while salty oblivion awaited others.
You've seen the refugees heading nowhere,
you've heard the executioners sing joyfully.
You should praise the mutilated world.
Remember the moments when we were together
in a white room and the curtain fluttered.
Return in thought to the concert where music flared.
You gathered acorns in the park in autumn
and leaves eddied over the earth's scars.
Praise the mutilated world
and the grey feather a thrush lost,
and the gentle light that strays and vanishes
and returns.

'Try to Praise the Mutilated World'
by Adam Zagajewski

PROLOGUE

Saignon

I OPEN THE SHUTTERS, expecting sun, but there is a dense mist shrouding the view. I get back into the Phwah bed, so called because my husband deemed it the most comfortable bed in the world, and that was the noise he made as he sank into it, luxuriating, beaming.

But now, I am sitting in it alone.

I love this room. It is like being in the clouds or under the sea, with its sky-blue walls and white, translucent, wafting curtains. It was nearly like being in an inkpot when my daughter Joanna and I first applied the blue ochre, but a day sponging white on top, before John saw the disaster, turned it into a triumph of interior décor.

So, here I am, in this room, on this bed, writing this, sipping my tea and watching the landscape reveal itself as the rising sun melts the haze. It is like that big scene in a panto. From my principal-boy days, I seem to remember it was called the revelation scene. No – transformation scene.

That's it.

Transformation.

There's a word that 'speaks to my condition' as we Quakers say. In panto, it is all done with dry ice and gauzes that slowly fly out revealing a jewelled cave, or Cinders in her ball gown, in a coach drawn by defecating ponies. Or a country scena, an ill-painted version of this. I half-expect Snow White to enter and sing a song about being lost and frightened. But no, there is no sound of an audience coughing its disapproval of the smog drifting, as it always does, over the front of the stalls. There is only the din of frogs, giggling and whoroping, as they do whatever it is that frogs do here in the spring. There are distant bells. The dogs across the valley greet each other and wake a frantic woodpecker and the bird that sounds like a telephone.

The bosky tang of fir and rosemary prickles my nostrils. Later, in the summer, the sweet, soft, lavender smell will take its place. But now it is this smell. Only this place, at this time of day, at this time of year, with this mist, has this smell. It has to be savoured now, this moment.

Now.

I am here now. The old sixties mantra.

The scene unfolds. Gradually, the lime tree in the foreground is lit from behind, so that its opening leaves shine fresh green, and crystals sparkle on the twigs. It is the first season since its partner in the garden was felled and it seems to be adjusting well.

The sun has really got into its stride now. Next the forest is illuminated, then finally the horizon, the backdrop, the spectacular mountains of the Ventoux and the Luberon and the vast, arching, blue sky.

Now the sun is streaming through the window, so I strip off, and run through some basic yoga poses, my naked body sapping up the warmth. I feel lithe and healthy, despite the sagging flesh, which, as no one can see it but me, is not a worry. The framework beneath still functions.

For which I am truly grateful.

As I am for many things. Just being here, for one. People have died, and, back in London, even now, a friend is in the painful process of making her exit.

Whereas, I am dressed and off to Saignon for breakfast.

Settled with my bowl of hot chocolate and warm almond croissant and my notebook, I drink in the sun on my face and the view of the sturdy – no – etched as it is by the morning light and shadows, majestic, Romanesque village church.

I marvel that just over a year ago I could not sit here without tears streaming down my face. I had to stop coming. This place, so potent to our relationship, both when my husband was alive and because of a note he had written that I discovered after his death, became anathema to me. So what has happened to change all that? To allow me to sit here with a smile on my face?

Alone. Content.

Even, I venture to say, happy. Now, this moment, anyway. Sanguine about what may come next and my ability to cope with it.

Whatever.

Your body was a temple to Delight;
Cold are its ashes whence the breath is fled,
Yet here one time your spirit was wont to move;
Here might I hope to find you day or night,
And here I come to look for you, my love,
Even now, foolishly, knowing you are dead.

From 'As to some lovely temple, tenantless'
by Edna St Vincent Millay

I

Provence

COPING AND HAPPY I was not, when, early in 2004, I arrived at our house in Provence. I had escaped after a disastrous Christmas, suffering from a deep depression. As was the weather. Alone, lugging my case, I wallowed through mud, down the track to the house. Scythed by a Mistral and drenched by the rain, I battled to open the heavy shutters.

Inside, the house was bleak. I struggled to light the wood stove – a job John had always done – and discovered the gas canisters for the oven had run out. Starving after the long drive through France, and desperate for something hot to eat, I went and got a new one from the garage. Carrying it through the garden nearly crippled me.

That night in the Phwah bed I tossed and turned in its vastness, kept awake by the aching absence, combined with the worrying presence of loirs scampering in the roof. These are pretty pests that eat through wires and beams and have to be got rid of. Not a task I relished. The house seemed to be conspiring to make me even more aware of how inadequate I was without John. Two years after his death. I felt feeble and stupid and utterly miserable.

Next morning the sun shone again with its usual brilliance, and I wandered the soaked and battered garden, performing by myself the ritual check that had always started our visits, when we listed the tasks to be undertaken to repair our beloved house after the ravages of the winter. The peach, apricot, quince, fig and cherry trees seemed to have turned into a jungle. A broken branch of the walnut was hitting the roof and dislodging the antique Provençal tiles; it was probably providing a highway for the loirs and squirrels I had heard the night before playing boules with stored nuts in the eaves.

John was besotted with that tree. When he was a child, every Christmas, his father brought home wet walnuts, and he and his brother Ray cracked them open, dipped them in salt and relished the delicacy, despite the inevitable mouth ulcers that followed. To have an endless supply growing in his garden was magic. But the walnuts were a sad disappointment to John. Each year there would be a huge crop but some nasty black blight always attacked the nuts and rendered them inedible. He even resorted to sending a question into the radio programme *Gardeners' Question Time*. On their advice he poured buckets of water on to the tree, to no avail. A year after his death, it yielded a treeful of perfect juicy nuts. They were stored in baskets, in the cellar.

Waiting.

Everyone had joked that it was a sign of divine, or leastways, a ghostly John's intervention, but I had rejected such comforting myths. I could not contemplate 'how-pleased-John-would-have-been'-type thinking. It seemed an impertinence to attribute thoughts to the absent John that I wanted to hear. The man could be unpredictable, bad-tempered and perverse. And I had no right to concoct a picture of him to bring myself, or anyone else, comfort. How often we do that when people die. 'How So-and-so would have loved that.' 'She would have wanted such-and-such', gradually shaping the dead person into a creature we want to be with.

I wanted to be with him all right. But not with some distorted invention. I wanted him with me in person, cracking the nuts, and dipping them in salt, and drooling. Or spitting them out and saying they weren't worth waiting for. Who knows how he would react? But dear God, I wanted to.

Now, as I looked at the buds appearing ready for another crop, a relentless, new season, I was beginning to suspect I never would.

The acceptance of that bitter truth was slow in coming. For two years I was doing well. I kept him with me as I relived our life together in the book I wrote. When it was published, the thousands of letters I received showed I had inadvertently tapped into a great pool of grief. It had not been my intention to write such a book. I replied as best I could to my correspondents; because many of them were keeping their despair secret, yet felt they could share it with a stranger. I arrogantly felt responsible for helping them. I, after all, was doing all right. On the road to recovery. Some of the people were still grieving personal tragedy four, five, even twenty years, later. I was mystified by this. My immediate searing anguish at John's death had, I thought, waned into something more benign.

Because he was coming back.

He'd often gone away. But he always came back. For two years I assumed that at any moment he would walk through the door and say, 'All right, kid?' I was expecting it during Christmas 2003. But I was alone in that belief.

The family all congregated at our house in Wiltshire to celebrate together. My daughters went to great pains to arrange a lovely time for my grandchildren and me. All was noise and excitement from which I felt utterly detached. I had known the same feeling when I had a mini nervous breakdown some years before. It is marvellously described by Sylvia Plath in *The Bell Jar*: 'I couldn't get myself to react. I felt very still and very empty, the way the eye of a tornado must feel, moving dully along the middle of the surrounding hullabaloo.' I tried to snap out of my stupor and join in the fun. I should be over it by now. All the books say so. And the time-is-a-great-healer merchants.

I looked round the festive table and realised I was the only one who had not moved on.

Two of the little ones were not even born when John was alive, and the other three could not remember him. The adults did. Stories were exchanged about his notorious bah-humbug attitude to Christmas, but the tales of his sometimes destructive behaviour were leavened with laughter. He had become a fond memory. An acceptable version to treasure and chuckle over. But it wasn't my reality. The imperfect one I ached for.

Mute with misery I was a death's head at the feast. Banquo's ghost had nothing on me. I couldn't join in the reminiscence. Relegating him to the past. I wanted him in the present, in the flesh. Especially the flesh, as it happens. To caress and cling to. As my daughters could to their partners. I did my best to smile benignly, as befitted my role of brave widow, while they chattered about their plans for their homes, their children, their future. Mine did not feature. I could see they were worried about me and didn't know what else they could do. They were sensible. They knew he wouldn't come back. And quite rightly, life would go on without him. Whereas, mine was on hold. Why? It would have been madness if voiced, even to myself.

I could not let him go.

He wouldn't like it. I had to wait.

The world outside the family had moved on, too. When it was mooted that a spin-off of *Morse* should be done and I was kindly consulted, I said how pleased I was, because all his work mates would be employed and Kevin Whately would have a lovely job. But I was gutted. Finally Inspector Mouse, as we called him, would also be well and truly gone. Bless him, he too would be as dead as a doornail. And I was distraught at the finality of it.

Surrounded as I was by evidence of my family's adaptation

to John's death and their healthy ability to move on, I was aware that my behaviour was out of line. I knew the danger signs. I was depressed. I was certainly depressing the hell out of everyone else. My daughters' profound grief at their father's death had mercifully mellowed, only to be replaced by anxiety about their disturbed mother. I felt ashamed but powerless to snap out of it. I was irritable with the children.

I was furious when one of my grandchildren, Charlie John, pulled a book from the shelves and left it on the floor. It was the poems of W. B. Yeats. Inside John had written 'I love these poems almost as much as I love you, December 1983'. Marked in pencil was the following poem:

> *When you are old and grey and full of sleep,*
> *And nodding by the fire, take down this book,*
> *And slowly read, and dream of the soft look*
> *Your eyes had once, and of their shadows deep;*
>
> *How many loved your moments of glad grace,*
> *And loved your beauty with love false or true,*
> *But one man loved the pilgrim soul in you,*
> *And loved the sorrows of your changing face;*
>
> *And bending down beside the glowing bars,*
> *Murmur, a little sadly, how Love fled*
> *And paced upon the mountains overhead*
> *And hid his face amid a crowd of stars.*

In Provence John would stand on the patio, gazing in wonder at the myriads of stars sparkling there that the London city glare obliterates. So perhaps this was a message. I needed to see those stars, where he was maybe hiding his face. I could hang on, stop him slipping away. Feel his presence. France had always been a haven of peace for us. That was what I needed. So off I went.

Which is how I came to trudge through the mud to be confronted by loirs, recalcitrant wood stoves, and all the rest of the mountainous molehills.

I was fourteen when I visited France for the first time. It blew my suburban mind. I ventured nervously from a pebble-dashed semi in Bexleyheath, where the regular fare was a joint roasted on Sunday, cold on Monday, shepherd's pied on Tuesday, and rissoled (whatever happened to rissoles?) on Wednesday, and the rest of the week was sardines or tomatoes on toast, Welsh rarebit and a nice bit of cod in a daring parsley sauce. Conversation at table was about how I was doing at school, or Dad at the factory, or Mum in the shop. Anything likely to be controversial was taboo. If the grannies were there, my contribution was limited by the injunctions 'Don't speak with your mouth full' and 'Little girls should be seen and not heard'. From there, via an au-pair job organised by my school during the summer holidays, I was catapulted into a wealthy, sophisticated, Parisian household. My employer was the epitome of French chic, with black hair oiled back into a chignon, crimson lips and fingernails, and couture clothes. The husband was a bigwig with the Comédie Française, so their guests were louche and exciting people who sat around arguing passionately, long into the night, about the arts and politics. It was a seismic culture shock.

I helped prepare the meals. Even salad was a revelation. No limp lettuce leaf and half a tomato here. I swung the salad dryer full of aromatic leaves picked from the garden, and watched while Madame dressed them with pungent olive oil that bore no resemblance to the yellow stuff I bought in Boots to treat my earache. I sampled frogs' legs, snails and dishes that aroused taste buds that had hitherto lain dormant. A different wine was served for each course to enhance the food. It was nectar for the gods. I had only previously sipped the sugary Barsac that Dad ceremoniously produced once a year at Christmas. The meals went on for hours and the smell of perfume, garlic and Gauloises made me swoon with delight.

In August we decamped to their villa in Fouras, which was then still a mere village near La Rochelle. In Monsieur's absence, no sooner had one lover departed than I put fresh, sweet-smelling linen on Madame's bed ready for the next to arrive. In between she would share her romantic secrets with me and stroke my face with tears in her eyes, muttering, 'Ah, la jeunesse.' She contrived a romance between myself and the student who sang with the café band. We danced under the stars to 'La Mer' and I still have a melting spot in my heart for the gentle Claude. France awakened me to the sensual pleasures of life. I have loved it ever since.

Numerous years and visits later, I went on a painting course in Les Bassacs, a hamlet in the Luberon, the name given to the valley between and including the Luberon mountains on one side and the Plateau de Vaucluse and the Ventoux range on the other. On the first day, under the tutelage of a professional artist, I attempted to draw a little flight of steps. It was the beginning and end of my artistic aspirations. I reckoned if Cézanne had had sixty goes at capturing the unique Provençal light on nearby Mont Victoire, on the evidence of my first attempts, I was not going to get far in a week. I bear the cross of perfectionism; being a good amateur painter held no charm for me.

So I downed my brush and basked in the sun, scenery and food. At night I guiltily joined my erstwhile fellow students around a candlelit table overlooking the pool, which in turn has a view of the valley and mountains beyond. Savouring the Provençal food and Ventoux wine, on a balmy night, listening to the cicadas was, I decided, my nirvana. I phoned John, stuck in London filming *Morse*, to wax boozily lyrical about the sun, the landscape, the poppies, the sunflowers, and the gracious local people. My daughter Ellie Jane was filming a *Bergerac* out there at the same time and also had a go at him. He reluctantly came over for the weekend. He instantly fell under the Luberon spell, which was to enchant him for what was left of his life.

We knew at once that we wanted to spend a lot of time there but the thought of buying a house abroad seemed a bit scary and grown-up, so we enlisted the help of our new friends Liz and David Atkinson who ran the painting course. They lined up several possibles and we came over to inspect them, eventually choosing one in the *commune* of Saignon, in a small *hameau* of five houses surrounded by vineyards, lavender fields and cherry orchards. It was a little way up the Grand Luberon mountain, so cooler than the valley in summer, where the temperature can hit over forty degrees.

The orchard below our garden was obviously neglected but our efforts to buy it were foiled by the complicated French inheritance laws. Instead we have, over the years, watched the cherry trees being strangled by ivy which every now and then John and various sons-in-law have hacked away. The whole thing is very Chekhovian. The upside of this neglect is the wealth of wild flowers to be found there, untroubled by vicious pesticides. Rare orchids, violets, primrose and most bewitching of all a carpet of sweet-smelling narcissi, which arrives to synchronise with the sunbeamed canopy of cherry blossom above.

Alongside the house was a less pleasing fragrance, given off by a field in which a flock of ducks, geese and chickens had killed the grass with their foraging. The French are not sentimental about their animals and the fowl were not a pretty sight. I tried not to worry about their mangy, grubby appearance; they were not pets, but had to provide eggs and eventually dinner. And the smell was tolerable when the wind was in the right direction. Anyway, the stink of the village septic tank, which was also in the field, made chicken shit seem like Chanel.

The smells we learnt to live with, the noise was more of a problem. The clattering of the cicadas is deafening. Sometimes they get into a throbbing rhythm that drives you mad. The frogs come from far and wide to the raucous orgies down by the stream. The dogs have a choral society to rival the Philharmonic. André's tenor hound usually starts the cantata, to be joined by basses and sopranos echoing all round the valley. This cacophony we could tolerate. But the cock went too far.

The sound of a rooster greeting the dawn might be considered picturesquely rural. But not if the bird is tone-deaf. This creature was all right with the cock-a-doodle bit, but its doo was teeth-clenchingly flat. It grated on our nerves so much that we seriously considered putting the house back on the market. Then a miracle happened. One day when Caruso, as we called him, had desperately tried to hit the right note for about half an hour, I put on a tape to drown the noise. It happened to be Mozart's Requiem. Instant silence. We went out to look. He was standing on one leg, neck stretched up, ear cocked (is that where the word comes from?) in the direction of the music. He stayed in this trance-like position all the time the tape played. It somewhat limited our selection of music, as Bach and Beethoven left him cold, but Mozart did the trick every time. John believed he was the reincarnation of Salieri, trying to learn from his rival's genius, but sadly it didn't improve the cock's musical ear. He continued to sing flat till he and all the rest of the coop were slaughtered by a music-loving fox one bloody night. When I expressed my hypocritical regret to the owner, she just shrugged and said, 'C'est la campagne.'

It was a phrase Christiane, our neighbour, who was to become a close friend, used often. Swarming bees, scorpions, hornets, vipers and mosquitoes were accepted with the same insouciance – working on the theory that they were harmless unless you annoyed them. A pretty good philosophy of life really.

Christiane was the first person in Saignon I managed to communicate with. She originated from the Basque country, so her accent was less impenetrable than the local Provençal dialect – think Cornwall. Always plumply neat, with cropped hair, a ready smile and quick wit, she subtly kept an eye on things. It was not a good idea to cross her. One woman moved into the village and, when the Romany pickers in their caravans arrived for the cherry harvest, she complained to the *mairie*. Christiane was incensed that these loyal workers, known and respected by everyone, should be so insulted. The woman, not the gypsies, moved on not long after.

Christiane liked a gossip and filled me in on all the villagers. In our first week in residence, we were alarmed to see a bearded tramp with a sack over his shoulder, carrying a gun, wandering in the orchard. At his feet were two slavering hounds. Dogs are not my favourite animals, especially in a country where rabies is endemic and there seem to be a lot of frothing strays, but Christiane laughed when I told her of my anxiety. The man was out hunting, one of two brothers who live together in the next house to ours. Gentle souls both, André and Denis have the grand surname Empereur and a big family tomb in the ornate Saignon graveyard. For years they lived in thrall to their mother, whilst they worked in the local glacé-cherry factory. Now they were on their own.

Denis tends the allotment that provides all their fruit and vegetables. During *la chasse* season, André and his dogs (who the rest of the year are kept in a pen with the chickens) catch rabbit and wild boar to store for their meat supply. Although they lived next door, it was many years before these timid men would talk to us, and then I had to guess at a lot of the conversation, although John, who refused to speak French, seemed to under-stand them more. We have never been in their house or they in ours, but I will sometimes find beans or tomatoes on my door-step, and I put any leftover wine or food on theirs when we leave.

John was not completely incognito in France – some of his programmes are shown, with a wonderful guttural French voice dubbed on – but our neighbours made no mention of his fame. The only indication we had that they knew we wanted to guard our anonymity was when some reporters discovered where we lived and ventured down the track. We were away. Sensing an invasion of our and their privacy, André got his gun and saw them off. We were never troubled again. Nothing was said by the brothers or us about it, apart from a mumbled 'merci' from me next time I saw them, and a lot of shrugging and blushing from them. I was told about the incident by Christiane, not by André or Denis.

When we first moved to Saignon, Christiane's husband Roget was the vineyard owner. Not as glamorous as it seems, because the local wine, in his own opinion, is pretty inferior stuff (it has to do with the soil), although he did once open a fragrant bottle that came from one secret field that was saved for family wine. Out in the sun all day, he was wizened and bent from stooping over the vines; a smiley troll. He always wore an incongruous naval peaked cap as he rode his tractor into town, laden with grapes for the commune co-operative wine collection. One of their many sons, Frédéric, was then a beautiful young man. He did all sorts of jobs for us, as well as sharing a beer with John in amicable silence. He usually picked us up at the airport in our car but one day an emergency arose and he sent Christiane and Roget instead. They trundled all the way to Marseilles in their ramshackle old jalopy, and drove us home at a sedate thirty miles an hour. Seeing sunbeaten Roget in his cap and Christiane in her best dress standing nervously in the arrivals lounge in a swirl of tourists was a touching sight. We felt so welcomed by what was, for them, a brave undertaking on our behalf.

Frédéric disappeared from our lives when he married an older woman. Apparently she has cramped his style somewhat, much to the dismay of the local lasses and my daughters and, I have to admit, myself. I miss the sight of his glistening bare torso rippling in the sun as he chopped the firewood. 'Yes all right, calm down, dear,' as John would sigh.

We were not the only people that spoke English in the *hameau*. Judith is one of those pioneering American women who feel drawn to Europe. She left her native land to come on her own, to a part of the world where she knew no one, and set up home there. I think she was relieved when I came on the scene and her brain could have a rest from speaking French.

We were both doing up our houses at the same time. Ours was in a dilapidated state, with no bathroom or kitchen. We had a lot of barbecues. Studying scripts gave John the perfect excuse to absent himself from dealing with French bureaucracy, and shopping for furniture in the searing midsummer heat, so I was grateful for Judith's assistance with crafty *maçons*, uncooperative France Telecom and dodgy electricians. We shared a phlegmatic plumber called Monsieur Montegard. He was baffled by our need to see numerous toilets and test their seats before choosing one. He took us to a huge warehouse and was visibly mortified when we got in and out of the baths to assess their comfort level. I saw him mouthing 'anglaise' to his fellow plumbers and his explanation seemed to satisfy them.

The French do like the English. Despite our football hooligans wrecking Marseilles. But it took several years before we were really accepted in the *hameau*. We didn't make a good start. Things have to take their time, like the seasons, but we were eager to make friends. So, in what, in retrospect, was a presumptuous gesture, we invited everyone in for drinks. A little research would have revealed that the whole concept was alien to them. The women didn't drink at all, and the men, apart from André, only with meals. Our elegant titbits were eyed with suspicion, and then totally spurned. The men did not utter a word to us but eventually made the best of a bad job and rabbited away amongst themselves. The women were just embarrassed, refusing to sit down or say much apart from 'non' and 'oui'.

The next day Christiane assured me that, despite their reticence, everyone was glad when we arrived, because we were not German or, even worse, Parisian. Their attitude to Germans was understandable. The wartime history of the area is somewhat ambivalent, and people are reluctant to discuss it, but there are some clues. In St Saturnin d'Apt there is a wall with bullet holes preserved to commemorate the occasion when the eldest son from every family was shot as a reprisal for a Resistance sabotage. You have to be French to understand their dislike of Parisians.

There is not much in the way of entertainment – the telly is awful – so friendship is important, if not given easily. We learnt to know our place and bide our time. John and I would listen to them, sitting in the sun, talking, talking non-stop. They had known one another all their lives, and do not have a drink to oil their tongues, yet the talk is as passionate as I remembered from my au-pair days. Especially over a game of boules.

At weekends, families visit and boules is played on the bumpy patch of ground that serves as a pitch: bodies contort as they follow a shot; emotional mumbled approval of a good move and the howls of despair at a bad one ring out. We would watch from a distance. Then John's father made a big break-through. He stood by the game, arms behind his back, watching intensely, nodding and shaking his head silently. Maybe it was his Lancashire cloth cap, similar to those worn by the old men of the village, but they invited him to join them. He played bowls in Stockport, so had a strong arm. For one radiant afternoon he had the time of his life. No one spoke the other's language but for two happy hours they gestured and grunted and laughed uproariously with each other.

Granddad took to France like a *canard* to *l'eau*. Strange for a man who was deeply suspicious of Abroad. Usually any variation from chip butties or pie and chips was greeted with 'aw no, not for me', yet in France he would try anything: crème brûlée and goat's cheese were downed with delight. He seemed to shake off all his English inhibitions and embraced the 'froggie' lifestyle. As did John.

John loathed public scrutiny, so that in England he was virtually a recluse. In France he was free to be himself, rather than some image based on the characters he played on television. This self was someone who liked the simple things of life. There, he could wander the lanes, and sit in cafés unaccosted. He could even join the crowds in a market without causing a commotion.

We were partial to a nice market and there are dozens of them in the Luberon. The biggest is on a Saturday morning in Apt, when the whole town is taken over with stalls. Just to walk amongst the sights and smells of fruit, goat's cheese, herbs, flowers, lavender, local wine and honey, and the spices in the Arab section, is an uplifting feast of the senses. In French markets you see proper shopping. Women with newly coiffed hair, arguing with the stallholders, sniffing, squeezing, prodding the produce. The Gallic shrug is much in evidence, as is companionable laughter when the deal is struck. Our shopping always ended in our favourite *pâtisserie,* where the girls would giggle when Monsieur Um Er arrived, so called because of John's solemn dithering whilst he chose his daily teatime gâteau.

We relished eating out without being stared at, although there are not that many grand restaurants in the Luberon. However, everything stops for lunch. Apt closes completely between twelve and three and everyone rushes home or to a café to eat. On one occasion we were lunching in the Café de la Gare in Bonnieux when a helicopter landed in the garden. Out stepped some electricity workers, who ate their three-course lunch with wine before setting off again to repair a fallen cable in the mountains. No wonder power cuts are accepted as the norm. Let's get our priorities right here. Lunch or lights? No competition.

What gave us most pleasure was being at home together. Without the pressure of work or our hectic city lives, we valued domesticity. The house, even after the building work, was unsophisticated. We shunned central heating, although winters can be cold. The ritual of lighting the stove was more fun than clicking a switch. The Man of the House allowed me to twist newspaper into complicated faggots, under his expert direction. He raked out the ashes and put them on our spindly rosebush, which didn't seem to like them very much. Then he would collect twigs for kindling from the cherry orchard, to go on top of the paper, carefully grading them upwards from small to large. Lots of manipulating of dampers and frantic blowing followed, whilst one by one he added the logs. His pleasure at the resulting fire was more than for any BAFTA award. If it didn't take, it was, of course, the fault of my faggots.

Our new kitchen was pretty basic. Except for the oven. He read somewhere that all the top chefs had a Lacanche. They cost the earth, but aiming slightly *au-dessus de sa gare*, he wanted one too. It is a monstrous iron thing that for some chichi reason doesn't have automatic lighting, so you have to fiddle around with matches, which, of course, you can never find. The oven takes ages to warm up and makes loud clicking noises as it does so. He defensively swore it cooked beautifully. Especially his signature dish. This was Elizabeth David's coq au vin, involving complicated operations with the giblets you'd do well to find in a British supermarket and a spectacular moment of flambéing the chicken in brandy.

I insisted on a dishwasher but he ignored it, preferring to demonstrate his washing-up skills. He even brought his own Brillo pads from London because he deemed the French version inferior. He was triumphant when, after searching the bric-à-brac stalls, he came home with a sink tidy. These were common when we were kids for collecting tea-leaves and potato peelings, before the dawn of waste disposers. He spent many a happy hour scouring pans and polishing glasses with his special linen tea towel.

I, in my turn, revelled in washing the heavy, antique sheets we used instead of duvets in the summer heat. The two of us pegging them on the line, to dry in the lavender-perfumed air, was marital bliss.

Our children were desperate for us to install a swimming-pool, but that would alter the whole nature of the house. It would become a poncey villa. Besides, we enjoyed our visits to the local *piscine*. An old-fashioned lido, it has three pools: for babies, youngsters and grown-ups. The changing cubicles are stalls with a wooden bench and tiled floor. You hand your clothes in on a heavy, steel, hanger contraption and are given a rubber wristband in exchange. Boxer shorts are forbidden, strangely, for the lads' skimpy trunks are much ruder. The water is crystal-clear and unheated except by the sun. The lifeguards are strict but friendly. No anti-social behaviour is allowed and the children are polite and solicitous of those younger than themselves and old codgers like me. There is a café on a gallery for spectators, where John would sit with a coffee and croissant, reading his paper.

Like the washing-up and the fire-lighting, the pool was a throwback to our childhoods. Labour-saving machines and sleek health clubs are an improvement, but we felt a deep, nostalgic joy in getting back to basics. Even though the basics – particularly in John's childhood – were, in reality, pretty grim. But it is different when you are doing things from choice, and with someone you love.

We had tasted the high life but we agreed we were never happier than when reading our books in the dappled shade of the two lime trees, lying side by side, on our special swing-back deck chairs that we bought in the Isle sur La Sorgue market. As I write, I have in front of me an antique toy donkey that he bought there for me, because I said it looked as though it felt lonely. Little did I think that, one day soon, so would I.

Now, between useless attempts to coax the stove into taking the winter chill out of the house, I made a desultory list of the jobs needing to be done. And stared at it. A lot. For the next few days I wandered round in a torpor of misery. Feeling sorry for myself. Wallowing in it. Conjuring up sad ghosts. The walls echoed with lost laughter: my dear friend Sheila Gish, arriving, dressed, as usual, in glamorous white, expressing her delight at the house with her distinctive chortle which, as Simon Callow pointed out at her memorial, spanned from middle C to top E – 'Ah hah' – now dead of a grotesque cancer; Clare Venables sitting by the wood stove, poring over the cryptic crossword, her fine brain utterly bewildered by the obtuseness of the clues – also gone; John stoically bearing my clumsy nursing when changing his chemotherapy bags. My mind was obsessing on death. I was aware that this wasn't healthy. Not two years after he's gone, for God's sake. But I had no desire to snap out of it. My wretchedness was changing from an acute condition to a chronic one, like a bad back that gives you an excuse for not participating in life. All the things that used to delight me had become a burden: shopping, cooking; even the sun hurt my tear-worn eyes. I wondered how I could still suffer from water retention when so much gushed from my nose and eyes.

I was on my knees in front of the stove, yet again struggling to light it, when a bird flew violently out of the flue into my face. It whirled around the room as I frantically struggled with windows and shutters to let it out. I hate fluttery things, be they man, flirty woman, or beast. Once, when the children were little, a bat flew into our house in the country. I hurled the kids upstairs, slammed the doors and phoned John in London to come and rescue us. He drove the hundred miles, detached a curtain to which the bat was clinging, threw it out of the window and drove back to London, muttering and swearing quite a lot. I managed to get this bird out on my own and, heart pounding, went to bed to keep warm.

The following evening my bird paid another visit. This time I was calmer. It turned out to be a baby, not very wise, owl. It perched on the door of the stove, all eight inches of it, huge eyes surveying the room and eventually lighting on me, peering over the back of the sofa. If owls can smile, it did. Certainly its head jerked to a jokey, quizzical angle that made me feel very silly. I opened the window wide, said, 'Go on, then, bugger off, you daft owl,' and, casting a disdainful look at me, it glided with an elegant swoop into the silent blackness towards those myriad stars.

That night I had a vivid dream that John was there with me. I reached out and touched him. I felt the roughness of his bristles. Saw the cleft in his chin and the scar. The silky receding hair, and his blue, blue, wryly smiling eyes. I went to hold him, but he turned deliberately and drifted away. I tried to call out to him but my voice wouldn't work. I woke weeping, hideously alone.

Knowing he had really gone.

Finally. For ever. Hiding his face amid a crowd of stars.

And knowing I had to get rid of this house.

It was a home that was meant to be shared. It was no longer valid. Nostalgia and happy memories weren't working for me. This beautiful place was holding me back. I needed to tear myself away; move on. Sometimes a painful wrench is necessary to mend a broken limb. The same for a heart. A couplet from a poem by Robert Frost, 'The Oven Bird', came to mind.

The question that he frames in all but words
Is what to make of a diminished thing.

What indeed? My mother's maxim 'Pull yourself together' had a lot to recommend it. Never mind therapy, religion, AA – eventually it is down to you. The decision whether to sink or swim is yours.

'Live adventurously', a Quaker advice, was also whirling around somewhere.

Well, what about it, Sheila? As John would say, 'Put your money where your mouth is.' Be a depressed widow boring the arse off everyone, or get on with life. Your choice.

If you are alive you've got to flap your arms and legs, you've got to jump around a lot. For life is the very opposite of death and you must, at the very least, think noisy and colourfully or you are not alive.

Mel Brooks

2

London · Liverpool

THE FIRST CHOICE I made was to put the house on the market. What would John think of me putting his beloved home up for sale? There we go again. What would he think? He's not here to think anything. It's down to me. So, come on. Get on with it. Phone the *immobiliers*. Dither, dither.

In the end, I got my friend Liz to do it. I just couldn't get my act together sufficiently to organise it. Then I fled back to London and sank into the Slough of Despond.

This wretchedness is beginning to sound remarkably like self-pity. I hope not. I have never wondered why sad things have happened to me; indulged in the 'why me?' syndrome. The death of my first and second husband from the same cancer; my grandson's brain tumour; my own cancer; other things – it's life. Or death. There is no reason, no punishing for past sins, no testing of faith, no lessons learnt. It just is. I'm not being picked on, it happens to everyone. I accept that. Nothing I can do. In Penelope Lively's wonderful novel *Moon Tiger*, the protagonist Claudia says: 'I think of how once I was brash enough to believe I could dictate to life, instead of which it has turned on me with its fangs bared.' Now, I was afraid that if I didn't do a bit of dictating I'd get bitten. Or become catatonic. Better to keep flapping and jumping. No time for self-pity. Busy myself with displacement activities.

One of these activities dismissed any claim to personal harddonebyness. A couple of young directors – a Jewish man, Tim Roseman, and a Lebanese woman, Rima Brihi – had interviewed people from both sides of the catastrophe of modern Israel and, helped by Robin Soans, had compiled the gathered material into a play. Called the *Arab-Israeli Cookbook* it centred on food because the writers discovered how important the preparing and eating of meals was to maintaining a simple routine – a semblance of normality – in the chaos of continual conflict. When I read it, despite being a bit old for performing in rooms above pubs, I had to be part of it.

It was damned hard work. Eight actors were called upon to play forty-three characters, and the research needed to fill in the background of the subject was demanding. We listened to talks by Jews and Palestinians desperate to let their voices be heard above the tumult of ill-informed world opinion, all of them quietly working to counter extremism and find a solution. My friend Thelma Ruby lent us films of her family who went to the Promised Land, full of dreams of setting up a perfect socialist state. I had seen the early Palestinian refugee camps when I visited Beirut in the sixties; miles of sordid plastic tents, children playing in raw sewage, desperate overcrowding. I was afraid then that the Jewish dream of a longed-for homeland could not be successfully achieved at such a cost. But I remembered too, as a young woman, meeting people who had gone to work in the early kibbutzim who were thrilled by the vision of making the desert bloom and living in peace after the Holocaust.

The most challenging aspect of the play for me was that, in the tiny Gate Theatre with the audience breathing down my neck, I had to prepare and cook an Arab dish ready for the cast to eat on stage, without poisoning them. (There were no understudies.) Compared to that, the task of playing five different characters was a piece of falafel. The horror of the blown-up buses, the endless waits at checkpoints, of cherished sons becoming suicide bombers, was starkly brought to life by the characters' testimonies, which we endeavoured to deliver with simplicity and honesty. It was a moving experience, every night, for us as well as the audience. Listening to the news about war zones, it is easy to forget that there are people trying to live their lives, eating, sleeping, teaching their children and making love. Everyday life continues, or tries to. Faced with the seriousness of the project it would have been churlish to moan abut the backstage conditions. Nevertheless I did.

I shared a cell, ten feet by eight feet, with two other actors – my daughter Abigail and Amanda Boxer – all our costumes for the numerous characters we played, plus the prop department. And a pigeon. He flew in one day and our bird-loving fellow actor and nutter, Amanda, persuaded us he should be made welcome. The lavatory was shared with the audience, and as I preferred not to meet them in the toilet just before trying to convince them that I was a tragic old Arab lady, the only alternative was to use another disgusting lavatory for the pub clients, who certainly had no intention of attending our moving evening. One had to be careful not to wet one's costume on the urine-drenched floor. When the lavatory suddenly started erupting like a Vesuvius-type bidet, we had to improvise reasons in the dialogue for soaking wet trousers and skirts.

Actors are asked to perform in conditions that would merit closure if animals were involved. What's more, though some, like me, whinge and moan, we still carry on doing the job. Usually for a pittance that a roadsweeper would laugh at. Or, indeed, in some fringe theatres for no money at all. I don't think the public realise, when they begrudge 'taxpayers' money' –

that bellyaching phrase – being used for theatre, how much the artists themselves subsidise the arts. Backstage conditions in most West End theatres are comfy for the mice and cock-roaches that live there, but freezing in the winter and boiling hot and airless in the summer, with toilet facilities only slightly better than those in the average fringe venue. Every time I go to a theatre and sit with my knees under my chin and have to queue for a drink or a pee, I darkly wish that, for all their beauty, these old theatres would be ripped out and replaced by something more congenial.

This discomfort in my working life, including film locations in cemeteries, pig farms, mental hospitals, morgues, and, in recent years, frequently inside coffins, has meant that, from the moment I made some money, my first priority was somewhere comfortable to come home to. It seems to be a human trait to make a nest. When I did the Quaker food run for the homeless, I was impressed by how doorways, and particularly the bull-ring at Waterloo, were decked out to create a personal space for each of the inhabitants. However temporary my base, starting with a rented basement room in Pimlico, it has always been my pride and joy and absorbed my attention and wages.

After John's death, I had no intention of moving home in London. We lived in a house of which he was never particularly fond, so – unlike France – there were no great happy memories to disquiet me. Then I was invited to a party by my friends Delena Kidd and Gary Raymond, in their house overlooking the river in Hammersmith. I have always felt a passionate attachment to the Thames. The Pimlico basement was near it, it ran past our old family home in Chiswick, and a house we once had in the country was close to its source. Delena and Gary had lived around the corner from me when I was married to my first husband, Alec Ross, and our children had grown up together. It felt like it would be a perfect life circle if we could be neigh-bours again, now with our grandchildren. That and glorious views of my comforting ever-flowing Thames. I asked them to keep their ears to the ground for any houses becoming available. A possibility of radical change had presented itself that was in keeping with my new resolve.

Delena was more diligent than I could ever have hoped. The residents did not seem to have John's and my grim tenacity in relationships. First, my friends located a couple discussing divorce and I kept an eye on their marriage for a few months, disgracefully unsympathetic to their misery. Then Delena phoned to say she had heard of another couple in difficulties. She brazenly slipped them a note asking if they were moving and, bingo, they were going their separate ways. I pounced and within days the deal was done.

So – a fresh start, in a house that John had no attachment to, and wouldn't even have liked. Planes roar over the Thames and cars hum on Hammersmith Bridge. John loved the tranquillity of our house in Wiltshire, but peace and quiet are anathema to me. I grind to a halt in the country, start to ache all over from inactivity. I don't care for hunting, horses scare me, and squelching over some drenched fields soon palls. Small doses of country life are therapeutic, but eventually, sitting looking at flowers grow stultifies me. The mooing of cows depresses me; but I find the sound of planes and cars reassuring. As I grow older I need to be in the city observing – if not always taking part in – seething activity. I want human beings around me. Lots of them. Not sheep and rabbits.

Not only would John not have liked the house, but, with the help of my daughter Ellie Jane, I set about decorating it in a way that would have made him very nervous. Minimalist verging on stark. It was my way of trying to accept his absence. Spring-cleaning the memories. Who was I trying to fool?

One day, surrounded by my new furniture and memory-proof white walls, I noticed on the ceiling the reflection of the river in the sun, dancing and flickering. And there he was, lying on a different sofa but with that beatific boy's smile, relishing the same image in the house he had loved two miles upstream. He would not be shut out. But now he was a memory rather than an expected presence and there was sadness in that. My acceptance in Saignon of his absolute absence made these seemingly unavoidable reminders difficult to bear in a different way. How was I to dismiss them from my mind?

It was a good time to take stock of my situation. At seventy-three I optimistically estimated that I might have seven more years of vigorous life left. Judging by how quickly the last seven had gone, time was short. What was I going to do with what was left?

I was doomed if the only option was to pursue the acceptable old-lady occupations. Grannying is fun but only a part-time job as their mothers want them back, especially as my rules on bedtime, sweeties and teeth-cleaning are apt to be a bit lax. All my daughters have somehow turned out to be wonderful mothers. Just as I followed Dr Spock they have various gurus whose methods of childcare they pursue. When I look after my grandchildren I do my best to adhere to the routines but I am easily hoodwinked into believing that 'Mummy lets us stay up till midnight/eat ice-cream after we've cleaned our teeth/swing on the chandelier'.

Joanna's Charlie, aged three, and Alfie, aged one, are be-witching children. To begin with I had some trouble connecting with Alfie. He would stare at me long and hard through his half-inch-long Thaw lashes, flicking alarmed sideways glances at his mother as if to say 'Is she safe? Who is this diddle-oh? Of all the nanas in the world why did you lumber me with this one?' One night when I was babysitting he woke up. He probably would have gone to sleep again but I seized the opportunity to get him up and do some bonding. Hearing

The Animal Boogie and the Ukulele Orchestra of Great Britain, Charlie too came downstairs and joined us for a bit of bopping. There being, by then, no likelihood of a return to bed, their parents came home to find us in a row on the sofa, eating chocolate and watching the late-night horror movie – their bedtime routine ruined. No, a reliable granny I am not.

I have tried entertaining à la Nigella and it ends in chaos and tears; garden plants die when I look at them: all suitable pursuits for the elderly, all beyond my capability. With a lifetime's experience behind me, I am most myself pretending to be someone else on a screen or stage. Undignified though that might be. Acting is what I am best at. Luckily for me it is a job that has no retirement limits; it can continue till you drop down dead as long as you can still remember the lines and not bump into the scenery – and as long as someone will offer you the roles.

Ellie Jane's partner Matthew Byam Shaw, a producer, suggested something that might suit me. I am all for nepotism but when my son-not-in-law suggested that the mother-in-law from hell in *The Anniversary* would be the ideal role for me I was momentarily taken aback.

In 1966 I had played the part of the feisty daughter-in-law in the original production with Mona Washbourne as the appalling mum. Then I played the same part in the film version of the play, opposite Bette Davis frightening us all to death both on screen and off. However, very soon after I finish in any play, my brain completely erases all the lines from my memory. It is probably a defence mechanism, as the amount of words I have learnt over the sixty years of my working life would, if retained, probably blow the system. So I had to re-read the script.

What I did remember was that the laughs were some of the biggest I can recall in a theatre, as well as gasps of shock at Mum's cruelty, and applause when anyone scored a point against her. Altogether, a total theatrical experience that engaged an audience on every level. Or offended some, which is also what theatre should do. Would it still work in a world that is less shocked by people behaving badly?

Well it did. We opened at the Playhouse in Liverpool, the theatre where John began his career straight from RADA, and it was a riot. I was in my element. Packed audiences howling with laughter and cheering at the curtain call. The audiences in Liverpool are marvellously uninhibited.

All my career I have loved working in the provinces, as we used to call Birmingham, Leeds, Manchester and their like. When touring a show pre opening in the West End of London, there are always dark murmurings about being 'OK on the road but what about in Town?' As though the audiences in London are not just different but in some way superior to the rest of England. More serious. More discerning. Nonsense. It either works or it doesn't.

Many times I have been tempted into dreary, worthy plays for the prestige they carry. The London critics rave, the people who read their reviews nod approval and laugh that special humourless 'haw haw' that says they understand an intellectual nuance, whilst secretly longing for the show to end, so they can get to supper, where they will pretend they adored it to their friends, and thankfully cross it off their list of things they ought to see. What I really love is hearing an audience genuinely roaring with laughter. Mind you, it is quite satisfying to make them sniffle too. I have been so helped by Frankie Howerd, Kenneth Williams, Eddie Izzard, Richard Pryor, Catherine Tate's old lady, Ray Cooney, Mel Brooks, Alan Ayckbourn and countless other mirth makers when times have been tough. Laughter is important. It is a genuine healer of the sad soul.

I remember the moment when I made the decision to use humour to get by. At grammar school we were asked to design a town. I was a diligent student and spent hours on the project, working out a Utopian existence for my inhabitants. There was a factory for employment, medical care, schools, art gallery, playing spaces, and a theatre, of course. And cows.

Miss Lewin showed my plan to the whole class, pointing a derisory finger at my field of cows in the centre of town. I had thought this through carefully; their milk would provide instant nourishment for all the children, who in those days had a little bottle a day at school. It would be fresh and warm, straight from my cows, which was one of my good memories of being evacuated, but the teacher had the whole class howling with laughter at the thought of these urban cattle. I was deeply hurt and not a little angry. A sulky, temperamental outburst was imminent, but hearing their amusement, I decided it was probably more fun than respect, and a better option was to abandon umbrage and go for the laugh. And that has usually been my choice ever since.

We came to London with the play, and its success continued. I don't have the courage to read reviews, but apparently mine were all wonderful. Matthew gave me a photo of my name in lights and I was pleased to see myself up there in action. On my own. Never mind that the newspapers used the same old sentimental guff about sad Sheila trying to forget her loss. People were paying to see me in a play, not just a widow of a man they loved. They wouldn't pay good money and sit through two hours of theatre for that. It did my ego no end of good.

The publicity interviews I most enjoyed were with Jonathan Ross and Paul O'Grady. No pseudo, cliché-ridden, brave-widow bullshit from them. Marvellous, disrespectful stuff. Their sharp-witted, slightly dangerous, public personae conceal two sweet pussycats who love their families and friends. I like them a lot. They made me feel attractive with their compliments.

Not that I watched the programmes to see if they were right. I never look at anything I have done and, whatever people say, I am convinced I look ugly. Sad really, that when I come across early photos of myself I am surprised how presentable I was when I was agonising over a funny nose and pointy chin.

One programme in 2005 I had to watch as I was dubbing the narration, a poem to mark the sixtieth anniversary of VE Day. My voiceover was interspersed with people's memories of VE Day and the war. I was moved to tears by one story of a man who lived, I think, in Clapham, where there had been a devastating bomb that killed many people, including children. Several days after, a German airman bailed out and landed near the bombsite. A wrathful crowd set upon him and he was killed. The man, a working-class Londoner, still visits the airman's grave every year with a bunch of flowers.

The terrible thing was that I understood the crowd's rage. I felt it as a child when friends, and fathers of friends, were killed, and bombs rained down on my home. That is not something I like admitting. I would prefer to be forgiving like that gentle man. To decide, as a little boy with his bunch of flowers, to defy the mob mentality, was so courageous. He did not care that he was reviled by his neighbours. Actors I'm afraid like to be loved. It is our job after all. In *Grumpy Old Women* I let rip at some pretty soft targets. Even with them, I worry lest I offend. Or hurt. When I did *Room 101*, where you consign to oblivion things you dislike, egged on by Paul Merton, I obliterated Chiswick Post Office, complaining about the uncommunicative counter staff. When it went out, I was distraught with guilt. For all I knew, the monosyllabic woman, grunting behind her reinforced glass, was stricken with grief over the death of her mother. Or maybe they cannot be held responsible for their catatonic state, having all been sent into a hypnotic trance by the constant repetition of 'cashier number one, please'? No, I don't have the courage of my condemnations.

When *The Anniversary* came to an end, the company were

all sad. It is a recurring feature of theatre and film life, that you become close to colleagues, the show ends, and you all go your separate ways. It can feel very bleak. All the razzamatazz stops suddenly on Saturday night, you pack up your make-up, and clear your dressing room ready for a new inhabitant, and that's it. Very often you face unemployment. Convinced that you will never work again. Certainly on the following Monday night, if like me you are on your own, come the time when you would be getting ready for the show and you remember hearing the audience chatting in anticipation on the tannoy, it can feel very lonely.

The Anniversary had bolstered my self-respect, given me confidence. Now, here I was in no woman's land, trapped between the past and the future, teetering on the edge of something unknown. I had been busy, busy, busy filling the chasm left by the acceptance of John's absence. For me work was an effective panacea. But hovering on the edge of my conciousness was another Quaker quote, one I had chosen to ignore: 'Attend to what love requires of you which may not be great busyness.'

If I should go before the rest of you,
Break not a flower nor inscribe a stone,
Nor when I'm gone speak in a Sunday voice,
But be the usual selves that I have known.
Weep if you must,
Parting is hell,
But life goes on,
So sing as well.

'If I Should Go before the Rest of You'
by Joyce Grenfell

3

Ramsgate · Herne Bay · Puglia

WHEN YOU ARE IN the doldrums, people usually recommend a holiday. Even doctors. 'You need a change of scene,' they say. Well, the curtain was beginning to fall on France. That was a step in the right direction. If you have a second home abroad, you feel duty-bound to use it. So you go there, rather than exploring other holiday possibilities. But now – 'the world is your oyster' as my dad used to say. Although then, never having seen an oyster, I didn't know what it meant. Now, having seen and indeed eaten one, I still don't. Unless it is the possibility that you might find a pearl. Which would mean eating a lot of oysters. Or taking a lot of holidays.

That was not an idea for which I could rouse much enthusiasm. Especially on my own. I have never been very good at holidays anyway. It was not part of my conditioning. My parents didn't teach me leisure. I never remember them going out or having friends round. Indeed, I don't remember them ever being idle. If my mother sat down for a rest, her fingers would be clacking away with the knitting needles. If my dad listened to the wireless he would be cleaning the cutlery or polishing shoes with his special dusters and brushes. Busy, busy, busy.

The curse of the Protestant work ethic sits heavily on my shoulders. I feel guilty reading a book, unless it is research for something. (I blame my childhood – that's what I always do when I can't explain things any other way – my children have started to do it about me, so it seems only fair. Ellie Jane, when shouting at her errant daughter: 'God, Mum, I sound like you.') My grandma would find me jobs about the house, muttering, 'The devil finds work for idle hands.' She didn't consider reading a library book a proper thing to do. That is probably why the only books in the house were my granddad's Harmsworth's encyclopaedias, the Bible, and *10,000 Answers to Your Children's Questions*, which didn't seem to have any of the questions I wanted answered. The Bible was better on sex, if a bit confused.

We went on only two holidays when I was a child. The first was to Ramsgate before the war. In retrospect it was not a joyful event but at the time I thought it was. Being turned out of the bed-and-breakfast lodging, after sad kippers, or congealed scrambled egg on soggy toast come rain or shine, seemed reasonable. When it pelted down, you traipsed round Woolworth's or sat in a shelter on the promenade and watched the rain drifting over the sea and played I Spy with Mum and Dad. I spy something beginning with G. Grey? Yes. But the cafés, with their fish, or egg, and chips, were the Caprice to a kid from King's Cross. The funfair was exciting, too. I learnt to love speed on the motorbike roundabout, squealing with ecstasy.

I was less enchanted by the dodgems, on which I shared a car with a friend of my father whose hand seemed to hold me in odd places. More groping happened when I was too shy to refuse to squash up to him in a carriage in the aptly named Big Dipper. Quite a lot of my holiday was spent avoiding being alone with this gross man. I can't pretend his wandering hands, or what he led mine to grasp, or what he showed me, scarred me for life. He was the first in a list of what I would come to call Dirty Old Men that merely slightly soiled my, and on comparing notes, most of my girlfriends', lives. We dealt with it by laughing, and by probably being quite cruel: 'Don't think much of that chipolata, mate.' No, no great harm was done, I just remember not liking it very much. Nothing was said. He was Daddy's friend and paedophilia was unknown to that six-year-old child. Probably to my father too. All in all, not a happy holiday memory.

Less disconcerting is my recollection of the only other childhood vacation we had, in Herne Bay after the war. The English idea of recreation was still a spartan affair; at least for the lower classes. The country was a gloomy place in 1946, with rationing still in operation, and gaping holes left by the bombing, and fathers who didn't return from the war. We were not a stylish nation, with our utility furniture, and the few clothes we could get with clothing coupons augmented by home-made frocks, made on Singer sewing machines, from Butterick patterns, or, in my case, adapted from my sister Billie's wardrobe. I blush at the memory of a bathing costume, knitted by my mum, which floated away from my body in the water and sagged to my knees when I got out.

Herne Bay seafront was not Cannes, but it had some rather pretty beach huts, one of which Daddy hired, so we could shelter from the unrelenting rain. There must have been some sunny days then, but I don't remember them. Even if there had been there was not much action with buckets and spades, because the beach consisted of unforgiving pebbles, unless the tide was right out, leaving a bit of hard sand. There was a tiny boy in the next beach hut, with a quiff of hair forming a question-mark – we christened him Nipper, after a popular strip cartoon – who could sprint over the stones to paddle in the sea. Dad would stagger after him, yelping and grimacing,

falling on his knees and crawling, an elaborate daily pantomime that had me, Nipper and the other kids bellowing with
laughter. Twelve-year-old girls were still children in those
distant days, and sharing a holiday with parents who had little
time in their six-day working week to frolic with their offspring
was joyous. Nowadays, girls would probably prefer to go off to
Ibiza with their mates but I wanted no more than to laugh with,
and at, my dad.

When I had a family of my own, regrettably I didn't do
annual holidays with them. Actors don't have set holidays –
just periods out of work. Anyway it wasn't part of my lifestyle;
a foible much resented by my now-grown-up daughters, who
take regular holidays with their children. When they complain
about this I remind them of one holiday we did go on, to Tenby.
The usual rain that drenched me in England followed me to
Wales, lashing at the hotel windows. In desperation, I stripped
them to their costumes, figuring that they were going to get wet
anyway, and made them play on the deserted muddy beach and
swim in the sea, narrowly avoiding being struck by lightning. It
was by mutual agreement that we came home early.

John had a similar virtually holiday-free childhood, so had
the same indifference or, in his case, aversion, to the concept.
He felt safer at home, which is why France was perfect for him;
it was abroad but home as well. He liked the familiar. He had a
habit on holiday of making the first chair he sat on his nesting
place. We went to Oman together, and, it being Ramadan, the
super-deluxe Al Bustan hotel was empty, so we were upgraded
to a luxurious suite, full of reclining couches, vast beds and
sumptuous armchairs. When we arrived after the long journey,
John sank on to a hard chair by the front door to have a fag,
and that became his haven. It took several days for me to prise
him off it, and several more to get him outside to the glorious
beach, and it wasn't until the last day that I forced him into the
desert to visit some bedouins that I had met. And of course he

found it fascinating. But the holidays were an ordeal for him, and therefore for me, trying to keep him happy.

We did have two blissful holidays after he found sobriety, one in Paris and the other in Venice. I loved both places, but now, contemplating this oyster world that had presented itself, they were both no-go areas. Too many memories. Must move on. Must move on.

So, holidays were not top of my wish list – unlike the young man I saw on television in one of the holiday programmes I had started to watch, who was thrilled to be paying his way as a rep because he could 'make a lot of money, get pissed every night, and shag a lot of birds'. On the historic island of Rhodes. I wasn't tempted to book.

Then two things happened to point me a way forward. I watched a reality programme on TV about families swapping places with each other on holiday. I am not a fan of this new genre generally, but sometimes the programmes can throw up truths about us and the society we live in. One family was middle-class, confident and used to holidays abroad. The other was dominated by a fat clumsy, woman, with two down-trodden daughters, and a monosyllabic, defeated partner, whom she bullied into staying at home for holidays, with the odd trip to, I think, Weston-super-Mare. Even there, she was astonished, when she was persuaded to take a coach trip, that it had more to offer than she had dared to seek. To begin with I was infuriated by her insistence that everyone bow to her will, and her total ignorance of the world outside her rigid confines. Then the other family began to give her daughters ideas, and the husbands too had stilted talks behind her back. Her world began to fall apart. Her grief was awful to watch. Her fear and loss of identity when she was forced to go to Thailand – the other family's choice of holiday – was desper-ately sad. She tried to cling to her old suffocating values, so obviously a product of her childhood; in the end her liberated family was lost to her, vowing to take more trips, have more fun, but she yielded only a little.

The walls we erect around ourselves, with bricks made of fear, are well nigh impenetrable. Cowering behind them, we become prejudiced, ignorant and inert. I recognised myself, and certainly John, in aspects of this woman. It takes a supreme effort to breach those barricades of your conditioning. That John became what he was, did what he did, was an achievement to be much more proud of than he was. To move through the various stages of life takes courage. And determination.

My inability to move forward manifested itself one morning, when I woke with my eyes glued shut by an eye infection and no voice. My body trying to tell me something? All a bit New Agey – but I think so. Then an email handed me a straw to clutch, from the most unlikely source: the *Daily Mail*. Not, I have to say, my favourite dispenser of distortion to the masses. Although, at the end of a bitter battle with the paper, I had ended up liking the editor Paul Dacre better than I did at the beginning. And if you are up to your neck, it's pretty stupid to reject a hand proffered to keep your head above water.

The travel section had asked me to write a piece for them. I wasn't a journalist, and certainly not renowned for my travelling, so why I don't know. But why not? It was a godsent opportunity to take a holiday under the guise of work, a chance to kick-start myself into enjoyment, without the obligatory guilt. I was offered a week in a luxury spa somewhere hot, or a cruise, with my family or a friend. Whatever I liked. I could hand-pick my oyster, which would definitely contain a pearl. All this was too cushy for my conscience. So I chose to write about holidaying on my own.

The letters I had received had brought home the problems this could present; and not only because lone travellers are penalised for their solitude with single supplements and silly rules. British Airways cabin staff, because they are not insured, are not allowed to help you put your luggage in the overhead lockers – not easy if you are old, or not very tall, and have no one to help you, unless someone offers, which nowadays they seldom do. Entering a hotel dining room by yourself can be a challenge after a lifetime with a partner to keep you company. It's difficult to make friends because overtures, especially from men travelling alone, may be suspiciously rejected. So, although a cushy mini break with a friend would have been more pleasant, I decided, as is my wont, to choose the hard way.

A trip to Apulia or Puglia in Italy was suggested as a destination. I had to look it up on the map. It is the heel of the Italian boot. Interestingly enough for me, it encompassed Foggia, where my first husband, Alec Ross, was stationed for a time, in the RAF during the war. His stories were chiefly of confusion and mistakes. The Italian campaign does seem to encapsulate the chaos of war, as well as the extraordinary self-sacrifice of the men taking part. It is difficult to understand the early devotion of the Italians to Mussolini. OK, so he built towns and roads and made the trains run on time, but couldn't they see what a strutting, ludicrous figure he cut in his bizarre uniforms? By the time Alec arrived, they had realised their mistake, strung him up from a lamppost, and joined the Allies against the Germans. The army, covered by Alec and his comrades in the RAF, worked their way up the leg of Italy, culminating in a bemused Alec and a fellow, lowly airman being ushered to the royal box when they attended the opera in Rome, and receiving the salutation of the audience.

Thank God it is not necessary to invade the beaches or parachute into Italy any more. Instead you take a plane from Stansted. Which for me was almost as alarming. The journey by road across London to get there is bad enough but air travel has become a miserable business. Airports are ugly and un-welcoming, with endless queues and no one telling you what is happening. If you dare to ask, you are subjected to people in dusty uniforms snapping your head off, and barking orders, forgetting that your money is paying their salaries. The latest con is security. Little old ladies are forced to remove their shoes, willy-nilly, although they can scarcely bend to take them off, let alone detonate a bomb in them. I once protested when a mother with a toddler and a screaming babe in arms was forced to hand over her jars of puréed food. The jobsworth barked that she could buy more in Duty Free. I wonder how much their sales have increased since this ludicrously over-zealous, mind-lessly applied, new regime was brought in? And I am sick of being asked, what would I prefer: being blown up? The old lady and the harassed mother are no threat to me, and any well-trained, intelligent, security person, using their loaf, should know that.

Budget airlines are the only ones to fly to Brindisi, the local airport in Puglia. I imagined that, for those prices, the planes would be falling apart, and the customers would be herded like cattle. My daughters didn't help by shaking their heads and warning me that I was in for a nasty shock. When I go to France my usual airport is Gatwick, where the BA special-services team that used to usher John through have become my friends, and do the same for me. So, since he died, I have never travelled without support. Stansted and easyJet on my own promised to be a rude awakening.

I was agreeably surprised. Despite an unbelievable low fare, as apparently easyJet reckon to make a profit of a mere £2.50 per person, Stansted was well organised and attractive, and I was very happy taking on board my own, delicious, Pret A Manger sandwich. Anything is preferable to those anaemic white things, warmed up in plastic wraps, with something sticky and a slither of pale pink stuff inside. The easyJet steward was camp and jolly and startled me by actually offering to put my quite heavy bag in the locker, a first for me. Perhaps I looked particularly peaky and scared. The shiny new plane was mainly full of Italian passengers, who were very exuberant, cheering and applauding when we landed safely in Brindisi.

I emerged from the small, haphazard airport to find no signs of taxis or buses. Gradually everyone disappeared, met by their friends and family. I had my first attack of lonesome nerves, wondering how to get to the hotel. The only Italian I speak is phrases from a revue sketch I once did, called 'Parlata in Italiano'. It was a send-up of Anna Magnani and Italian opera and films, so I had perfected Italian phrases that meant: 'Don't leave me alone in this life!', 'Assassin!', 'I hate you!' and '*È morto!*' delivered like Callas in *Tosca*. None of which proved much use here, marooned in Brindisi airport. But Latin learnt at school and possibly something in my genes from Dad's Italian childhood, makes me understand the language quite well. My accent being good from the sketch, I asked, 'Masseria Torre Coccaro?' and was answered with a torrent of information, from which I gleaned they had a hotel bus. With a bit of mime and putting 'a's and 'o's on the ends of words, like telefono, I managed to persuade a man to phone the hotel, and indeed, after some time, a people carrier arrived. I was triumphant. Not much to achieve really, but alone I did it.

We drove through groves of gnarled silver-grey olive trees, writhing above a carpet of blazing red poppies, yellow daisies and blue cornflowers. On one side are miles of sandy beaches and coves, with only the occasional car parked on the grass beside the unspoiled coastline. Remembering the same impression of Balinese beaches in 1970 which are now solid stretches of tourist hotels, I wondered if I was lucky to come here before, surely, such perfect beaches suffer the same fate. I had left behind a wet, cold London in April and here, three hours later, the sun was shining in a cloudless sky. Despite some flutters of anxiety, it was a cheerful start to my lone ranging.

The approach to the hotel was impressive – through an olive grove that led to a gate in a tall wall, blinding white in the sun. Once through the gate we drove through luxurious gardens to be greeted by the owner of the hotel, Vittorio Muoli. Despite its five stars, no intimidating smooth operator he, but a shambling bear of a man in plimsolls and shirt-sleeves, shyly proud of what he has created, with the aid of his staff, all drawn from local villages. Vittorio told me that three years ago, this *masseria* had been a working farm.

My room was cool and welcoming, with a private patio, but once I had unpacked I stood there, wondering what to do next. My mouth is dry and I feel absurdly apprehensive. This is a holiday, for God's sake, not a first night. I don't have to prove anything. Just enjoy myself. How could that be so frightening? I forced myself out of the safety of my room to look around.

The *masseria*s were originally built as fortresses to protect the inhabitants from Turkish pirates and their like; most of the hotel was adapted from original buildings from every period of history. There are even caves used by ancient dwellers that had been converted into atmospheric sitting and billiard rooms. One has become a spectacular Aveda spa. To kill time – a dreadful phrase to use, especially when supposedly on a blissful break – I had a steam bath.

I am very partial to steam baths. I seek them out wherever I go. In my touring days in the fifties and sixties it was always comforting in winter, when the digs were freezing, to escape to a Turkish bath in those towns that were blessed with such indulgence. These old-fashioned baths are rapidly being re-placed by upmarket, swanky spas, which are to my mind nowhere near as invigorating. Gone are the salt rubs and the scouring with loofahs by muscly ladies. This one at the *masseria* though was a unique experience. There is something primeval about sitting alone, stark naked, in an underground rocky cavern, that gradually fills with hot steam, seemingly from the bowels of the earth. I felt disembodied. I could be anywhere, any time. To bring me down to earth, I had a massage, given by a girl who lacked the brash confidence of the army of dubiously trained beauty therapists who have sprung up back home. No aimless chitter-chat: 'Where did you go on holiday this year?', 'What do you do? Actress? What would I have seen you in?' It was more of a quiet, soothing stroke, really. Which was just what I needed. A sweet young girl, innocent of feminist sisterhood ideas, nevertheless gently caring for an agitated, older woman. For an hour, and for a fee, but the female bonding was welcome and surprisingly real, considering our only communication was with smiles and gestures.

Squeaky clean and feeling relaxed, I wandered into a garden created in Roman times. Ancient pillars line paths that wind through well-tended beds of vegetables and salad. The soft perfume of old-fashioned roses, jasmine and orange blossom fill the sunlit space, enclosed by the stone wall that has, with a bit of help, survived the centuries. In the centre is a well, feeding an elaborate irrigation system that is still partly functioning; they were clever with water, those Romans. I found wild caper, aromatic herbs of all sorts, fig, prickly pear, apple, apricot, quince and peach trees. No one was around. I sat on a stone bench, as many others must have done over the generations, and enjoyed the results of man's imagination, skill and weeding. From the primitive caves to this majestic garden, to me with my marvellous mobile phone, sitting here feeling sorry for myself. What a piece of work is man. And what a letdown I am to the human race for not valuing it.

Full of resolve, I marched back to my room, donned my bathing costume and kaftan and set off for the pool. It is made to look like an oasis, surrounded by palm-tree umbrellas. There is a bar to slake your thirst after a swim in the crystal-clear blue water. Well, that's the theory. Hovering at the entrance, I cast my eye round the sun-basking customers. They were all ravishingly beautiful. They were all with someone. The loungers are double size, based on the assumption that no one would be fool enough to venture here on their own. I spied one at the back, near the entrance, and slunk towards it.

It was too much to hope some nut-brown youth was going to leap on and lie beside me, gazing into my eyes. Or even a grey-haired old codger. There were one or two of them, but they were all clambering on to couches with ladies much younger than I. So, I spread out my books and my swimming goggles in the empty space, took off my kaftan, and lay down very quickly, because when you lie flat the slack of your skin drops back and you look smoother than when you're standing up. Not that anyone noticed.

Waiters were circulating, serving drinks, but none looked my way. It is a proven fact that after fifty women do dissolve. The one hour I spent by that pool, totally invisible to the waiters, will be added to my dossier of evidence of this disappearance phenomenon. My absence allowed me to gaze at the other sybarites. Obviously very rich, or with a rich man. It was, after all, an expensive hotel. Several, by the look of it, were on their honeymoon. How perfect. Lying hand in hand, on a sunbed, planning your life together. Occasionally a svelte girl would sashay down to the pool, dive in and emerge, glistening and bursting with health. I remember that feeling, when you know your body is in tiptop condition, and you are brown and bleached in the sun. You look your very best.

I don't look like that any more. It is only since John died that I have noticed. He thought I was beautiful and never stopped saying so. Was it because he was too vain to wear glasses? Or because he loved me? If he had been there, I would not have thought twice of bounding down and plunging in for a swim.

Without his loving gaze, I recognise the stark reality of the damage wrought by gravity. Germaine Greer and fellow feminists notwithstanding, I do not love what has happened to my buttocks. I would happily have forgone the experience that is supposed to make me proud of my wrinkles. If only for aesthetic reasons, I could not contemplate limping my sagging flesh down to the water. It could wait until dark when everyone was gone. So I cowered there, sneaking envious looks over my book at the nuzzling couples, feeling old, isolated, voyeuristic and thirsty.

The book is a vital weapon for the lonely. Especially in restaurants. That evening, I contemplated room service, but dolled myself up and, armed with a paper and a book, braved the stares of the guests. The *maître d'* was startled, even alarmed, when I said I wanted a table for one. If he had been busy, I have no doubt that rather than waste a table for two, I would have been refused entrance, as I have been on other occasions, but I was lucky. He found me a seat near the door where the waiters push in and out. I thought to object, but the hush that descended on the room intimidated me, and I ordered a large gin instead.

When the woman at the next table, sitting with her husband, sent a sympathetic glance in my direction, I looked at my watch and did a shrugging mime of being stood up by the vacant-chair person. It somehow seemed less shaming than being on my own. The secret was out the next night, however, when the same thing happened. So I resorted to Miss Havisham mode. If they think I am odd, I will damn well give them odd. I giggled out loud over my book, scribbled in my notebook and surrounded myself with bits of paper, drank a great deal and even did a bit of humming. It was a good ploy and I quite enjoyed myself.

In an effort to meet some of the other guests, I signed up for a cookery course. In the event I was the only one who did.

Everyone else had better things to do, or maybe the English translation of the leaflet about the cuisine I was about to master didn't sound overly tasty: 'The Puglesci don't throw nothing away of lambs and butcher's kid skins, prove our recipes of baked lamb's head, the quagghiaribde, a muffin filled of pluck, united scarmonza cheese'. I was particularly apprehensive about handling pluck.

As I was the only pupil the tutor, Liberata, so called because she was born in 1945, decided to teach me in the hotel kitchen, rather than the special classroom, with – first – a walk round the garden to meet the happily frolicking ducks, chicken and turkeys. I couldn't look them in the eye, as she gleefully pointed out their plumpness. We picked pungent herbs and she showed me a thousand-year-old olive tree that still bore an annual crop. Then in the kitchen she tried to teach me how to knead and cook bread, and concoct a kind of Lancashire Hot Pot made with mussels (*tiella*), which tasted, frankly, pretty disgusting. The pasta was slightly better although a bit grubby after I had fingered one shell shape to her ten. I shall continue to buy ready-made pasta however, as I reckon life is too short to mould a shape that's going to be eaten and is only a texture with tasty sauce when all is said and done. Well, mine is anyway. She assured me that in that region, all women still bake their bread and cook everything, even if they go out to work, although as yet few do. I will not be following their worthy example.

The chefs and waiters working in the kitchen were fascinated by my ineptitude and we made gesticulating jokes. Several spoke English, as waiters often do, because they work internationally. It was the most fun I had had since I arrived. It certainly eased the dining-room situation, because that night I got special treatment, as well as chats whilst they were serving me.

I was beginning to do a John. I had found a comfort zone; I

had got out of my room, but I was in danger of not venturing out of the hotel. I was quite happy reading in my Roman garden, swimming late at night and teaching a bit of English to the cleaners, in return for a smattering of Italian. However, it seemed silly to come all this way for that, and anyway I had an article to write.

I went into pull-yourself-together mode, and jacked myself into action. I could source only one guidebook. In order to get the job the translator must have had the gift of the gab, but not in very good English. Maybe it was the same person who did the cooking-course leaflet. He boasted that Apulia has 'land humpy, sheer, barren and avaricious, a suggestive scenographical effect'. Sights were frequently called 'homonymous'; that I could only suppose meant 'harmonious'. However, the pictures displayed an area of amazing diversity: prehistoric caves with wall paintings, Greek and Roman ruins, baroque, classical, Byzantine: you name it, Apulia's got it.

Trouble was, I had wasted so much time dithering I had only a few days left. I thought it best to recruit a driver rather than hire a car and drive myself, because when I am finding my way, and working out which side of the road I'm on, I miss so many of the sights. I justified the expense as necessary for my work and set off with a knowledgeable local man called Antonio at the wheel.

At the Masseria Maccarone, an olive mill that incorporates a museum, I was greeted by a member of the Marquesa family, which has lived in this gracefully proportioned palace for generations. He, to put it baldly, or in this case luxuriantly, tousledly, grey-headedly, is a dish. Tall, slim, aristocratic and dressed in Armani-style casual that only Italians seem to really get right. Think José Mourinho, totally elegant, but seeming not to have bothered much (not Italian, but you get the picture). He speaks halting English with a bewitching accent. I rack my brains to remember any phrases in the sketch with which to dazzle him, but *ciao, bambino* doesn't seem appropriate. I gush my profound admiration of his ancient oil mill, which works on exactly the same principle as the high-tech modern version. I wax lyrical, during a tasting to demonstrate the subtle variation in different oils. On leaving, he presses upon me four beautiful examples, one a numbered bottle of a limited edition. I thank him profusely, with lots of *molto*s and *bellissima*s. He kissed my hand, and I would have replied, 'Will you marry me and let me live here in your palace and I will grind your olives for you', only the sketch dialogue didn't run to that.

Apulia produces 70 per cent of Italy's olive oil and one-tenth of all Europe's wine, so I asked Antonio the driver to take me to Locorotundo, which yields a very tasty white. He took me to a café he knew, where an Anna Magnani look-alike was preparing the lunch. After my lesson, I watched with a newly expert eye as her deft fingers moulded pasta shapes with lightning speed, interrupted occasionally by vociferous exchanges with her clients that sounded like declarations of love and threats of murder, but were in fact about the weather and the neighbours. I decided I had underacted in the sketch. My reward for finishing a vast plateful was to be crushed on to her ample bosom in an emotional embrace.

I was beginning to like these people very much. And the region they inhabit is not only beautiful but also full of fascinating architecture and art. Cursing my stupidity at actually wanting to 'kill time' when I arrived, I was now in a frenzy to see more. With Antonio and my guidebook's help I endeavoured to cram in as many homonymous and suggestive sights as I could in the time I had left.

I felt I was discovering new territory. Everyone knows the Forum in Rome, but how many have visited the ruins of Egnatia? No one on the day I was there, and it was much more evocative for being grown over with grass and wild flowers. Antonio showed me several archaeological sites, undiscovered, or at least unmarked, in olive groves and fields. Centuries ago, families of workers thought this was the be-all and end-all, they were important, and their work vital. Yet here I was, sitting on a broken wall of their house, not even knowing who they were. Civilisations come and go. I wonder what will survive of ours.

But some of the grander buildings bygone Italians laboured to build are still there, intact. I'm grateful to them for that. I know of no other place with such infinite variety. Lecce is a stunning feast of the baroque, and it has rightful claims to be called the Florence of the South. In every town there are unexpected gems that Antonio dismissed with a shrug of indifference.

At one of the few touristy spots, a marvellous set of caves, the Castellano Grotte, I became involved in a little human drama. In a party of children, one small boy caught my eye. With his skinny legs and huge brown eyes and shabby clothes he was unlike his boisterous mates. Memories of my evacuee days were stirred by his pathetic attempts to be one of the lads. His clumsy jokes, and stone-kicking, to court favour, were rejected, and he stood, numb with longing, on the periphery of the group. An unattractive large boy said something to him and suddenly he was galvanised into violent rage, punching the fat boy in the face; the latter behaved like a footballer and made a terrible fuss, although clearly not greatly damaged. The teacher in charge grabbed the scraggy kid by the arm and shouted at him in fury, then addressed the others, obviously telling them to have nothing to do with him. By this time, I had built a whole life history around him. My heart bled for this little lad, wide-eyed and isolated, as the others made a show of having a good time without him. The mob loves to ostracise an outcast. I catch his eye and smile and nod. He is baffled. After a lot of face-pulling on my part, he smiles tentatively back. Desperate for an ally, his eyes follow me around.

The caves are stunning, full of stalagmites and stalactites, and curious rock formations. There are pink, yellow, purple and rainbow crystal formations, rock worn so thin as to imitate a veil, alabaster towers and a sparkling white cave that Aladdin would have been amazed by. As each wonder unfolded, I demonstrated my awe to my new little friend, with open-mouthed gapes and thumbs up and silent clapping. Other people must have thought me insane, but I was determined he would have fun, despite his tight-arsed teacher. I hid behind stalagmites, and suddenly jumped out as he approached; I even descended to poking my tongue out at his teacher behind her back. He probably thought I was some gnome that inhabited the magic kingdom, but he knew, I hope, that this strange creature liked him, even if his friends didn't. I was relieved to see that, eventually, one small girl with plaits, seeing him smile and probably look less dangerous than he sometimes did, sidled up to him and whispered something. Hopefully, 'Don't worry, I'm your friend.'

As the tour ended, I prayed to the gods of the cave to give him a break, blew him a kiss and disappeared from his life. As I was leaving it occurred to me that the encounter wouldn't have happened if I hadn't been alone. I probably wouldn't have noticed him if I had been chatting to a companion, and certainly wouldn't have behaved in such a weird way. It made my visit to the caves a richer experience, sharing it with him and – who knows – maybe, in the future, he will imagine some friendly sprite is on his side.

That evening I went to Ostuni to taste the nightlife. It is a white town, on a hill, overlooking the sea. The odd trendy bar is making an appearance, but most of the locals prefer to do the evening promenade, thronging the streets, eating ice-cream and gossiping. The youngsters were obviously sizing one another up in their latest finery. I sat in a café, watching, and felt no threat and saw no drunks – a bit different from noisy youngsters reeling round Liverpool on a Saturday night. Even the beach discos are well behaved. There just seems to be no tradition of associating a good time with getting paralytic. There were people of all ages, milling around, inclusive of small children and the aged. Perhaps it's the still-potent religious ethic, the climate, slower pace, or strong family tradition. It is probably claustrophobic if you live there, and most of the girls are fairly restricted, but it's extremely attractive to observe.

As I wandered up the hill, I turned a corner into a small square, and saw the sweetest little pink curvy cathedral tucked away in a corner. This is a girly building, small, decorated with filigree lacy stone and pretty as opposed to beautiful. I went into a nearby shop to ask if I could get the keys to look inside, but the priest had just left, I was told, on his bicycle, which evoked some giggling, suggesting a bit of a character. I vowed to go back, and get inside this entrancing building. Into the museum too, where the 25,000-year-old remains of a pregnant woman are to be found, one arm under her head, the other protecting the baby in her womb. Flints and horse and ox teeth found with her suggest a huntress. Now, there's a source for speculation.

Now I had started, the whole area stimulated my imagination. Because it is relatively unbesieged by tourists as yet, I could breathe in the atmosphere of ancient sites and buildings and reconstruct the past without crowds and gift shops intruding. I wandered around delving into alleys and courtyards and, in the absence of a decent guidebook, trying to find out answers to my questions by myself.

Boredom, loneliness and depression are all banished, once I get interested in my surroundings. The desire to find out, learn things, discover fresh fields and pastures new, leaves no space in my head for anything else. As long as I don't allow 'if only' to enter my mind, I am utterly consumed with an almost obsessive drive to learn – my brain spirals into negativity if I don't give it work to do. Maybe I need busyness. A bit frantic perhaps, and not a desirable way to live or holiday for most people, but it works for me.

My mother, who hates thunder storms,
Holds up each summer day and shakes
It out suspiciously, lest swarms
Of grape-dark clouds are lurking there;
But when the August weather breaks
And rains begin, and brittle frost
Sharpens the bird-abandoned air,
Her worried summer look is lost,

And I her son, though summer-born
And summer-loving, none the less
Am easier when the leaves are gone
Too often summer days appear
Emblems of perfect happiness
I can't confront: I must await
A time less bold, less rich, less clear:
An autumn more appropriate.

'Mother, Summer, I' by Philip Larkin

4

Hammersmith · Chiswick

CURIOSITY MAY BE THE antidote to many ills but it requires application and a constant fund of new activities to occupy the mind. The trouble is, I have little self-discipline. I need someone wielding a whip to lash me into action otherwise I just flop. Once started there is no stopping me but it is the getting going that is the problem. John was always appalled that I left learning lines until the last minute whilst he pored over a script for days. This book would not be written were it not for a bullying editor and a Rottweiler agent reminding me I have a deadline to observe, for which I have been paid money in advance, that I have already spent.

Returning from my holiday in Puglia to an empty house was a bit of an anti-climax. My cat was as pleased to see me as a cat will deign to be. Wanting a job, I offered to do some babysitting but my daughters have tightly organised lives that cannot schedule in a part-time grandmother. Especially one as inept as I. On top of their jobs they ferry kids to music, nursery school, football, ju-jitsu, sleepovers and what have you. Their days are, of necessity, carefully planned, so when I swan back in after a stint working or a jaunt abroad I cannot expect to disrupt the whole routine. On my return from Puglia I felt pretty redundant. After the newspaper article was delivered, I sank into the usual occupation of out-of-work actors – waiting for the phone to ring. And watching the telly.

Which can be painful. I eye beadily the dozens of suitable roles that I haven't been called upon to play. If the chosen actor is bad, I feel resentful; if she is good, I feel worse. Best to avoid drama. Yet reality shows upset me more. The incitement to hatred of Big Brother is shocking. Poor little Jade Goody has been falsely built into that modern phenomenon 'a celebrity', only to be vilified later, because, as a product of our society and education, she is ignorant and inarticulate – qualities that usually, nowadays, are considered preferable to anything that smacks of that dirty word 'élitism'. God forbid that we should value intelligence and knowledge. This feisty kid coming out of an appalling childhood of neglect had nothing to offer but her personality, which suddenly people decided they didn't like. So she is as thoughtlessly destroyed as she was created.

And yet I crouched on my sofa, watching the programme, transfixed. The inmates of the House have become increasingly more disturbed series by series, until we, the audience, are no better than the people amusing themselves by watching the insane in Bedlam. I watch it, and yes I often do, with my hand over my mouth from embarrassment. One insomniac night, I lighted upon a studio chat show, with a cross-section of the audience, discussing the previous day's happenings. The character judgements were illuminating: 'She's a fat cow', 'Peter fancies Liz', 'She's evil'. A singularly unattractive obese cretin said grandly of a nubile young blonde on the show 'I'd certainly shag 'er', as though bestowing the ultimate accolade: the great British public at their most erudite.

Almost more sickening was a programme in which Donald Trump set about testing young people for the honour of being employed by him. This nasty tacky man, with his silly blow-dried hair and slack mouth, was treated like a god. I suppose he is an idol of the modern religion of materialism, with its tenets of greed and determination, never mind who or what needs to be trampled on to get to the top rung of a rather dubious ladder. If they were lucky, they too could live in a palace of bad taste, and have Barbie look-alikes for partners. I wanted to punch his vacuous pampered face. Instead, I took it out on a chap who made the mistake of climbing up on to my balcony, and – whilst I was sitting looking at him – had the nerve to try to force his way into my house. I leapt up and screamed, 'Fuck off, fuck off, fuck off.' I think even the all-powerful Trump would have backed off and slunk away from this raging old dervish, leaping about shaking her fists.

After he had scuttled away, as I struggled to open the door to pursue him, I was a bit surprised at myself. I like to think of myself as a pacifist, but deep down is the same gutter-snipe aggression I discovered as an evacuee, that will lash out if roused. John had it too. Usually a gentle soul, he could be a snarling animal if challenged. Would I have pushed that fellow over into the river if I had got out on to the balcony in time? I like to think not. But I was incandescent with fury not just with him – silly, scared creature that he turned out to be – but the whole Trumpery of our values, at least as shown on reality television. Maybe that is why the public loved John so much: because, on the whole, he played decent men who aspired to be that old-fashioned thing, good.

I still, three years after his death, could not watch him on the box. It was even worse now I knew he wasn't coming back and I would never see him walking and talking in real life again. I had to speak about him a lot on the book tour for *The Two of Us* and there was an increasing danger of me becoming a profes-sional widow. A role I was not eager to play. I had done daughter, wife, and mother. Now I wanted to be Sheila. Whoever she is. Before I know what I want, I must know who I am. Sounds like a cliché at best – at worst, a ludicrous lack of insight on my part – that I have reached my seventies without knowing the answer. The truth is, this is the first time I have been absolutely on my own, able to behave as I choose. To be what I like. Not in relation to someone else. Not trying to be what they want me to be. As an actor too, so much of my efforts are focused on honing my effect on others. It's a hard habit to break.

As an ageing woman, unless I am recognised from the telly, I am invisible. There is a strange dichotomy in my life. The actor that slaps on the make-up and borrows a designer outfit and jewellery to appear on the Jonathan Ross show is a very different creature from the drab old thing trudging up Chiswick High Road, doing her shopping. If people do recognise me I sense their disappointment, verging on indignation – 'Aren't you Sheila Hancock?' When I am not recognised I am, like all older women, overlooked – as by the pool in Puglia. I find that quite difficult. How can I value myself if people I encounter don't think me worth noticing? Except as my trumped-up *alter ego* on their telly. One day, when the phone showed no sign of ringing, I forced myself up to Chiswick High Road for lunch in the new, trendy Fishworks. My self-esteem was not high when I entered, but it was on the floor when, after curtly taking and delivering my order, for a solid hour I was resolutely ignored by all four of the young waiters. There were no other customers so they were having a ball, flirting with one another, loudly commenting indiscreetly on previous clients, and wondering why they were so 'empty'. One pair of eyes momentarily flicked in my direction as he was giving me the bill, whilst continuing his badinage over my head. I blurted out, 'Oh hello. I'm here. I thought I was invisible.' Thus confirming their assumption that I was a daft old bat.

It comes to us all I suppose, even the most powerful. I was invited to the Woman of the Year lunch – an uplifting occasion, to be surrounded by women who have achieved much from all walks of life – I am always flattered that they should include me. The guest of honour was Margaret Thatcher. Having toured Britain with the RSC in 1982 and seen the devastation wrought by her policies, I felt I could not stay to give her the required ovation, so I made an excuse and quietly left. When I saw the event on the TV that night, I was ashamed of myself. Here was a woman who, whatever you thought of her, gave her whole life to fighting for what she believed was right and now she was a lost, bewildered old lady muttering, 'They told me not to speak.' How tragic has been her ousting by her party and her subsequent distress. And with what glee her former party faithful kicked her out – all those wimpish men fed up with Mummy knowing better.

The sight of this once-sharp mind reduced to confusion made me anxious about the future. From my window I can see a block of flats where my mother lived after my father's death. Or I could see it. The construction of a monstrous new block is gradually obscuring the gracious 1930s building that housed my grieving mother. Aesthetically offensive though this is, I am glad. Because when it has disappeared, so will reminders of the guilt about my treatment of this lonely widow.

My mother and father retired to a caravan in a park near Eastbourne. A suitable retirement for a couple who had led a gypsy existence, moving around the country working in hotels, pubs, factories and shops. They loved it. Dad worked in the club bar, and Mum joined the Women's Institute, becoming their local chairperson. I took her to Eastbourne to get an outfit for her proud trip to the annual rally at the Albert Hall. Life was good for them. They were busy doing things they enjoyed, instead of just slaving to provide a living and a good upbringing for their kids. It lasted only four years. After a jolly night in the club, where Dad demonstrated his high-kicking routine to the customers, he died in twenty minutes in my mother's arms, of a coronary.

She never shed a tear in front of anyone. The funeral and wake were organised and she agreed to come to London to help me with my baby. I got her settled in the tiny flat. Her whole life continued to be dedicated to the care of others. Once it had been my father, my sister and I. Now it would be my then husband Alec and me and baby Ellie Jane. At a time of erratic earnings, I could not afford childcare, so she was constantly on call – a bit different from my sporadic grannying. No child ever had such spotless shoes and white socks. I was grateful, but less tolerant, of an ever-present granny, than she had been of the two that were inflicted on her during her married life. Our lives and lifestyles were worlds apart. My child's behaviour appalled her. Dr Spock was the very devil. Never mind permissiveness and cuddles, what about discipline and nice manners? She had a point. Good manners might make life in our crowded world more tolerable. But, back then, her pursed lips irritated me. When Ellie Jane had eventually gone to bed, at the time she chose, à la Spock, I wanted to have a quiet chat, or maybe a flaming row with my husband, without her condemning eyes on me. Many is the night she must have sat alone, maybe weeping, behind that mercifully disappearing window. Maybe it is justice that I am sitting alone, imagining her sitting alone. Or a gift in the shape of a warning.

Once I belonged to a group that REALLY HAD THE WORD. I fought like hell for them.

But ANOTHER group came along and exposed the word of MY group as shallow and degenerate. They had a BETTER word.

So I quit the first group and lost all the friends I had made.

And I joined up with this NEW group. I fought like hell for them.

But ANOTHER group came round. They exposed the word of MY group as false and materialistic, THEIR word was VERY much better.

So I quit the second group and lost all the friends I had made.

And I joined up with this NEW group. I fought like hell for them.

Then this one guy came along and proved that there wasn't ANY word at all . . . that I should go off as an INDIVIDUAL and GROW!

So I quit the last group and lost all the friends I had made.

And now I sit home alone all day and all I do is GROW.

It would be nice to join up with some others who feel the way I do.

'Groups' by Jules Feiffer

5

Budapest

NO ONE WAS GOING to tell me what to do next. So in the absence of any work, if I didn't want to stagnate, I had to do something myself. Anything. So I booked another holiday, this time in Budapest with a travel firm called Solo. I chose them because they provide trips for people on their own, which do not penalise them for their single state. Solo has no truck with 'single supplements' and, in addition, plans your trip for you. A relief. I could not possibly have got it together sufficiently to do all that myself. I wasn't very excited about going anyway. I had no great burning desire to see Budapest, it was just the only destination still available for that week. Also it occurred to me that the sort of people that needed to go on a singles holiday would possibly not be a barrel of laughs. Would they all pathetic loners, desperate divorcées and wretched widows and widowers?

I was told to look out in the airport for the tour manager, wearing a red tie, standing by Boots the Chemist – the red tie sounded a bit Butlins. I watched for a while, peering from a café on a balcony, ready to scarper if my fellow travellers looked dodgy. The dozen or so people gathering below appeared harmless enough so I ventured to join them for a closer scrutiny. They were all fairly normal – in fact, they seemed more suspicious of the arrival of an actor than I was of them. Mike the tour manager greeted me with a firm handshake and introduced me to the others. They had mostly been on many of these holidays before, some already knew each other from other trips, but they soon started chatting to me, instructing me on the tricks of the trade.

Rule number one: however long the journey, only ever take hand luggage, and of course it must have wheels. With careful selection and washable clothes you can manage, and thereby avert the check-in queue, and the heart-stopping vigil at baggage reclaim. They patiently waited whilst I alone checked in my unnecessarily large bag.

Mike shepherded us on to the plane and by bus to the hotel. It was lovely to be looked after. The hotel was some distance from the centre of Budapest, and a bit like an airport lounge, with bags from all the groups staying there piled in the lobby. There was a mess-up over our rooms, but we had the luxury of having a drink while Mike sorted it out. The staff did not seem overly pleased to see us, but this onslaught of tourism is a relatively new experience for them.

I knew almost nothing about the country beyond the Hungarian blouse I had as a child, which I wore for best. Whilst Mike fought a protracted battle with the hotel manager I sat on my case and leafed through my guidebook to find out more.

It seems Hungary's past history is muddled and tempestuous. The land has been conquered and split up numerous times by various factions. Romans, Attila the Hun, Goths, Longobards (whoever they were), Avars, Magyars, Turks (they get everywhere), and the inevitable Habsburgs (as do they). You name them, they've been there, and left their mark. Poor little Hungary, right in the middle of mainland Europe, has been pushed and pulled hither and thither, usually managing to back the wrong side.

I have never really understood why the shooting of some archduke by a Serb started World War One, but Hungary was right in there, fists flailing, siding with Germany. Wrong. After the war, the Treaty of Trianon punished them, reducing their territory by half, bits going to Czechoslovakia, Romania, Yugoslavia and Austria. As World War Two approached Hitler promised them a bit back if they supported Germany. So they did. Wrong again! They ended up with Budapest virtually destroyed, after a six-week siege between the Germans and Russians. The latter took over, and imposed a particularly nasty brand of socialism on Hungary. This continued until 1991, when the last Russian soldier left, trying to sell his uniform to buy a loaf of bread. A sorry tale all round.

When eventually the rather rudimentary rooms were sorted out there was a panic to dump our bags in them and get aboard the coach for a tour of the city. We were introduced to our guide – a plump, rather dour little woman – who I hoped would fill in the gaps left in my sketchy knowledge. Unfortunately she had a voice that sent me to sleep. She explained that there were two parts of the city, Buda and Pest, on either side of the greyish yellow Danube, linked by several bridges. Sights flashed by outside the bus window as she droned on mechanically over the mike. I jerked awake at one point to hear her point out the Chain Bridge.

'This bridge', she told us, 'was designed by the man who built Barnes Bridge in London, of which it is a copy.'

'Excuse me,' I interrupted. 'Don't you mean Hammersmith Bridge?'

'No, it is Barnes.'

'Sorry, no. I live by Hammersmith Bridge and have a picture of the old one and it is exactly like that.'

'No, it is Barnes. That is what I am told.'

'By whom?'

'The Authority.'

'Well, tell the Authority they are wrong. Barnes is a railway bridge and quite different.'

'*It is Barnes,*' she said implacably.

By this time the rest of the group were shifting uneasily in their seats. They were quite prepared to take her word for it, not to mention that of the ominous Authority, and as far as they were concerned it didn't matter if she said it was like a flying elephant – they just wanted me to shut up.

Which I did for a while as she maundered on about the crumbling grandeur we could glimpse briefly as we sped past in the coach. Many buildings looked badly neglected, and she pointed out bullet holes and blast damage, both from the war and the uprising against Soviet domination in 1956. I longed to hear more about that but I held my tongue because it seemed she had learnt the script given to her by the Authority, parrot fashion, and any divergence threw her into a flap. I even suppressed my curiosity about the wall she fleetingly pointed out as being part of the Jewish ghetto, before she quickly moved on to point out another obscure statue.

I was glad when we were allowed to get out of the coach at the Hungarian National Museum, where we could go off on our own. Before we were released she told us, looking warily in my direction, 'This building is based on the famous British Museum in London.'

'Yes, yes you're right. I can see that. Well done, the Authority,' I said over-enthusiastically, trying to make up for my previous indiscretion. Everyone looked relieved but I noticed no one offered to accompany me round the museum.

We didn't have very long to investigate, for our zealous Mike and my friend the guide were keeping us on the move. One interjection of mine that the group did come to appreciate was prompted by my need for regular shots of caffeine. They would urge me to bleat at regular intervals 'a cup of coffee wouldn't go amiss' or 'I need sustenance, my blood sugar is falling'. If I hadn't we would have dropped dead of thirst and starvation, so frantic was the schedule.

Good restaurants were thin on the ground. Goulash and dumplings and stuffed cabbage, badly cooked, were the standard offering. That first night we went to a huge basement café, where only one man was eating – no surprise there, the food was dreadful. He had chosen to sit by the toilet, the door of which did not swing closed. Each time one of us came out he barked 'shut it', the only English phrase he knew, acquired, presumably, specially for his self-appointed doorman role. I doubt if he had learnt it from *The Sweeney*, but I made several visits to the toilet just to relish the incongruity and imagine how Jack Regan-Thaw would have laughed. I contemplated teaching him 'you're nicked' to add to his repertoire.

Dinner gave me my first chance to talk properly to my fellow soloists. They were a fascinating lot, all with stories to tell. For several of them, Solo had provided life-changing opportunities. The pretty woman who had lost two husbands to cancer had made lasting friends. The neat, elderly spinster whose youth and middle age had been sacrificed to a demanding mother had found a new lease of life after her parent died. There were two solitary years before she plucked up the courage to embark on a weekend Solo trip, since when she had been on sixteen tours all over the world, to make up for lost time. I struck up a delightful friendship with a bluff northerner who reminded me of John's father, a good-looking man whose jokes about people from 'oop north' being more down-to-earth than us snotty southerners belied a person of sophisticated tastes in theatre and music. He kept himself to himself most of the time and it was difficult to tell if that stemmed from shyness or an independent spirit.

I liked them all enough to brave an outing the following evening that, as described by Mike, did not bode well. In my impecunious early theatrical life I had worked as a serving wench at a medieval banquet junket attended by drunken businessmen, so an Authentic Hungarian Folk Evening sounded ominous.

My worst fears were realised. Somewhere in the woods above Buda, we sat uncomfortably in a kitsch imitation hunting lodge, with girls in rumpled national costumes serving truly revolting watery goulash and disgusting wine, and things made 'with every part of goose'. One of the dancers was distressingly like Freddie Mercury, and I mused that all of them had seen better days, only to end up performing on a pocket-handkerchief stage to indifferent tourists, in a travesty of their folk history. There but for the grace of god . . . ? Except I would be hard pushed to think of an English folksong or dance that I could do. 'Greensleeves'? 'Roll Out the Barrel'? 'The Lambeth Walk'? 'The Hokey Cokey'? A gruesome thought but better than sitting at home doing nothing, as I well knew.

The next night a few of us went off on our own, finding a charming pavement restaurant near the Octagon. We were having a quiet chat when a familiar English sound assailed our ears. A party of baying English stags appeared, naked apart from togas made from bedsheets that they had presumably not brought from home. The locals watched in bewilderment as they reeled past, bellowing, unsuccessfully holding together their travesty of Roman nobility. We kept very quiet hoping nobody would know we were British. *Et tu, Brute.*

Going around in coaches with a group of my fellow Brits meant that I was not coming into contact with any local people. Also being hurried around on pre-planned timed visits with the others meant I was tempted to gossip rather than really take things in as I had in Puglia when I was alone. So I decided to leave the group for a bit, to get my own take on this history-heavy city.

Budapest

Anyway I preferred the rattling trams to the soporific coach. The transport system is wonderful in Budapest. They have restored some of the original 1898 stations, which are charming to wait in. It is a chance to have a good peer at the residents. They are not ravishingly beautiful. Their diet does not make for lithe bodies and glowing skins. They look a bit glum, and many bear a striking resemblance to Les Dawson. Mind you, no one's at their best on a crowded tube train. Nor, as I discovered when I made it to one of Budapest's famous Turkish baths, are they much better naked.

I was now in my element. Especially in the glorious baths adjoining the Art Nouveau or Secession Gellert Hotel, all stained glass and wrought iron, one time haunt of rich Jazz Age clients in the twenties. The dumplings had done no favours to the bodies of the present-day bathers; I felt positively svelte in comparison. They took their pleasure rather morosely but I wallowed in the hot steam, cold plunges, bubble pools and mock-Roman swimming-pool. My enjoyment was only slightly marred by the martial attendants, who huffed and puffed in frustration when I didn't immediately understand their complicated orders about towels and cubicles. Their native tongue seems to bear no resemblance to any other language on the planet and most Hungarians do not speak English and are reluctant to speak German. I was disconcerted when, having explicitly described with my hands my request for a massage, a very large man with a bald head led me to a hard bench and ordered me to strip and lie down. This gentle giant proceeded to give me one of the most soothing massages I have ever had. That'll teach me to judge by appearances. And his name was George. Perfect.

Refreshed, I went up the nearby funicular railway to Castle Hill, to visit the Royal Palace. All of this area was ruined when the German army holed up there during the siege, hiding in caves and starving. This fascinated me more than all the rebuilt

79

glories of the churches and palaces that our tour guide fa-
voured.

The Liberation statue, high up on Gellert Hill, intrigued me
too. My guidebook told me that the statue was in the process of
being sculpted as a memorial to the regent Horthy's son when
the Russians invaded. They commandeered it, slapped a massive figure of a Soviet soldier holding a red flag in front, and lo –
a memorial to their great victory in 1945. The soldier was
toppled during the 1956 uprising, then recast and replaced,
only to disappear again when the Russians left in 1991.

There are statues and monuments everywhere in Budapest. I
usually had no idea who or what they were because even if
there was an explanatory plaque – which there frequently
wasn't – it was in Hungarian and therefore completely incomprehensible to me. It was frustrating: I felt I could only skim the
surface of the complex history they commemorated.

On the day the group was going to Heroes' Square, which I
knew to be full of statues, I decided that even the guide's dull
explanation would be better than nothing. Anyway I didn't
want to appear stand-offish, so I went along, determined to
behave well and not ask too many questions. So I was silent as
she reeled off all the worthies that were, or had been, depicted
in the square. It seemed that once a hero not always a hero in
Budapest. The omnipresent Habsburgs had been there – but
they were turfed off by the Communists in 1946. Stalin made
an appearance and was of course now gone. The unknown
soldier was the only person with any staying power – better to
be anonymous than put yourself about too much in this
country.

Our guide explained that the impressive space had been
created in 1896 to celebrate the millennium, 1,000 years since
a gentleman called Árpád led the Magyars to defeat the
Hungarians, which someone decided is when Hungary proper
started. Here we are on shaky ground again. They aren't really

certain of the date. Scholars say it was either 893 or 895 but they couldn't finish all the statues in time, so they changed the date to 896. I couldn't stop myself. I blurted out that I had read somewhere that a Hungarian professor had said, 'We Hungarians like to celebrate the 51st, the 101st and the 1,001st national anniversaries.'

To which the guide said, 'No, it was built in 1896.'

I tried to explain, 'Yes, I know – that was a joke.'

Suddenly she was Edith Evans as Lady Bracknell. 'A joke?' Clearly the concept was entirely foreign to her.

She continued her spiel, pointing out the magnificent group of Árpád and his warriors on over-excited horses.

'Very butch,' I muttered.

Ignoring me she identified Rydwan, the god of war, who was stark naked, in an iron chariot, drawn by two open-mouthed horses scandalised by Mr Rydwan's prettily raised arm.

'Very camp,' I said, having become the horrid naughty girl in the class who taunts the teacher.

'What is this camp?' she snapped.

I demonstrated the pose. 'He looks as if he is saying, "Get me, ducky".'

To which she replied po-faced, 'This is a statue. It does not talk.'

There was no answer to that.

By this time everyone was really fed up with me. I have always been bad at being in a group. I don't like doing what I am told. I am opinionated and argumentative – altogether a thorough nuisance. I would not like to be in a group with me. So for everyone's sake I decided to go off on my own again, along Andrássy út.

The view of this boulevard from Heroes' Square is breathtaking. It has at various times been called Stalin, Hungarian Youth, and People's Republic Avenue. It is a spectacular vista, wider and longer than the Champs-Élysées, and dare I say, potentially more impressive. Many buildings are in a terrible state, but work is going on and I watched mature trees being planted to restore its avenue character. A walk along it sums up the cultural life of Budapest. There are embassies, book shops, cafés, that have long been meeting places of intellectuals, the magnificent Opera House, which rivals that of Vienna, opposite which is the erstwhile home of the state ballet company. There are art galleries and an art college, the homes of Kodály and Liszt. Nearby is the academy where they, and Bartók and Solti, handed on their skills to others. Along this road have walked people who care about and contribute to the elevation and joy of the spirit. They represent everything that makes *homo sapiens* sapient. I marvelled at how far that grunting ape has evolved, as I walked along Andrássy út.

Until.

On this same road, I discovered evidence of the very worst of human endeavour. I looked up at one of the splendid houses that line the avenue, and saw the word TERROR reflected on the wall by the sun, from a canopy attached to the roof, with those letters cut out. Shocked, I went into the house, number 60, and was confronted by an art installation involving a huge Russian tank and a wall reaching to the roof, covered in black-and-white reliefs of hundreds of faces, headed by the word 'victims'. There was no reference to this museum – for that is what it was – in any guidebooks I saw, nor had it been mentioned by Mike or our Hungarian guide.

This building had been the headquarters of the police of the Hungarian Nazi Party, the Arrow Cross, who called it the House of Loyalty – that much-maligned word, debased nowadays by loyalty cards to Tesco and such like. Though perhaps it is good that it should be trivialised, or reassessed as a virtue, if it leads to such malign vendettas as those pursued here against anyone not 'loyal' to their group. When the Arrow Cross vacated the premises after Germany was defeated, the Com-

munist secret police, the ÁVO, later renamed the ÁVH, en-
thusiastically took over the interrogation, torture and killing
facilities. And now, in recognition of the building's terrible
history, it has become the House of Terror Museum.

I was not sure whether I was comforted or troubled by the
museum managing to tell its sordid story with such artistry. All
is atmospherically lit and soundscaped. Thus suffering is
transformed into something beautiful. It made me uneasy to
swing between admiration and revulsion. Perhaps that was the
idea.

There is one brilliantly conceived room containing 800 of the
dossiers compiled by ÁVO on their fellow citizens. They are
stacked on shelves, they paper the floor, the walls, the benches.
The warped bureaucratic nightmare swallows you up, whilst
you watch a film of the so-called trial of Imre Nagy. Although I
could not understand what they were saying, I was mesmerised
by this example of a travesty of justice. People shouting and
vindictive, with this bewildered man seeming to have no one on
his side. It was reminiscent of McCarthyism and the House
(that cosy word again) Committee on Un-American Activities,
when people in the United States, particularly in the film world,
were bullied into admitting they were in, or had been involved
with, the Communist Party. But in the US, although some
people were imprisoned for their beliefs and their refusal to
betray their friends, and although careers were ruined and lives
blighted, no one was actually hanged or shot. In Hungary, at
the same time, you were. For *not* being a Communist. 'Lord,
what fools these mortals be!'

If the film of Nagy's chaotic trial shocked me, the lift into the
basement was even more chilling. Here is no attempt to beautify.
The re-creation of the coal cellars used to imprison, torture and
kill is graphic and squalid. The solitary-confinement cell, the
floor space 60 x 50 cm and only 180 cm high, with two light
bulbs to shine in the prisoner's eyes, day and night. The wet cell,

where they were forced to sit in freezing water. The foxhole, a pitch-black concrete hole, where curling up in a ball, for days on end, was the only option. The treatment room equipped with instruments of torture that defy the belief that they were being used during my lifetime, beneath this street of culture. That is the crux. During my lifetime. And the gallows, a primitive noose imported from another prison in Kozra út that was still in use in 1985.

I was shaking when I surfaced. As a Quaker, I want to believe that 'there is that of God in everyone'. Looking at the faces of the men in the gallery of victimisers, I found it hard. How could this happen? I had some sympathy with a curt comment from a fellow countryman in the visitors' book: 'It should be in English.' Maybe he was as uncomprehending as I. He got short shrift from the next entry. Someone, obviously equally upset, wrote, 'It is, you prat. Leaflets in every room. We are not the master race you know.'

I went back to the hotel and tried to shower away my horror. Then I took a walk by the Danube. I was puzzled by three more sculptures. First, a row of shabby shoes cast in iron, fixed to the esplanade. Worn high heels, crumpled boots, the laces left undone as though just taken off and abandoned. Mysterious and disturbing. There was an inscription – in Hungarian. Puzzled, I went towards the parliament building, and here was the sculpture of a man, sitting staring at the river, obviously depressed, and what looked like a verse written out in front of him. Close by, was a strange little bridge over nothing, with a solitary man standing on it, looking into space. My guidebooks were no help at all, and we were departing the next day. I was tantalised that I was going to leave with so many questions unanswered.

That night, our last, I was having a farewell drink with some of my new friends when my bluff northerner started making derisive remarks about 'pakis'. I was stunned because it was so unexpected. He was a good, funny, kindly man, no ranting BNP maniac.

I considered keeping my mouth shut but with the visions of what hatred of people who differ from you in race or belief can lead to still fresh in my mind after the House of Terror, I turned on him more angrily than I should have done. He was upset. Then he explained that he had never had his ideas questioned before, because all his friends felt the same. He described how Halifax, where he had lived all his life, had been transformed by immigration, and how difficult it was for him to accept.

The next day, as we parted, he graciously thanked me for making him think. The truth was he had made *me* think even more. Was I doing the same thing? Just reciting the liberal hogwash that all *my* friends concurred with? Had I really thought it through for myself?

On the day of our departure I got into conversation with a young woman in a café. She told me she was a tour guide so I asked her about the Terror Museum.

'I would rather not discuss it,' she said. 'My grandfather was imprisoned there for three months.'

She was a university student, intelligent and knowledgeable, and I thought perhaps she could help me understand Budapest better. So when she told me she was about to lead a group on a tour focusing on classical music I wangled myself on to it and stayed another week. I had unfinished business in Budapest, and I reckoned a few concerts would feed my soul.

For the time being, I decided not to scrabble in the filth of 60 Andrássy út, but to explore Budapest's revival of the good things of life. We went to a concert in the Congress Centre, opened in 1975, where Lang Lang was playing Rachmaninoff's Concerto No. 3. The last concert John and I ever went to together was this Chinese pianist's English debut at the Albert

Hall. John had been recently diagnosed with cancer, but we forgot it all, swept away by this star shining so brightly.

Equally uplifting was the glamorous but shabby home of Liszt, hopefully due for restoration. Kodály's, near by, reflects his devotion to Hungarian folk art in the ornaments and books. He worked out a system to make it easier to learn to read music, with the result that at present 60 per cent of Hungarian children sing in a choir. I wish it were the same in our schools. Imagining how barren my life would be without music, it infuriates me that children are not given the chance to appreciate it as I was, a working-class girl, by my teachers. The same with Shakespeare. One of the best performances of a Shakespeare sonnet I have ever witnessed was spoken by a tearaway black girl, backed up by a rap chant. She thought Shakespeare was rubbish, until my daughter Ellie Jane opened her ears to the music of the language in one of the drama workshops she leads.

In a conversation about Kodály with one of the group, a professional who had spent a lifetime working in the service of others, I rather flippantly suggested that perhaps rap was our modern British folk music. I was shocked by the polite but deeply felt diatribe my remark unleashed: 'They are not British. Anyone can come to our country and claim to be British. I find that unacceptable,' and more in the same vein. It transpired that several of the group abhorred the idea of a uniform euro, despite our trouble with the forints. They had a profound love of German, French, and Italian composers but didn't want any part of the European Union. Keep ourselves to ourselves was the theme. Keep out people who abuse our hospitality. In fact keep them out even if they don't.

These were cultured, well-read people so their attitude startled me. What resentment is lurking deep in our psyche. The places they lived in had, unlike my friend from the north, been unaltered by immigration. Yet they were really angry. It all added to the angst I was feeling. Something about this city generally and in particular the Terror Museum had affected me deeply. Everyone must find the museum upsetting but I was disproportionately shaken. I couldn't get it out of my mind. Was it because of my synchronous wartime childhood? Or the awareness that blind hatred is still bubbling beneath polite surfaces?

I have always believed that if you are frightened of something inside or outside of yourself it is best to confront it. Plunge right in and find out all about it and the fear will dissipate. But in this case, why probe old wounds? Perhaps it is best just to hide them beneath a bandage and hope they won't fester. I had discovered ugly blemishes in this city. Would it not be best, like my fellow travellers, to forget about them and enjoy the lovely things? But it seems to me that if you go to a country and don't look at its past, it's like not taking into account your own. It's blinkered and superficial.

I plucked up the courage to tackle the young guide again about her grandfather being imprisoned in 60 Andrássy út. She told me he would never talk about it and she (unlike me) had the decency to leave well alone. She reasoned, 'At a time of fear and intimidation, even best friends and families betray one another.' Many of the people who had persecuted their neighbours were now in public office, and successful in all walks of life, recanting their previous beliefs. She quoted Péter Esterházy, 'In 1989 it was suddenly rush hour on the road to Damascus.'

She was perplexed about how you deal with the past. It is all the vogue now to say sorry for historic crimes committed by our ancestors – slavery, colonisation, Catholic orphanages. The list is endless. What does it achieve? Closure? That is a favourite word nowadays. If only. I had accepted that John was no longer going to come back, but was the subject closed? Forgotten? No way. She protested, 'My generation has done nothing wrong. We want to move on.' So I understood when, as we passed the ghetto area, her only comment was that more Jews survived in Budapest than in any other city. No mention of the 600,000 I knew to have been murdered in Hungary, plus half a million gypsies and numerous political prisoners and gays. I did not demur and spoil the lovely holiday of music and beautiful churches by unwelcome dispute. I dutifully joined the group at the baroque splendour of St Stephen's Basilica. It boasts a very important relic – the mummified forearm of King Stephen. There is actually a Chapel of the Holy Right Hand, which is taken very seriously by the devout. As these things are. But I had had enough. I was baroqued out.

I signed up for a walk to explore Art Nouveau and Bauhaus in Budapest. As a girl who left school at fifteen and had no further conventional education, apart from two wasted years at the, then, toffs' finishing school, RADA, I have an excuse for my ignorance of many subjects. So, it is with only slight shame that I confess I did not know how to pronounce Bauhaus, let alone know what it was.

The first building our guide showed us was in a run-down area on the Buda side, that had me agape. Maybe it was the surfeit of grandeur that made the austere simplicity of Vár-osmajori Jézus Szíve Plébániatemplom so moving. This church, designed by one Árkay Bertalan in 1933, the year of my birth, is made seemingly of rectangular and square stone boxes, straight lines and flat surfaces, apart from some perfectly proportioned arches in the porch. Its walls shone pinkish-white in the sun. Inside was an oasis of calm. Beautifully lit by sunlight from angled plain windows, all was wood and stone and simplicity apart from a stunning modern stained-glass window behind the rudimentary altar. The atmosphere was the most holy of any of the numerous churches I had visited. In a side chapel was one small blaze of light – a dazzling window designed by, of all people, Le Corbusier. He, I had heard of. I knew his influence had been blamed for the monstrous estates thrown up after the war and for the dirty concrete of the National Theatre. This glorious window made me think there must be more to him than his reputation suggested.

We visited an area where some neglected but elegant modernist houses took me back to my childhood. When I lived in Bexleyheath, I regularly passed two, or was it three, strange, obviously grand, houses that made me want to be rich when I grew up so that I too could have a balcony (a luxury unknown in Bexleyheath) in a house that looked like a ship. White, with angled walls and curved windows, they seemed other-worldly, but I now saw they were modernist in design. In Bexleyheath. How on earth did they land there amongst the pebble-dash?

Johannes Schuler, the young architect who took us round, had a convert in me. I suspect he was a bit taken aback by my childish enthusiasm and whooping around but he actually liked answering questions. He was disparaging about the restoration of the city, which in some cases is a matter of painting over the dirt and scars, and scornful of new buildings that were being thrown up. However, he recommended a visit to one that he admired: the Holocaust Memorial Centre, which opened in 2004. No one wanted to come with me – 'too depressing'. But I needed to go. Having suppressed thoughts of the war for most of my life, something about this city made it imperative that I should not allow myself to forget what happened.

The Holocaust Memorial Centre was the only place in Budapest where there was heavy security, and I was searched before going in. When it opened, on 16 April 2004 on the sixtieth anniversary of the ghettoisation of the Jews, there was a bomb threat, and sharpshooters stationed on the roofs. It is nice to think that the police were protecting the Jews, which is a change from their wartime history.

It is indeed a splendid building. The modern part is all strange angles and jarring shapes, to depict the twisted horror of the Holocaust, but the contrast of grass and pinkish shades of pastel stone and marble makes it extraordinarily peaceful. The new construction incorporates a synagogue that was used as an internment camp to herd Jews before disbursing them to the camps in 1944. It was left derelict and empty during the Communist era, but is now returned to its past glory.

There were two exhibitions taking place. The main one using film and sound, started with a touching reminder of Jewish life before the war: Jewish men and women working with their neighbours, singing and dancing, celebrating weddings. Then we traced the yellow stars, the exclusion laws, the imprisonment under the Arrow Cross Hungarian Nazis. With the arrival of the Germans in 1944, and in particular Eichmann, occurred one of the quickest exterminations of Jews in any country. In fifty-six days, 437,402 Jews in Hungary were rounded up by Hungarian army and police, and deported to camps, mainly Auschwitz, and most of them murdered.

I knew the stories of people crowded and locked into cattle trucks for days on end with no food, water or lavatories, but here was an exhibition of graphic photos of these events from an album discovered by Lily Jacob, a prisoner at Auschwitz. When she heard the sounds of the US troops liberating the camp, Jacob dragged herself, suffering from typhoid and weighing only forty kilos, to the SS barracks, in search of something to keep her warm. There, she found an album, which presumably the owner had forgotten to destroy before he fled the approaching liberators. In it were 200 photos, some of them of the family and friends she had lost.

Two photographers had been given permission by the SS to photograph the arrival and selection process of some of the Hungarian Jews arriving at Auschwitz. These two men clambered on wagons, and moved in and out between hordes of bewildered men, women, and children, to take their dreadful photographs. What can have possessed them to record such shameful events so proudly and meticulously? The rows, five abreast, awaiting selection, women and children one side, men the other. Babies struggling in their mothers' arms, small frightened children gazing with big eyes at the man with the camera. Indolent soldiers, sloping around watching, whilst their superiors waved their hands, making life and death selections of who would be worked and starved to death, and who sent straight to the gas chambers. One shot is carefully composed to include a lorry, which is parked alongside the queue, loaded with canisters of zyclone gas that will soon choke to death most of the people that they are photographing. A perfectly framed wide shot shows women massed in regimental lines, with recently shaved heads, their dirty frocks covering their shaven pubic hair, trying desperately to retain some dignity in front of a camera. In one photo, an older woman in glasses is standing tall, looking defiantly into the lens, surrounded by younger frightened women clutching children, and one suspects that she knows the building behind them is the crematorium. God knows what our gallant photographers hoped to achieve by that compositon, but not, one suspects, the study of a noble woman. There is an eerie calm in most of the pictures. The prisoners surely cannot have known what was happening; although, in one shot, an old lady is struggling violently, with three men trying to quieten her.

The other exhibition in the museum was the story of the fate of the Roma. One of the most shocking photos, which will be engraved on my soul for ever, is of a group of young naked Roma women, arms folded over their bare breasts, or holding on to one another, as they stumble down a heap of earth, with a row of SS men, uniformed in greatcoats, helmets and boots, in the background waiting to fire their bullets into the soft womanly bodies.

During that week I read a book called *Fateless* by Imre Kertész. It tells the story of a young Jewish boy from Budapest.

It brings to bitter life the squalor of that time. It proves how impossible, even if you were not one of the people who herded the prisoners to the depots, it would have been not to see it happening. Or, indeed, watch, while some were marched to the banks of the Danube, murdered and pitched into the river. That was what the row of shoes I had seen was commemorating. I could not fathom what they were, for who could readily imagine such an event, on that very place that I was walking, on that sunny day? Not in some bygone primitive age but when I was ten years old.

Kertész, and Primo Levi, write of how the human spark could survive in the camps. Not always nobly, but merely to survive was noble. Trying to create order out of chaos. Organising yourself. Dividing your ration of one lump of bread to last for two meals. On the marches, and endless standing out in the freezing cold as punishment or torture, placing yourself in the middle, so other bodies helped to keep you upright. Resting on work parties, when the guard looked the other way, if only for a minute, to conserve some of your skeletal energy. When the transports arrived, the prisoners on duty, forced to unload the half-dead arrivals, whispered warnings to the youngsters that they must say they were over sixteen and healthy so as not to be gassed straightaway. And never to say if they were a twin, lest Mengele should use them for his vile experiments. When you are dying, as even the living were, there is no great selfless friendship. If your friend died on the bunk beside you, despite the stench and the lice, you kept it quiet for as long as possible, and ate his paltry ration as well as your own.

I left the Holocaust Memorial Centre depressed by the depths of depravity to which man can descend. The fact is that there are always amongst us people who will use warped idealism to excuse bestial behaviour. Devotion to a group, a cause – the

Budapest

perfect Aryan society, unified Germany, or Hungary, jihad. To obey orders, no matter what. And there are others who are prepared to turn the other way.

The question in my mind is would I be either of these? I was once a Young Communist; I too wanted to impose my version of a better world. I have also kept quiet when it would have been better to 'speak truth to power'. Or would I, please God, if really tested, be like the local people in the testimonies, who smuggled food into the Jewish and Roma ghettos for their neighbours? Who hid people in their lofts and cellars?

Honourable, too, were the people like Bartók and Solti, who left their homeland in protest or Prime Minister Teleki, who, when he could not persuade his country not to join Germany in attacking Yugoslavia, committed suicide. Surely as a public protest, not as a way out. The evocative statue I had seen of the sad man staring at the Danube was Attila József, a poet who wrote inspirationally about his homeland, and also killed himself in 1937, when he was just thirty-two years old. The shame and despair about the way their country was going was unbearable to them all.

More recently in a speech on Holocaust memorial day Ferenc Gyurcsány, their less than perfect prime minister said, 'We let their hands go. We were not courageous enough, and we were not strong enough to keep them, to keep them with us. We let the evil be stronger than ourselves. We let this happen as Hungarians, Slovaks, Czechs; we let this happen as Europeans.'

The last statue that had puzzled me, the lone man on the bridge over nothing, turned out to be Imre Nagy, the man I had seen in the mock-trial film in the House of Terror. He was a committed Communist, who was horrified to see the excesses to which Communism led his country. When Khrushchev denounced Stalin in 1956, Hungarian students and factory workers rallied, leading to a full-scale uprising. Imre Nagy joined them, which led to his trial as shown in the House of

93

Terror, and two years later, his execution. The revolution was quelled by the arrival of Russian tanks. The students on the radio appealed for the world to help them. But we didn't: 2500 died, 20,000 were severely wounded and 200,000 fled their native land, to become exiled in countries hopefully more welcoming to them than we sometimes are towards our asylum seekers.

We must protest, even – maybe especially – us oldies. Not just about pensions and the NHS, but on behalf of those who are 'not like us' – cocklers dying in our sea, and a lorryload of Chinese suffocating to death because of our ludicrously inefficient asylum system. Age is no excuse for opting out. When you are old, there is more free time to engage in a fight. At worst, it is something to pass the time if you are lonely. We can even protest online. A click with a mouse seems a poor substitute for marching to Aldermaston but perhaps more befits our years. But voices must be raised.

The past in Budapest feels very recent. They prefer to forget the pain but the monuments are there if you look. There is a wonderful sculpture of a weeping willow, the leaves engraved with the names of the dead, on the site of one of the gates to the ghetto, paid for in part by the film star Tony Curtis, an American Hungarian Jew. I hope there will not come a time when that is removed like so many other memorials in the city.

I identify with Budapest. Here is a place desperate to move on. Wanting to obliterate its past. But underneath there are unresolved questions; lurking fears and uncertainties. They haunt me too and fill me with melancholy.

If life seems jolly rotten
There's something you've forgotten
And that's to laugh and smile and dance and sing.
When you're feeling in the dumps
Don't be silly chumps
Just purse your lips and whistle – that's the thing.

And . . . always look on the bright side of life . . .
Always look on the light side of life . . .

From 'Always Look on the Bright Side of Life'
by Eric Idle,
from Monty Python's *Life of Brian*

6

Gatwick · Antibes · Africa

I HAD TO GO to France to check on progress of the house sale. Having now faced my fear of flying budget airlines I deserted BA for the much cheaper easyJet to Marseilles. I regretted it when they announced that the plane was postponed for two hours.

No reason was given for the delay, no one to ask, just wait and put up with it, in the lounge packed with furious adults and fractious children. I chose to pay £19 and wait in the special lounge where at least I could sit down. Not as swish as those of BA, but better than the seething ghastliness downstairs. After about half an hour, suddenly my flight was flashed up to depart in fifteen minutes from Gate 12. The friendly woman on the desk phoned to check this sudden change and yes, it was correct. I tore over, only to discover not a soul in the waiting area and the door locked. In desperation, I pushed the emergency button and it opened, setting off a loud alarm. I ran down to the plane, to be confronted by a startled captain and crew who, when they realised I wasn't a suicide bomber, told me they were going to Ireland, but I could join them if I wished.

Returning to the holding area, I again pushed an alarm to get out. No one arrested, or even looked at, me as I emerged, klaxons blaring. I decided to try Gate 11, from where the plane had been previously planned to depart. Sweating and panicky, I rushed up to the girl on the desk, who was reading a magazine, and asked if I could go to the plane. It was some time before she tore her eyes away from the page, and looked at me with studied indifference. Eventually she sighed, 'It i'n't even 'ere yet.' I burbled out my story, and insisted that the information board said it was, and was she sure? Was I still at the wrong gate? Maybe it is because easyJet are not responsible for ground staff at Gatwick but she could not have been more uninterested. She could barely be bothered to mouth her monosyllabic replies, and looked at me with cold disdain. Eventually she ordered me to stand outside the door and wait. There was an empty lounge with seats beside her, but she drawled that it was 'against the rules' to wait in there or where I was standing. She insisted that I move ten feet away from her.

This two-year-old, nasty piece of work, in her uniform, was thoroughly comfortable with the discomfort of a distraught old woman. Her look towards me was a mixture of malice and smirking superiority. She was enjoying herself. She continued to sit, relishing her authority to force a growing crowd of confused people, including screaming kids and fragile old folk, to wait in the corridor, merely shrugging if anyone asked what was going on.

When her co-worker arrived, she laughed and joked with her, occasionally glancing at me to see if I was watching what fun she was having, and how little she cared about all of us standing hot and wretched in our queue. Never once did she break off her conversation to give us information or even to explain the misinformation. After about an hour, the phone rang, she tidied her desk, and without looking up summoned us in, with a languid reluctant flap of her hand.

I seemed to be the only person in the docile queue that was hopping mad at our treatment. If others had backed me up we could have started a revolution and forced her to use her phone to get some information rather than having giggling conversations on it with her friends. Instead of which I ended up feeling like a troublemaker and the girl, unchallenged, would see no reason to behave differently in the future. Something in this girl's background, or psyche, or life experience, made her vindictive, which a little bit of power and a uniform had unleashed. In a small way, admittedly; Budapest, this was not. But she could not imagine the difficulties of the woman holding a tiny baby, whilst trying to stop a toddler running away. She was devoid of empathy. An actor like me is inclined to overdo the empathy because it is part of our job to put ourselves in other people's shoes, but I believe that lack of it is at the root of a hell of a lot of problems.

Arriving in France, with all this whirling around my brain, as things tend to when you have no one with whom to talk it out of your system, I was struck by the difference in empathy levels. It was a bit late to start appreciating my way of life in France when I was planning to leave, and anyway all country people are more empathetic than townies, but in Apt, where I do my shopping, the streets are pristine, because people do not toss cigarette packets out of car windows or sling down their empty fast-food cartons – and not just because they don't eat much fast food. As for the dreaded mobile phone – in Apt I see scarcely anyone babbling mindlessly into one, oblivious to the irritation, or in my case apoplectic rage, of the trapped listeners forced to eavesdrop on their tedious lives. Are these babblers not aware of the world around them?

Similarly the people at the airport, using their wheelie cases as mowers, or others whirling around knocking everyone flying with their rucksacks. They don't need to contain bombs, they have always been lethal weapons. The cyclists on pavements, the women barging their way through with battering prams, all have no sense of the space around them, or of the sensibility of the people within it. Lack of empathy. The same applies to the vomit and the urine in the streets of Liverpool and elsewhere that our fellow citizens inflict on the rest of us during their desperate weekend revelry. All of which rumination depressed me unutterably. Particularly the realisation that I am becoming the sort of dreary old fart who moans that it wasn't like this when I was a gal. But it wasn't.

In Saignon I lay in the Phwah bed, staring at the ceiling, imagining John's usual, 'Yes all right, dear, calm down, calm down.' I tried to stop thinking of the brilliantly cutting things I should have said to the hapless airport employee. Yes, she was becoming hapless to me now. My empathy vibes were flowing again. Pretty soon my rage had ebbed and left me feeling guilty. After a sleepless night I felt old and tired as I arranged for a man to fell and trim some trees in the garden to neaten it up for prospective buyers. Next morning the dishwasher broke, forcing me to unload it and wash up using John's old Brillo pads and linen cloths. Beset by gloom, I decided to drive to Antibes and visit my sister.

My sister Billie is a character. For a while, she worked in a charity shop in Oulton Broad and a report by the district manager described her as 'a lovely sprightly little lady with blue hair'. At the time, it was an effort to be sprightly, as she had recently lost her husband of fifty years, and was wretched at the thought of spending the rest of her life in the Broads: a bleak and watery place in which to end one's days alone. Especially someone with her history.

So, she sold her house, put her agoraphobic cat in a basket, and they both moved to Antibes. She was seventy-nine. Her body is now bent forward, possibly aggravated by her propensity to race through life like a bulldozer, always leaving me and everyone else trailing a few yards behind her. She will chatter away at a rate of knots to anyone, including total strangers, her thoughts running ahead of her voice, so the sense is sometimes garbled. Malapropisms abound. She will tell you long stories about Gaby, Vicky, Zizi, Tom, Dick and Harry, forgetting that you have no idea who they are. The period of childhood during which I lived with her I spent in monk-like silence, because I couldn't get a word in edgeways. But I worshipped her.

As a child she was small and chubby-cheeked, with beautiful nut-brown curls, whereas I was lanky and thin with mousy straight hair. She was vivacious, funny and talented. I was sullen, dull and studious. My huge feet didn't dance, but hers twinkled and twirled to the delight of all who beheld her. When we lived in a pub in Berkshire she went to dancing classes at the Italia Conti school in Holborn, travelling up in the guard's van, and met at the other end by a couple who thought she was so brilliant and adorable that they begged to adopt her. When she won a scholarship for full-time training at Conti's, my dad got a job in the Carpenter's Arms in King's Cross to be near the school. We both went to Ely Place Convent because they let her have the afternoons off to attend classes in tap, ballet, acrobatics, modern dance, singing and acting.

Although we spent little time together when I was young, she is the only link that I have left to my childhood. Budapest had sent thoughts of the war whirling round my brain and I wondered whether, being seven years older than me, she would remember it more clearly and perhaps shed light on why it was that I still found it so disturbing. What happened to *her* during those years? And how did she feel about it?

Her career was very different to mine though we both went on the stage. She went into what was called 'variety' and I opted for mainly 'straight acting' – the very names demonstrate which was the jollier option. Billie's stories are hilarious and always guaranteed to make me laugh but this time I wanted to discuss her wartime experiences. I knew she had been right in the thick of it – I could remember my parents' worry – and I wanted to know how badly it had affected her. On the face of it, it was a dreadful experience for a teenage girl. But not in Billie's version.

It is difficult to keep her on track as her brain darts all over the place, but I did my best to cross-examine her. My repeated 'and how did you feel about that?' was laughed off or met with a blank stare. I had to glean for myself what this young girl might have gone through from the funny stories she told me.

Her first job at the start of the war, when she was about fifteen, was in the pantomime *Jack and Jill*, put on by the impresario Jack Hylton at the Palace Theatre, produced in rather a hurry in an effort to keep his precious showgirls out of battledress. These languid lasses were reluctant to do much more on stage than pose sulkily, especially when they saw the tatty costumes, inherited from a touring panto, that they were expected to wear. In one number they donned pink taffeta short dresses, poke bonnets, white socks and patent shoes, rather disturbingly pretending to be children, singing Jack and Jill to sleep in a forest. Surely some confusion in plots here. Undaunted, they stood in showgirl poses, singing a ditty that went:

> *Hush, hush do not make a noise,*
> *Lightly tread upon the air.*
> *All the little girls and boys,*
> *Make no sound.*

(Billie demonstrates the cloying harmony.)

> *Ah, ah, ah, ah*
> *Ah, ah, ah, ah*

(Re-enacted by Billie, my sister and the rest of the chorus enter, fingers on lips, creeping on their toes.)

Ah, ah, ah,
Ah, ah, ah.
Hush, Hush, Hush.

Whereupon my sister and the rest of the young dancers broke into a spirited tap dance. At the dress rehearsal, Mr Hylton woke with a start in the stalls and, brandishing his whisky bottle, shouted, 'Jesus Christ, what's that? Get 'em off. The bleeding babes are meant to be sleeping.'

There was little thought to protect youngsters in the theatre in those days and they were not well looked after. The showgirls were higher in the pecking order than the chorus, and would force Billie, being the youngest in the company, to break the rule and go out between shows to get buns from Maison Bertaux. If she refused, her head was pushed into the trough of water used to extinguish incendiary bombs. Our union Equity would have something to say about that nowadays but Billie seemed quite sanguine about it. 'That's how it was.'

She had no rest during the show as the chorus dressing room was miles from the stage so they were forced to sit on benches in the wings, waiting for their next entrance, and had to use the time to knit for the troops.

Conditions were pretty vile in the theatre in London during the war. Rats from the bombed sewers roamed the theatre, and audiences prepared to brave the air raids were sparse. The fifteen-year-old Billie learnt to dodge the bombs and told me horrific stories as though they were nothing special. On one occasion, they heard that a bomb had fallen in the Pall Mall area. One of the girls' parents had a pub in an alley there. After the show, Billie accompanied her to see what had happened. The pub was completely destroyed by a bomb. The two girls rushed around London trying to locate her family. The parents were in a rest centre, but they found her brother's mutilated body in a temporary morgue. Yet they were back next day, giving it their all at the Palace Theatre.

The whole company showed great resilience. Billie roared with laughter as she told me about a rather camp chorus boy in the show who was sitting on a lavatory, with his trousers down, when a bomb sliced the house and left him, stranded, revealed to the world. Valiantly rescued by a butch fireman on a ladder, he was devastated that his hair was such a mess.

She appeared in a couple of other shows before gradually the theatres in London closed down, unable to compete with Mr Hitler's firework display. So Billie volunteered for ENSA. The initials stood for Entertainments National Service Association but were more commonly interpreted as Every Night Something Awful.

The headquarters were based at the Theatre Royal, Drury Lane, where people were teamed up and formed into acts and shows. Billie was paired with her kooky friend Bobby Pett, into what was known as a 'sister act'. They joined the cacophony of rehearsals, grabbing any space they could backstage, in the bars, or the stalls, to create a performance. When I was doing the band call of *Sweeney Todd* in the same dress-circle bar and heard for the first time the huge orchestra playing the magnificent score of Sondheim's music, I couldn't help thinking of my sister and Bobby, working out their dance steps, as they hummed a melody, and clapped out the beat.

The two girls first of all toured all over England, and were then told to congregate at Drury Lane for an overseas assignment. They were taken to Liverpool, where they boarded the *Andes*, a luxury-liner-turned-troopship, crowded with hundreds of men, two nurses and them. They were much sought after, particularly after they gave a performance of their new act, which involved stripping off different layers of costume until they were left in very snazzy corsets. The nurses felt considerably disadvantaged in their uniforms.

During the long time at sea, my sister complained to the captain that the man steering the boat wasn't very good, as they were zigzagging all over the place. It was only when they arrived that he explained they had been dodging U-boats, the German submarines. When she went up the gangplank at Freetown, my sixteen-year-old sister was confronted with, in her words 'my first sight of a man's willy and it was black'. They were helped on shore by semi-naked black residents.

After several performances in Freetown, they embarked on an odyssey, on which they were the first white women to set foot in certain areas of east, west, north, south and central Africa, covering as much ground as any redoubtable Victorian woman explorer. They travelled by small plane, train, but mostly in an open jeep, through the bush to remote camps. They wore masks over their faces with the eyes cut out to protect them from the red dust, frightening the natives to death. Their lavatory was the side of the jeep, with a sergeant keeping watch for curious villagers, snakes and wild animals. The first place they slept in was a mud hut where they hung their washed undies up on a string line that a thief hooked out of an open window; they had to sew up the front of some men's pants to wear. The bush radio soon spread the story, so they would be greeted by 'Oh, you're the girls with no knickers.'

Their attempts to give the women-hungry troops something pretty to look at were slightly marred by Bobby being violently carsick, and often being carried off the jeep comatose, and both of them being bright yellow from the anti-malaria drugs. They learnt to rig up a shower with a tin can and string, and to make up in the jeep wing mirrors. Then they leapt on to the platform composed of oilcans and planks to perform their seductive numbers. The arm gestures were altered to wage a constant battle with greasepaint-loving mosquitoes. One night, in the languorously sophisticated song, 'I'm Blasé', Bobby frantically walloped at a swarm of flying insects with her long cigarette holder, and disappeared down the back of the stage. A couple of soldiers hoisted her back, replaced her bent cigarette in the holder, and she continued undaunted.

They suffered from sandfly fever, malaria, dysentery, and the wonderful Bobby eventually died very young from TB, which Billie is convinced started during their months in Africa. On one occasion, an army doctor gave Billie an overdose of smallpox vaccination and she contracted a mild case of the disease – she bears the scars to this day. The rest of the company had to continue and left her for a month in quarantine, in a hut guarded by an army private. Another time, they gave a lift to an airman going to Accra, and the day after they arrived had to have a series of painful injections in their stomachs, as he had developed bubonic plague. No wonder, considering many nights were spent throwing things at large rats approaching their beds.

They always had guards assigned to them, as they were such a curiosity, both with the troops and the Africans. In Tobruk, their protection was provided by German prisoners. In one village, Billie ventured out alone and was surrounded by children pushing and prodding her, trying to pull out bits of her hair. She was rescued by a man in a grass skirt and painted mask, who turned out to be the Oxford-educated local witch doctor. He told her, in perfect English, that it was best to stay in the army camp, to which he escorted her back.

Billie has an ancient leather writing case on which she wrote the names of all the places she visited. There can be few people that have travelled so extensively in Africa, especially in those days before proper roads and towns. It was a remarkable achievement for a girl of sixteen. She makes it all sound a great lark, even the fact that, after one horrendous journey, when for once she was billeted in a comfortable hotel in Nairobi, she couldn't stop shaking and crying for two full days. 'What a bloody waste,' was her only comment.

By the same token, she is vague about the sex-starved men who must have become enamoured of her. One clue came, when in the writing case I found a signed card saying, 'I thank God that he left the door of heaven open long enough to let an angel out.'

'Who was Paul?' I asked.

A quick glance at the card, a shrug, 'Gawd knows.'

Once a very handsome ex-serviceman came to our house to pick her up on a motorbike. Billie, in a tight skirt and pert little hat, was appalled, and palmed him off with me, then a twelve-year-old girl. I was thrilled to ride pillion down to Hastings but I doubt if he was as happy. Although he did return to take me to several speedway races. I have loved the smell of diesel oil ever since.

After the war, my sister played the music halls with various sister acts. Then, when playing in the chorus of the Folies-Bergère at the Prince of Wales Theatre in London, she fell in love with one of the three Barbour brothers, who performed an act on stilts. She and her husband Roy then formed their own act, dancing on stilts and big wooden boots, and manipulating puppets, which my brilliant sister made, as well as juggling and – as if that wasn't enough – occasionally a dog and a chimp joined the act. They toured in a beautiful old caravan. Eventually television killed variety theatre in England and they moved to Paris, where they lived for twenty-odd years.

She was of an age during the war when many of her friends, people she worked with and those she entertained in ENSA, were killed, but none of this has blighted her life. In Paris their flat became a meeting place for performers of all nationalities. It was tiny, but Billie managed to rustle up splendid meals for all and sundry. They travelled throughout Europe. I loved visiting them when they were in theatres like the Lido. The productions were spectacular and the nudes ravishingly beautiful. The same girls that sat in the flat, stuffing themselves with food, or that would be backstage, leaning stark naked against a wall, chatting casually to my brother-in-law, transformed into goddesses on stage. One Casino de Paris show was one of the most ravishing pieces of theatre that I have ever seen. It starred Zizi Jeanmaire, and was designed by Erté with costumes by Yves St Laurent. The music was written by Serge Gainsbourg, Michel Colombier and Michel Legrand. Breathtaking.

Some of the places Billie performed were surprising. I visited her when she and Roy were playing a club in Marseilles. I had gone to tell her I was expecting my first baby. All the lovely artistes were thrilled for me, and one exceptionally pretty sweetie insisted on taking me to buy a baby outfit. It was years later that Billie happened to mention that she was a transsexual, as were the entire cast. Some had had the operation, some not, but all were exquisite.

My sister is without any racial or sexual prejudice. It just doesn't occur to her. She has worked and lived with so many different races and creeds, and does not regard anywhere as her home. She has mostly lived in France, but her French is still far from perfect, although she has smatterings of many languages, usually with reference to digs and tempos. She was in many countries at crucial times of their history – South Africa in 1953, Israel in 1961, Yugoslavia in 1963, Thailand in 1966, Iraq in 1978 – yet when I question her about the political situation in the countries she visited she is indifferent. She was in Vietnam in 1967 when the use of Agent Orange was at its peak. US troops and Vietnamese civilians were dying in their thousands, but her main objection was that the audiences were stoned out of their minds. She couldn't allow herself to contemplate why that might be.

In 1964, three years after the Wall went up, she and Roy played the Friedrichstadtpalast in East Berlin next door to

Brecht's Berliner Ensemble theatre. Brecht was dead by then, but she regularly met 'his nice wife', when they ate together in a canteen. Helene Weigel must surely have adored Billie's blithe spirit. When the Swedish pop band were sacked on the first night, she thought it was a shame because they were rather good and didn't think that they were 'a bad influence'. When she saw the police searching the dustbins of her flat, she took it all in her stride, and still left her radio out for the concierge to listen to forbidden programmes. She had smuggled it through the Wall, although some magazines had been confiscated. Checkpoint Charlie, that monstrous imposition on people's liberties, was a 'bloody nuisance' to Billie because of the queues, though she was pleased that a poster of their act was stuck on the infamous Wall. She thought it rotten that the principal dancer in the company couldn't perform in West Berlin. Not because of the fundamental injustice but because she'd miss out on the better money in the West. I dare say the dancer made the best of a bad job, too. There is a marvellous acceptance of the status quo amongst variety artists because of the peripatetic nature of their job.

My sister and brother-in-law entertained in Saddam Hussein's Habbaniya Tourist Village in 1981. It was later an army camp, and is now a refugee centre, but then it was an exclusive retreat frequented by Hussein's élite, including his infamous half-brother, the intelligence chief Barzan, his much-respected uncle, various relatives and, on occasion, his vile sons – 'But they weren't vile then, they were young and very polite.' She is not sure if she met Hussein himself as there were so many doubles. Billie had no idea of what they were up to. They treated her with great courtesy, which was all she cared about. She did a daily kids' entertainment and on one occasion told a noisy pushy child to shut up and sit down. The next day a man in a jeep, carrying a gun, drew up beside her, demanding an explanation of the incident.

Billie gave him a mouthful: 'He's spoiling it for all the others. You need to teach him some manners.'

'Oh really?' The onlookers held their breath.

'Yes, I've told him he can't come to the show again if he doesn't behave.'

The man spluttered a bit, but when it looked as though Billie was about to have another go he said quickly, 'Thank you – you did the right thing.' And drove off.

The child turned out to be a close relative of Hussein. Presumably his minion was more frightened of Billie than he was of the boss.

One farcical event happened when my sister arranged a Christmas party for the children, for which she made a red costume and a white cotton-wool beard for some poor Arab to play Santa Claus. It was such a success that she was made to repeat it on New Year's Day despite her protests that it was not done. She seems to have thoroughly enjoyed herself at this place, christened Paradise Prison by the staff, despite making sure she talked critically only in the open air, in case her bungalow was bugged. Even this didn't unduly worry her. 'That's the way they are.'

My sister has pranced gaily through a remarkable life, quite unaware of her uniqueness. She drives me mad, as sisters do, but I am inordinately proud of her. Her attitude is so different from mine; she makes me feel very boring as I angst my way through life, while she just accepts everything at face value. Folk can be black, white, purple, gay, transvestite, transsexual, whatever they like as long as they are nice and a good audience. If the lighting is good and the sound system works on the makeshift stage, a group of filthy mud huts in a clearing is 'lovely'. Her life has been, and is now, fun, despite considerable hardship.

After probing her memories, we went for a walk along the front in Antibes. I noticed a young woman, spread-eagled on a lilo, floating in the sun. I remembered the bliss of doing that when your body was beautiful and you didn't care about the two old biddies staring at you.

'I wouldn't do that now. Would you, Bill?'

'Why on earth not? I come swimming here all the time.'

Bold, brave, regardless Billie.

When I first came to East Anglia in 1964, I was twenty-five years old. I did not notice the huge skies. I had no time to stand and stare . . . I could not give in to wonder because there in my mind's eye was I. Like all young people I was preoccupied with inventing myself . . . I walk the same paths now that I walked twenty-five years ago, but now I am not aware of the figure I am cutting. I neither expect nor hope to be noticed. I am hoping only to take in what is happening around me . . . I want to be open to everything, to be agog, spellbound.

From *The Change* by Germaine Greer

7

Thailand

INSPIRED BY MY SISTER'S insouciance I resolved to make a positive effort to, as she, my mother and Monty Python would say, 'look on the bright side'. My glass in future would be half full rather than half empty. It is patently a happier way to live life, so it is absurd not to make an effort to do it. But I needed to work at it as if I were playing a part. It seemed sensible to start the exercise with a complete change of scene, where old bad habits could be more easily broken.

After my not altogether successful attempts to be part of a group holiday, I decided to go it alone; put myself to the test of going a long way, to a different culture, and be open to the lovely things it had to offer. To give in to wonder and not to allow thoughts of self, or darkness, to get in the way. Just to take in what is happening around me, without suspicion. Tomorrow fresh woods and pastures new with no mucky mud.

Someone suggested that I go camping – get back to nature. I had only ever camped once, if you discount revue with Kenneth Williams. I was in the Brownies. Again, the group thing didn't work for me. I seemed the only one of a dozen over-excited nine-year-olds that found the whole thing appalling. Eating a burnt sausage, with the scorched fingers that had held it on a stick in the bonfire, dancing round a papier-mâché toadstool, chanting twit twoo. Sitting cross-legged in wet grass, round a damply smouldering bonfire, singing:

> *Kookaburra sits in the old gum tree*
> *Merry merry king of the bush is he,*
> *Laugh kookaburra, laugh kookaburra*
> *Gay your life must be.*

Whatever this kookaburra thing was on, it was having a damn sight better time than me. The jolly ditty was sung as a round, and I always got lost, ending up mouthing silently like John Redwood, lest Brown Owl strip me of my singing badge.

An article in a travel magazine proposed a much better idea. A luxury spa in Thailand; massage, reflexology, saunas and fabulous food. With my penchant for spas, what could be more ideal? Even the suggestion that it was 'best for couples in search of peace and seclusion' didn't deter me. I visualised brushing up my meditation techniques in this Buddhist country and you don't need a partner for that. With the help of a few nice pills and ciggies I had spent a lot of the sixties in a trance, but despite the counsel of the Maharishi I have never quite got the hang of meditation. I always end up with my brain in a frantic whirl rather than in a state of bliss, but it is never too late to learn and I could do with some of the old peace and love now.

The plane trip was a dream. Beautiful Thai maidens in iridescent silk gowns, catering to my needs. It was worth every penny of the extra fortune to go business class. The only snag was I had a terrible hacking cough, not helped by the plane air-conditioning, but soothed by the fragrant tisanes created somehow in mid-air by the diminutive ministering angels.

There was a small wait in Bangkok when some passengers left and others boarded. I had foolishly broken my rule of hand luggage only, so, after landing in Chiang Mai, I followed the crowd to baggage reclaim. I waited to spot my bag on the carousel. Cases came and went, heaved off and away by happy travellers. They dwindled to nothing and still I waited, panicking now. Perhaps it had been mistakenly taken off at Bangkok when a lot of people disembarked? Eventually it was just me, with a thumping heart, standing by an empty luggage belt. My bag was missing. And by then there was not a soul around to ask for help. I searched for anyone in authority, but the place was deserted. Eventually a tiny bow-legged chap scuttled through. I forcibly stopped him and mimed bags being lost. It scared him to death. When I showed him my ticket, he pointed into the distance and scampered away, darting terrified looks over his shoulder. I followed the direction of his finger, out of a door, down a long deserted corridor, and eventually into another room, where, miraculously, my bag was sitting all on its own, on another belt. There was still no one around, so I picked it up and struggled out of the airport.

Outside, I could barely breathe. Chiang Mai reminded me of London before the clean air legislation. The whole place was enshrouded in a filthy fog. In the taxi to the hotel I was like Mimi dying of consumption in *La Bohème*. Seeing the hordes of battered old cars belching exhaust fumes, I could understand the reason for the air pollution. The streets were crowded with ramshackle houses and what looked like shops piled high with junk. This dilapidation continued until we came to an ornate entrance. Then we entered another world. My hotel.

A very rich man has bought fifty-two acres of derelict paddy fields and woodland and commissioned a young architect to re-create a village based on the old Lanna designs of north Thailand. He used local craftsmen, and gathered up antiques, and even whole houses, and reconstructed the ancient way of life, with the considerable bonus of also incorporating every modern convenience and luxury. My wooden villa on stilts had an indoor and outdoor Jacuzzi, my own private steam room, a huge plasma TV screen, surround-sound music, and a balcony and terrace overlooking a rice field. From my garden I could walk on illuminated wooden boards, through the growing rice, passing the odd water buffalo, to have a cocktail in the bar. Luscious flowers and jungle trees abounded. At night the Thai frogs made even more racket than the French ones. They were enormous, probably very well fed with titbits from the choice of French, Thai and American restaurants that the hotel provided – oh, and a few hops away in the private shopping area, they could have Chinese or Indian. As I lay supping a glass of chilled white wine in one of my jacuzzis, which changed colour as I soaked in the fragrant water, I muttered John's mantra, 'Oh yes, this is the life, I tell you.' It may be a bit Disney, but it was the most beautiful and luxurious hotel I have ever visited. No, I wouldn't allow myself to worry about the living conditions beyond the gates. I was here to shamelessly indulge myself. Starting with a massage.

Since John's death there is an aching void in my life of physical contact. I long for caresses. At my age, I'm not likely to get them. Being pampered in a luxury spa is a very acceptable second best. Reflexology, shiatsu, hot-stone massage, fragrant oils, a feast of sensuality. Following Germaine's advice I was certainly 'agog' at the beauty of the Thai people. The girls are tiny and full of grace. They could not be more different than the Hungarians. What a varied species we are. Most of the staff had not yet mastered perfect English, despite having lessons in the hotel. Listening to them talking together is like a hearing a group of Marilyn Monroes, sexily breathy, with lots of soft aahing, up and down the scales. No wonder Western men adore them. They seem to genuinely want to make you happy. They glow with goodwill. It's not just routine 'have a nice day' stuff. They were worried about my cough, and brought potions to my villa in their free time. After I had been there for several days, gardeners I had never met would point at their throats and signal sympathy for me. One day all the staff were dressed up in national costume to process for a wedding, and as they passed me, they all did the hands-together prayer-and-bow gesture, which brought tears to my eyes. I learnt to return the compliment. It didn't feel silly, just a lovely expression of respect.

The Thais have a tradition of trying to inject fun into everything, including work. It even has a name – *sanuk* – which could explain their childlike spirits. They are never snappy or rude. I wondered if it was their training that made them so constantly sweet-natured. Or fear of losing a good job. Nope, I was not going to dwell on what they went home to each night when they left this rich woman's paradise.

I was made to wonder at their sunniness when I visited the pool. It was not a pretty sight. The pool itself was, of course, ravishing, but sprawled around it were depressed middle-aged men with shorts tucked below their pot bellies, chattering on mobiles or reading papers, whilst their honed and over-smoothed wives, wearing elaborate jewellery with their bathing costumes, stared into space beside them. They clicked their fingers at, and were graciously served by, exquisite Thai girls and boys whose smiles never faded.

I was delighted to discover I had progressed since Puglia. No cowering in my kaftan; like Germaine, I now 'neither expect nor hope to be noticed', which is either a huge self-confident step forward, or a surrender to the inevitable. Either way, I had a nice time sunning myself by the pool, thankful that I wasn't one of those bored wives ordering yet another gin. Better to be on my own than that.

However, after a few days I did crave some company. I decided to expand my culinary repertoire, and take another cookery course. As in Puglia, I was the only one. The tutor took me to the huge market in town to purchase our ingredients. I sympathised with the hapless woman in the reality-television show, forced to swap Weston-super-Mare for Thailand. The huge fried frogs, and piles of pigs' heads were hard to take, as were the birds in cages you could pay to release – a particularly nasty form of begging for a Buddhist country, which cost me a fortune. But the vegetables, fruit, and herbs were pleasing to work with, and, with the teacher's help, I conjured up a passable Thai curry and salad, as well as a dubious-looking banana-and-coconut pudding. They looked very pretty, when garnished with flowers, but it all tasted a bit like Jo Malone soap.

The lone dining was still a bit of a problem. I wasn't yet able to be myself. It was still easier to pretend to be a character. I found myself adopting a role dictated by my clothes. Because of the sun, I sported a straw panama-style hat, one of John's silk shirts, over a long cotton skirt to avoid mosquitoes, and canvas plimsolls for negotiating the rice fields. Sometimes I even held a parasol. The archetypal dotty Englishwoman. Helping some of the staff with their pronunciation, I had transmuted from Miss Havisham into Anna in the court of Siam.

Pampered, fed and watered, I wanted for nothing. The real world was shut out. The Terror Museum was pushed from my mind. When some shocking film footage of American soldiers in Iraq dragging into their compound a young lad who had been throwing stones, and beating the hell out of him, whilst the man operating the camera, presumably to entertain his friends, breathed 'yes, yes' orgasmically into the microphone, appeared on my super state-of-the-art TV, I simply turned it off.

I had been given a few introductions by one of my daughter's friends, who once did a bit of gardening for us and has since made it big in the Far East by dreaming up a deluxe guide to everything trendy in various places. An up-market *Rough Guide*; a brilliant, wittily accomplished idea that has provided him with an elegant lifestyle. Thus I stepped from the swirling mayhem of mid-town Chang Mai, into a cool, elegant shop selling designer furniture and ornaments of exquisite taste. This was run by one of his acquaintances who, coincidentally, turned out to be a woman whom I had known in England when she worked for a training centre for actors, of which I had been a co-founder. She too had found her feet in Thailand, after various adventures, including being in a relationship with an African headhunter. We met up with others in a thriving gourmet restaurant run by a Dutch friend of hers. It always seems to me a strange existence, to live in a foreign country but cling to one's fellow countrymen and way of life, whilst usually slagging off the homeland, as depicted by the international *Telegraph* and *Daily Mail*. This group of people in Thailand were providing much-needed employment for the locals, but admitted that they didn't really know them any better than I. It is a wonderful life, great food, perfect weather, no responsibility for the country's political or – in the case of Thailand – human-rights misdemeanours, but it makes me uneasy. I am too grim a person to be on perpetual holiday. Though of course I was changing all that, wasn't I?

As someone who is frightened of all big four-legged things, and quite a few small ones too, and wouldn't dream of mounting a horse, I had been persuaded by one of my pals on the staff of the hotel to book for a trek on an elephant, followed by a trip on a raft. I resolved to try it – face my fears and all that. I was once recruited to lead an elephant into the ring when I worked with Bertram Mills's circus, because the said beast had started trying to step on the feet of the previous girl, whom for some reason he had taken agin (as the non-forgetting elephant is wont to do). Actually, he needed no leading, having done the act for years, and I grew rather fond of him, but certainly never contemplated riding on his back.

The animals at the camp I visited were refugees from the collapsed logging trade and seemed to be enjoying their new life. These diligent creatures work for fifty years, cared for by one man who trains his son to take over. Then, they are retired into the wild, where they can live for another eighty years. Not a bad life really. The mahouts, as their owners are called, very obviously adore their animals. I enjoyed the sight of a very large beast lying in a shallow river, eyes blissfully closed, mouth definitely smiling, whilst a handsome young boy clambered over her, scrubbing and rinsing her languorously splayed body. During a demonstration of logging an over-eager baby elephant kept dropping his logs, and his mother thwacked him out of the way with her trunk, and tidied up after him like a fussy housewife. By the time we were ready to start the trek I had decided they were very nice animals and I wanted to get to know them better.

So I was almost eager to mount, especially as it was made easy by getting on from a high platform. I settled into a rather wobbly seat contraption. It was very, very, high up. I nearly panicked but, once in motion, amazingly, I felt no fear. The creature moved so carefully and solidly, I soon had absolute trust in it. I took off my shoes and put my bare feet on its back and felt the power of its giant muscles. This was it; this was happiness. I laughed out loud with excitement. I patted and scratched his neck to show my appreciation of him, and he acknowledged this with a backward swing of his trunk. Going down a steep hill was a bit challenging, as was traversing a very narrow path along a sheer cliffside, but the animal was deft and placed his feet with infinite care. I wanted to ride bareback, like the mahouts, using my feet behind his ears to give directions, but was told I needed proper training for that, which I made a vow I would go back and get one day.

I fell in love with these majestic beasts. I want one of my own. If I have to sacrifice my car to save the planet, this is the perfect mode of transport for my aching bones and he would cut a hell of a dash in Chiswick High Road. Even the waiters in Fishworks would notice me. And it would cheer people up. Elephants have ludicrous faces and from behind they are even funnier, like fat-arsed gentlemen in ill-fitting grey combinations, and they fart and poo a great deal. But they walk like models, and mine felt gentle and utterly reliable. Plus he would be company for my cat.

After some time wading through rivers and plodding up and down rough terrain, we arrived at a hill-tribe village. The women and children were dressed in brilliant dresses and ornate jewellery. They sold their wares in a dignified take-it-or-leave-it fashion and despite their homes being primitive, with no modern amenities, the place rang with their laughter as they greeted the mahouts. They looked pretty happy to me, on my brief visit. The little boy who waded up to my raft and bartered skilfully with me to get a good price for the hat he was selling, splashed around in glee and triumph when he clinched the sale, as proud as my grandson Jack when he came top in physics. At a time when we in the materialistic West are questioning some of our values, these people, usually not Buddhist, but with strong – albeit to us, strange – spiritual beliefs, living in a hard-working community, seem to have found an enviable lifestyle; at least preferable to the polluted, increasingly westernised development in Chiang Mai. Which is all right for me to say, ensconced in a palatial mock-up of their lives, with all mod cons.

Spaced out after all the cosseting in the spa, I was in for a rude shock in Bangkok. On arrival at the airport I was arrested. As I showed my passport at check-in, all hell broke loose. Two men in uniform were summoned and they gesticulated and shouted at me before forcing me across the concourse into a small room where even more very cross men arrived. I had no idea what I was supposed to have done, as they didn't speak

English and I had only picked up Thai words for greeting, thanks, and pleasure, none of which seemed appropriate in the circumstances. I was thoroughly body-searched and then one of the men gave a solemn-sounding speech and handed me a paper to sign. I had read too many stories of people unknowingly confessing to drug offences to comply. I tried to indicate that I demanded someone who spoke English to attend. Eventually they all left, shutting me in the room alone, with someone outside peering through the glass panel of the door, presumably to check I didn't escape.

I was there for about two hours, my mind filling with stories of foreigners languishing in ghastly Thai prisons for years on end. Finally a Thai guardian angel in a suit arrived. He explained that there were irregularities in my passport. Firstly, my tickets were in a different name to that in my passport. I pointed out that although it was in my married name of Thaw, on another page, admittedly in very small type, it said 'professionally known as Sheila Hancock', the name in which my tickets were booked. He tried to explain this to the now quite big group of uniformed men. Clearly they were not happy about a woman having a working life with a different name, and I didn't look like their concept of a prostitute. The most heinous crime however, was that I had entered the country illegally. I had not registered with immigration and had my passport stamped accordingly. I must therefore be a drug smuggler; presumably, since I had got myself into this situation, a pretty incompetent one. I could think of no explanation for my crime. My translator pointed out that I was in serious trouble, the solution to which was either to leave the country immediately, which they would permit, as they had found no drugs on me, or go to gaol.

Suddenly it dawned on me what had happened. In my muddle over the lost bags in Chang Mai, I had somehow wandered out of the airport without going through the usual passport checks. I had gone down a deserted back route to find my bag, by which time no one was around and in the absence of anyone to tell me otherwise I had just gone through a back door out of the airport. The translator took a deep breath and tried to explain this to my fierce guards, perhaps suggesting that I was obviously a scatty old Englishwoman, unlikely to be a threat to the moral fabric of Thailand. After a heated discussion, he informed me I was very lucky that they were trying to improve their image – you could have fooled me – and if it had been Cambodia or Vietnam I would definitely be incarcerated. I had to have photos taken and fill in a form with his help, and was instructed to report to them when I left the following week. I now had a criminal record in Bangkok.

If I thought the air in Chiang Mai was bad, that was before I took my first filthy breaths of freedom outside Bangkok airport. The police and many civilians were wearing smog masks. I sank, choking, into a grubby taxi. The driver eyed me in his mirror. 'Hello beautiful. How old are you? Seventeen?'

When someone thinks it a compliment to make that joke it confirms that you are looking very old indeed. His chatting-up was marred by calling me sir and picking his nose throughout. Of course he tried to persuade me he knew a much better hotel than the one I was going to. I had had enough. I got incredibly grand, even at one point saying, 'Now, look here, my man,' until he grumpily dumped me at the hotel. My first grouchy Thai, doing the usual city things. I knew where I was with him.

So far I was not enamoured of Bangkok, and the posh but soulless hotel didn't improve matters. The clientele were busy having business meetings all over the foyer and those that were not were very unattractive. As I waited for reception to get round to me after dealing with their preferred male clients, I saw one gross European man sprawled on a sofa, his eyes closed, being fed cake by a very young Thai girl. He didn't speak a word to her, and she admired her new trainers as she tended him like a robot. Obviously business was not the only occupation of the hotel guests. That night in the restaurant, I shrivelled with embarrassment for a ludicrous American, sporting a walrus moustache, white hair in a pigtail, and a highly coloured silk shirt that would have looked beautiful on a lithe young Thai lad, but was obscene stretched over his fat belly. He was dining with three delicately pretty Thai women, whom he was leaping about photographing along with the food, with his big expensive camera. They tittered and smiled to order, but when he turned his back to change lenses, the looks between them showed their distaste.

The Thai sex trade started in earnest during the Vietnam War, when American troops used the country as a break from their nightmare. Now men flock over from everywhere, to enjoy the favours of these beguiling women – and, tragically, children – seeking supposed oriental subservience after tiring of us fierce feminists. I am told that, after marriage, these yielding damsels, by tradition, expect to control the household and the purse strings. I profoundly hope that when these men get their trophy wives back to Essex, they discover they have wed little viragos. Most of the women here that are for sale do not end up with a very good deal. But I wasn't going to dwell on that. I could avoid the red-light district, and would ignore what was going on in the hotel.

I arranged to be taken on a tour in a car. My driver and guide was a charming man called Anan. We paid the obligatory visit to the royal palace of their adored king. I refused to contemplate what would happen if he fell foul of one of the many coups and murders that bedevil Thai history. When I seemed underwhelmed by the garish delights of the Grand Palace and the numerous temples, he took me to the new Siam Paragon, without doubt the most dazzling shopping mall I have ever visited – all designer labels, expensive cosmetics, gourmet food hall, numerous restaurants. I asked Anan to have a Japanese meal there with me. At first he was reluctant, but eventually he relaxed. Over the sushi he told me that he has twin boys who have attended all-day nursery since four months old, so that both he and his wife can work to make ends meet. He has high blood pressure, and is surely not in the ideal job, coping with tetchy tourists and nightmare traffic jams. I felt guilty that I had breezily commented that a £300 designer handbag was cheap compared to England. He had just smiled and nodded politely. It is a wonder he didn't hit me, knowing what that sum would have meant to him.

As we drove around, I was disappointed to see that, apart from the temples, the city is beginning to look like anywhere else, all modern hotels and office blocks built in the nebulous Western style. Bangkok is obviously attracting a lot of foreign investment and its buildings and transport are being upgraded. The prime minister, who was then the billionaire Thaksin Shinawatra (until recently he was in exile in the UK and is now facing corruption charges back in Thailand), was on a mission to transform the country. I had got there too late. I would have preferred it when it was the Venice of the East, before the canals had been filled in and turned into ugly roads.

'Let's take tea in the old Oriental Hotel and pretend it's the old days,' I suggested to Anan.

He looked embarrassed, 'I'm not allowed in.'

Me, even more embarrassed than him: 'Nonsense. Take off your cap and badge and take my arm. They will think you are my toy boy and in Bangkok they won't turn a hair.'

I don't think his grasp of English was good enough to quite understand me but, when I explained I didn't want to go in alone, he nervously did as I suggested. Unusually, I was really glad to be recognised by the manager because it meant that for once in his life Anan was treated with courtesy.

This, at last, was the old Bangkok. Even here, I would have preferred it to be more decayed, as it was when Hemingway,

Conrad, Noël Coward, the young Gore Vidal et al., wrote and caroused in its faded grandeur. After the war, a group of local people rescued the hotel from dereliction. One was Jim Thompson, an ex-pat American, who fell in love with the country and set up a cottage industry for producing the exquisite Thai silk. He became quite famous. There is even a rather tatty Thai restaurant in Tooting named after him. He incorporated several of the original Thai wooden houses to create a superb residence by one of the canals, on the opposite side of which were the houses of many of the people who wove his silks. He rejected air-conditioning and modern cooking stoves, entertaining royally in an elegant version of real Thai customs, although, strangely, he never learnt the language. His house, which I visited, is crammed with antiques and vivid paintings, which are very decorative, but make me long for Turner. I loved the feel of his house and garden though. It is a happy place and I wished I could have visited during his lifetime when it seemed to be perpetual open house. He went for a walk one day, whilst staying in a friend's house in the Cameroons, and vanished off the face of the earth. There are all sorts of theories about what happened but, judging by a few clues and photos, I suspect he was a bit of a gay kooka-burra, and that could have had something to do with it, in those unenlightened days.

Anyway, he would hate it now. Noisy motor boats roar past his house; everything that he relished and admired about life there has virtually disappeared. At least in the big towns. When I return to get to know the elephants, I will explore the parts of Thailand that have not been overtaken by so-called progress. Anan has promised to take me, because he said our trips have been like a holiday to him. He certainly made my stay much more enjoyable.

On my last night I had a pedicure and the girl was quite nasty; it was a relief. All the sweetness and light was beginning to pall. It is too good to be true. It makes me suspicious because, I suppose, I am by nature cynical and churlish, however much I try not to be. The over-the-top luxury, and the relentless charm, which in the wily city felt more like servility, makes me feel guilty. I know there is dire poverty in Thailand. Anan is struggling to exist. I know there is corruption and unrest. I tried my damnedest to put it out of my mind and go with the luxurious flow, but it is against my nature to be so incurious.

Neither look forward where there is doubt, nor backward where there is regret. Look inward and ask yourself not if there is anything out in the world that you want and had better grab quickly before nightfall, but whether there is anything inside you that you have not yet unpacked.

From *Resident Alien: Quentin Crisp Explains it All*
by Tim Fountain

8

Bexleyheath · Berkshire · Dorset

MY SISTER IS TOTALLY absorbed in the now, and in Thailand I had tried to follow her example. But I find as I grow older, I am more interested in the past. My own and the world's. Maybe because my future is limited. I believe that at the outset of Alzheimer's you forget recent events but remember clearly things and people from long ago. Seems sensible. To mull over what's happened. Try to understand it. Get it in perspective. Maybe even relive it, bring back people from your childhood, so that your daughter becomes your mother. The recent past is difficult to untangle. It is only in retrospect when the blood has cooled, the heart stopped speeding, that you can calmly consider what happened. Just as history is reinterpreted when looked at from a distance, and you can see what was important. Or view it from a different angle. When I was young, we only learnt about kings and queens, now there is a whole working-class and feminist perspective to examine. I suspect that my childhood affected me for the rest of my life, and my childhood took place during a war, the same war that was experienced in Budapest. Perhaps that is why I can't let these events go; it is a symptom of old age. I needed to look at them more closely; try to understand the disquiet triggered by the Terror Museum that would not go away.

I first became acquainted with fear on the day I saw my mother cry. It was when the wireless told us that we were at war with Germany. As I watched her clinging to my father, muttering 'Christ not again', I was very afraid. I was six years old and adult tears were unknown to me. I did not understand that my mother had already lived through one world war. Up until then I had known only peace so I didn't know what war meant. I could think of no words of comfort. Or comprehend why they were needed. As my mother wept I could only close my eyes tight and clench my fists and teeth, a technique I cultivated to great effect over the following years. I remained frightened for much of the duration of the conflict, which ended when I was twelve. And maybe for the rest of my life. Not all the time of course. I also tasted joy during those days. That has been less easy to sustain. Tranquillity, a valuable ingredient of childhood development, was non-existent. And has been ever since.

I can remember vividly some of my feelings as a wartime child, but the sequence of events escapes me. Except for my sister all of the people whom I knew then are dead or have disappeared from my life. Certain incidents stand out as mile-stones, however, with all the distortions that time may have wrought. That I still feel shaky and tearful as I recall some of them seems to prove their veracity.

The temporary crack in my mother's calm, coping façade was soon mended and she set about reorganising our lives and home to deal with potential bombing and invasion. We soon had an Anderson shelter in the garden, six foot six by four foot six with a wooden floor and paraffin lamp and candles. Dad constructed frames to fit into the windows at night as black-out, which it was my job to put up – maybe curtains would have been easier but he liked to be different. Brown sticky paper was crisscrossed to my father's design across the panes, to prevent flying glass. Dad joined the ARP (Air Raid Precautions) as a warden and taught me how to rotate the wooden rattle to be used to warn people of a gas attack.

We had to practise putting on our gas masks and Mum made natty leatherette cases for them that weren't as awkward to carry as the square cardboard boxes we were issued with. I found these rubber acrid-smelling masks horrific, and it took a lot of threats to make me put mine on. I felt claustrophobic and suffocated but the alternative fate described to me by my desperate father forced me to comply. It also terrified me. As did his instruction on how to work a stirrup pump and use buckets of sand to extinguish the deadly incendiary bombs that were coming our way. He made me recite my identity number CJFQ29 stroke 4 in case of somehow being separated from my parents. It was engraved on a disc around my neck and on my memory to this day.

My mother learnt how to create tasty dishes out of nothing. With rationing she had to. It is staggering to contemplate that I now eat more in one meal than our ration for a whole week. Each person had four ounces of butter, one ounce of cheese, one egg, and about one chop of meat. I remember beating the butter with milk, and something else – maybe margarine – to make it stretch further. In addition we children were given nasty glutinous cod-liver oil and a spoonful of orange concentrate. And every day at school we had fat little bottles of creamy milk sucked through a straw. As I had constant styes in my eye, I also took Yeast Vite.

The whole of our garden, and indeed the local park, was turned over to growing vegetables. I loved working in companionable silence with my father, digging and seeding. We marked the rows with a piece of string, fixed either end by a bit of wood pushed into the ground. Then Dad trowelled out a little trench, or dug a big one if it was potatoes, and I was allowed to scatter in the seeds, or plop in the potatoes or beans at regular intervals, push over the earth and jump it down flat. My favourite job was collecting caterpillars from the cabbages, and blackfly from the Brussels sprouts, and drowning or squishing them. They were our enemies, and I was quickly learning the desire to eliminate insects and people who threaten.

The sweets ration was a measly eight ounces a month, for which we had a book of points to manage our allocation, so the choice between sherbet fountains, a bit of austerity chocolate or barley sugar was a serious business. Maybe my adult gluttonous inability to take merely one or two chocolates but instead devour the lot, however large the box, in one sitting, stems from those parsimonious childhood decisions. I can remember on one occasion, hearing on the grapevine that a shop some distance away had Crunchie bars, rushing over on my bike and queuing for ages, then sitting on a wall outside with my trophy, sucking the chocolate coating very slowly and poking my tongue into the melting honeycomb interior. No sweet has ever tasted so sublime since.

Clothes too were rationed, which resulted in a lot of 'make do and mend'. I don't remember buying any new clothes during the war, but I did enjoy a dress made out of barrage-balloon silk, which at least wasn't a hand-me-down. Less pleasing were some rather smelly big mittens, made from the fur of an unfortunate rabbit that also supplied us with several dinners.

The first few months after the declaration were known as the Phoney or Bore War. Not a lot actually happened on the home front, but the threat was in the air. The adults whispered a lot and looked tense when listening to the wireless news. There was talk of sending the children away. The government was insisting on the necessity of getting us out of danger. A mass evacuation was planned called Operation Pied Piper. An unfortunate choice of name, considering the fate of the children in that story.

Operation Pied Piper was not a popular proposal. The country was divided into three categories: reception areas, which would receive evacuees; danger areas from which children and mothers with babies would be evacuated; and neutral areas, which were neither. Straight off, 200 reception areas asked to be made neutral and no one asked to be made reception. Not a situation likely to make the evacuees feel welcome. The people in the danger zone did not want to relinquish their children, to send them into the arms of strangers, anyway.

Some children were sent abroad. A risky project, with U-boats already marauding the waters around Britain. One heartbreaking tragedy happened when the SS *City of Benares* was torpedoed, and 256 people died, 81 of them children. After the ship went down, the children were tossed about in lifeboats in storm conditions. When rescuers arrived they were faced with one boat full of 19 dead children and others barely alive, after twenty hours in the raging sea.

When I set out from King's Cross station to be evacuated, I can remember the train being crowded with labelled children, clutching gas masks and suitcases or bundles, sometimes just paper parcels. But I do not remember the selection process, in which local people picked the prettiest and cleanest first, leaving the less attractive to deal with the humiliation of rejection, so it can't have been too bad for me. There are heart-warming tales of kids from the slums landing up in middle-class homes or even aristocratic palaces, and tasting luxury for the first time in their lives, although a lot of them were thrown out, when they were discovered to be lousy and not toilet-trained.

I ended up billeted on Mr and Mrs Giles, an elderly childless couple. Despite previously only ever having lived in the staff accommodation of the hotels and pubs in which my father worked, latterly my home had been a semi-detached, pebble-dashed, two-bedroom-plus-boxroom house in Bexleyheath. Somewhat overcrowded, with two grannies, my parents and my sister and I, but you could use a bathroom and toilet if you were patient. Baths were only once a week, the regulation five inches deep and had to be shared, so that for the last one in it was freezing cold. But it was a proper bath and a lavatory, indoors, with a chain to pull. The Gileses' cottage had no such comforts. There was a ghastly outside lavatory; but the tin bath put in front of the black kitchen range, I quite enjoyed. Constantly topped up with water from the kettle on the big iron hob, it was much warmer than the baths I was used to.

The Gileses had a snappy little Pekinese called Dainty that I fear was easier for them to deal with than a twitchy, miserable seven-year-old girl, but they did their best. My relationship with Mr Giles was very like that portrayed in *Goodnight, Mister Tom*, in which John starred on television. John, being nine years younger than I, did not remember the war, so I was able to help him with my experience. We agreed that the sense of abandonment I felt then was much the same as he did when his mother deserted him.

To begin with, Mr Giles never spoke to me, even when we ate together. One day, while I was playing in the garden, some cows got in. I screamed the place down, as these huge creatures lumbered around in a panic. Mr Giles rushed out, clay pipe hanging from his mouth, whipped me up in his arms, took me indoors and drove the cows away. From then on, I knew he was on my side. I may not have my parents, but he would protect me. Slowly, a shy, warm relationship developed between us, which looking back probably gave him some pleasure, despite the disruption to their placid lives.

However, with the best will in the world, they were not equipped to deal with the psychological problems that beset a child wrenched from her home and parents, whom she feared were in danger of being killed by gas, or bombs or invading Germans. And I, in my turn, could not discuss with them the problems I was facing at the local village school.

Before I was evacuated, I attended a primary school, imaginatively led by Miss Markham. She was one of several big, slightly butch, women teachers that nourished my childhood. With fifty-odd children in a class, she and her tiny staff managed to keep order by the sheer brilliance of their teaching skills. I had a tendency to get over-excited and the punishment was to 'see Miss Markham'. The agonisingly long wait outside her door was doubtless intentional, because, by the time I got into her room, she needed to say nothing to increase my regret at disappointing her. The contrast at the village school I attended in Berkshire was incomprehensible to me. The headmistress doubtless had a name, but I remember only that I called her Miss Greenbum. Her method of punishment was the cane. The thought of a big person assaulting a little one was revolting to me then and it still is.

In class, except when writing, we had to sit in silence with our arms folded. Art was endlessly drawing flags with a ruler, which merely taught me the right way up for a Union Jack. To this day I obsessively doodle flags on my scripts. It was very hard for the reception towns to assimilate thousands of strange and troubled children, and it was made clear to us what usurpers we were. The locals were already doing joined-up writing, but I was still just printing. As were many other evacuees, or vaccies as we became known. We were held up to derision, inferior beings that we were. Originality and creativity, as learnt from Miss Markham, were worthless commodities to Miss Greenbum, and what few compositions we did were judged for the neatness of their writing and accuracy of spelling, rather than the use of imagination.

Also, we were deemed dirty. Some of us were. The whole school was made aware of it when the weekly Flea Inspection revealed our crime. On one occasion, nits were found in my hair, and when another teacher tried to take me to the cloakroom – to wash my hair in carbolic soap and vinegar – I bit her, which earned me two strokes of the cane on my hand in front of the whole school. I hated that woman and the local kids, who smelled blood when they sensed my inability to defend myself. To get to school, I had to cross an area of grass where they would lie in wait for me. I would hide behind some little hillocks on the perimeter, until I thought the coast was clear, then pelt across, arriving at the school panting and sweating. And sometimes bruised.

I do not remember exactly how, whether it was the biting of the teacher, and the cane, or my face too being painted purple when I contracted impetigo like them, but over time I became friends with the Jones family, the local outlaws. They taught me far more than Miss Greenbum. What I learnt from the Joneses was that even the most savage enemies can become friends – a valuable lesson for a wartime child who is being taught to hate. And self-sufficiency.

The Joneses were a large, very obviously poor family. They had no bikes or toys. None of us had Game Boys or TVs to distract us. Amusement was improvised from nothing. The wall of a house was good for complicated hand- and headstands. A ball thrown against it with variations of clapping, twirling, between your legs, backwards, underarm, overarm, behind your back, could occupy several hours. An iron girder in a barn was a hair-raising setting for an acrobatic display of somersaults and tight-rope walking. Haystacks were slides and cosy dens. Trees were swings and climbing frames, requiring the careful skill of a mountaineer to reach the summit. Food was provided by scrumping apples, blackberries, raiding turnip fields and, I'm sorry to say, the bun shop near the school.

Mr and Mrs Giles had no idea of what I got up to, but when they saw I was beginning to have a good time, they allowed me a free rein. From cowardly wimp, I emerged as the Joneses' favourite clown, up for anything, and in turn protected by them. In our dens I told them stories, something I suspect no one had ever done. I led them in songs and wild dancing. From what I observe, that kind of playing is dead and gone. Dangers imagined and real nowadays restrict children's freedom to roam. Gangs still exist, providing – as they did for me – a substitute family, but the crimes are more serious than our occasional shoplifting. The Jones boys had knives, but they were used for cutting wood for lighting a campfire. And skinning rabbits. Very nasty.

Nature became a solace and delight. As I got bolder, I often wandered off on my own, putting frogspawn in jam jars or sitting in the sun reading. If Proust had his madeleines to remind him of times past, I have watercress. We picked it from the beds in the stream at Ewelme, tied it in bunches and sold it. An evocative flower for me is the cowslip. My mother came on a visit, bringing me a new frock made from two of her old dresses. It was blue-and-white check cotton with a panel inserted in the bodice of sky-blue linen. A sash that tied at the back gathered in the full skirt. Wandering around in my new finery, on a perfect English summer's day, I saw a field of delicate yellow in the distance, and when I reached it, discovered it was not the usual buttercups, but a carpet of exquisite little flowers, which I later discovered were called cowslips. I gathered two bunches to give to Mr Giles and my mother, and made for the cottage. The sun on my face, the breeze blowing my new frock around my bare brown legs, the hum of insects, the scent of flowers, made my spirits soar into what I recognise, looking back, as transcendence. I had never had a feeling like it in my short life. Breathtaking, wonderful. A magic moment for me alone. I did not, could not, explain it to anyone but kept it close to my heart. Maybe it is such epiphanies that people regard as union with the divine and make for religious conversion. For a seven-year-old girl, it was a precious secret, and a state of consciousness to be sought ever after.

When nothing much happened for some time, a false sense of security prevailed and I and many other evacuees were returned home – just in time for the Blitz. We were subjected to a relentless nightly bombardment. Bexleyheath was situated in 'Bomb Alley'. It was in the middle of prime targets Vickers-Armstrong, Woolwich Arsenal and the docks. Behind our house was a searchlight and a deafening ack-ack gun; above our heads, a skyful of barrage balloons; and along the road, black containers for creating a smoke screen, and concrete blocks and barbed wire ready to lay across the road to bar the way of approaching tanks. Our house never took a direct hit, but was constantly blasted, so that in the end my father gave up repairing damage. He put a tarpaulin over the roof, and boarded up the broken windows. Anyway we spent most of the time down the shelter.

To begin with, when the air-raid warning went, I would turn off the gas and water and put on my siren suit over my pyjamas. This was an all-in-one trouser-and-jacket garment copied from that sported by Churchill, which he wore with a homburg hat and bow tie when visiting bomb sites. I then lead the way down the garden with a masked torch. Inside the shelter, we would light a candle and read or play cards and board games, whilst the raid raged above us. In the corner were our bags, packed ready in case our house was bombed or destroyed by an incendiary fire before I could get to my stirrup pump. Sometimes my mother nervously allowed me to watch the dogfights between the Spitfires and hordes of German planes. The average age of the Battle of Britain pilots, many of whom were killed, was twenty-four. We thought they were wonderful. And they were. They saved our skins. Hitler must have wrongly thought we were well defended, such an incredible fight they put up. Ducking and weaving and twirling in the sky, little cotton-wool puffs of smoke and trails from their exhaust creating complex patterns. At night the searchlights criss-crossed the darkness, every now and then picking up a plane in their beam. If no bombs fell, it seemed so remote it was like being at the pictures.

Most of the time when the raid was overhead, the door of the shelter was firmly closed. Eventually we stayed down there all night, on bunks built in by my father. With the help of earplugs, I could sleep through the loudest incidents, even a landmine that exploded a few doors away and the dreaded ack-ack gun. My poor mother, who before the war would hide in the cupboard under the stairs in a thunderstorm, must have suffered dreadfully; although the only time I remember her demonstrating her terror was one night when she struggled on to her bunk in the dark, and a terrible hissing and squawking filled the shelter. It was the next door's ginger tom, who was lucky to escape with his life when my frantic mother beat at him as though he were the Führer himself.

My main fear was that a German airman would bail out in our garden, for of course he would be a murderous villain – all Germans were. I had a good look round when I crept out of the shelter to go to the lavatory under the apple tree, making sure the searchlight was not in action before I crouched down. Sometimes the sky glowed red with fires from London or the docks.

In the morning we would emerge, blinking, to survey the damage. Sometimes we crunched across debris and glass, the smell of cordite twitching our nostrils. Then the search for shrapnel, shell and machine-gun bullet cases and – biggest prize of all – a piece of bomb. No more cigarette cards or stamps for us, this was far more exciting. My father would arrive home and report on his night as a warden. I think he rather enjoyed the fact that he was in charge of his post, giving orders to a doctor and a bank manager. The war was a great leveller. No room for class distinction when you are fighting a common enemy.

Whenever we could, we still went to school. In a crocodile, protected by one of the mothers, wearing our tin helmets and carrying our gas masks. When we got there we went down the big shelters, where we did lessons. We seemed to be underground most of the time.

Later, for some reason that I have forgotten, I was evacuated for a second time. On this occasion I went to a distant relative in Crewkerne in Somerset. It was less of a culture shock, as I had already learnt about country ways in Berkshire, and was a much tougher cookie, having survived previous evacuation and the Blitz.

This time I didn't go to school at all and, by some miracle, was allowed to visit my best friend, Brenda Barry, who had been evacuated to Dorset. Best friends are very important to little girls; they are a source of delight when things are going well, and anguish when they fall out. Which they do a lot. 'You're not my friend any more' is a sentence that chills a young girl's heart. Through these relationships you learn about jealousy, rejection, and the pleasure of shared confidences and aspirations. Brenda and I dreamed of being film stars, and marrying Tyrone Power and Robert Taylor. Brenda was shorter than I, with curly dark hair and laughing eyes. I loved her very much.

I don't know how I got to Dorset but, having been parted, we were thrilled to see each other again. She was living, along with her two older sisters, near the village of Langton Matravers. Their cottage was called Sea Spray and stood in the middle of nowhere, a tiny, tumbledown, stone house with no electricity or water. It was a beautiful summer, so drawing water from a well and, in the warm night, reading by mellow paraffin lamp, was no hardship. It was bliss.

We talked and talked, pouring out our sad little souls. We fantasised about the tales of smugglers and searched for the secret tunnel we were convinced went from Sea Spray to the beach. We became the characters in an Enid Blyton adventure. We had a real life escapade when Brenda's sister jammed her finger in an ironing board, and we had to run over fields in the dark to fetch a doctor, there being no road to the house. We went to Corfe Castle and pretended to be artists, sketching the village. But the night that thrilled me most was a visit to Dancing Ledge. The Isle of Purbeck has a rocky coastline and many of the cliffs by the sea have been quarried for the beautiful stone. Dancing Ledge is one such. There is a steep cliff with caves, and sticking out – as the name suggests – is a rocky ledge upon which, when the tide is out, the sea thrashes, throwing up dancing spray. On this ledge is a roughly rectangular deep hole that fills with water, which is left as the tide ebbs, providing a perfect swimming-pool.

It happened that the tide was out after midnight, so one moonlight night we were allowed to run down the grassy slopes, and clamber down the cliff for a swim. We were alone in the vast shadowy world, apart of course from the smugglers, and their confederates, who were doubtless bouncing about in boats in the roaring sea. We stripped off our clothes and leapt into the black pool, seeming cold at first but actually quite warm from the hot sun that had shone on it all day. We thrashed about, whooping and laughing, exhilarated and fully alive. Then we lay on our backs, floating hand in hand in the velvet water, quite still, staring up at the thousands of stars in the huge sky. The sea crashed against the ledge beside us, and we felt tiny, absorbed into the elements, but made safe by our clasped warm hands. I shuddered with amazement. Shared with my best friend in all the world. A double delight.

Elated by this happy memory of the war, the phrase 'lighten our darkness' kept going round my head. Then I remembered it was our nightly family prayer: 'Lighten our darkness, we beseech thee, O Lord; and by thy great mercy defend us from all perils and dangers of this night.'

Well, something did defend us, all our family survived the war and I should rejoice. And perhaps revisit those good times instead of dwelling on the sadness. With this intention, on impulse, I booked into a hotel in Dorset and the next day I drove to Langton Matravers, left my car and set off across the fields to search for Sea Spray.

It took me a long time to recognise it. It has been tarted up to provide a second home for 'someone in the music business'. I got this from a gardener who was tending the immaculate lawns and flowers. No smuggler would venture into this blue-shuttered, tastefully extended house. It is very attractive but not the wonderful primitive place of my memory. Central heating and electricity are *de rigueur* now, I suppose. The owners have even laid an asphalt road to drive their car to the door. So would I, if truth be told.

With some regret for progress I set off towards the sea. The scenery was the same as I remembered, but my feelings as I slithered down the steep incline were not. It wasn't helped by being one of those days of relentless drizzle, so the ground was soggy and sticking to my trainers. I remember skipping down as a child, but by the time I arrived at the sea I was red-faced and puffing, a bit concerned that, on the climb back, my romantic journey might end in a heart attack.

Dancing Ledge was totally different. It is now part of a World Heritage coastal walk. Groups of hearty hikers march along, there is a fence all around the cliffs because nowadays there must be no risk, and steps have been carved to reach the ledge. It is a hell of a drop – when I looked over I was amazed that two nine-year-old kids had managed to get down there. Now, there were climbers with harnesses and people holding ropes at the top lest they fall. How on earth did we manage it? I think there was a rickety iron ladder, but it is still a very long way down and nothing but a rocky ledge below. The danger of that climb in the dark must have made our nerve ends tingle, adding to the sensuousness of the experience. What brave little girls we were.

No longer so brave, I crept down the steps, which were hairy enough for me. Inevitably, the magic pool was not as I remembered. The water looked black and full of bits. Floating in it now would not be at all the same. There was the usual litter scattered around, and people dismally sheltering from the rain in the dank caves. Needing to get my breath back, I too sat under a rock, eating a KitKat and looked at my guidebook.

My childhood reverie was shattered when I read that at this place, which brought such joy to the nine-year-old me, ten-year-old boys were used to work in the quarry. An old quarry-man said, 'They wass cheap, plenty of 'em and more where they cum vram', which put me in mind of a shocking documentary made in Palestine – that we looked at whilst researching for the *Arab-Israeli Cookbook* – about the training of children as suicide bombers; the adults who trained them to kill themselves and others had said something very similar. How ill we treat our children in the world, not just in olden times.

After clambering back up the hill, I drove around for a while in the pouring rain. Everything I came across conspired to obstruct my search for loveliness. There were notices warning of 'tanks crossing' and I remembered that the military still own a lot of this beautiful area to use for practice manoeuvres. In 1943 the army commandeered a picturesque little village called Tyneham, turning out the inhabitants, supposedly for a short time. The villagers left a touching notice on the church door: 'Please treat the church and houses with care, we have given up our homes, where many of us have lived for generations, to help win the war to keep men free. We shall return one day and thank you for treating the village kindly.' They never have been allowed back and the village is in ruins.

It was in this area, around Studland Bay in 1944, not long after I was there with Brenda, that Monty, the King and Eisenhower gathered to watch rehearsals for the Normandy landings. A couple of months before – some miles along the coast from our beautiful Dancing Ledge – at Slapton Sands the Americans had staged a similar rehearsal that ended in disaster. Through criminal mismanagement the boats were torpedoed by German U-boats, men were trapped below decks or drowned, dragged down by their waterlogged heavy clothes and lifebelts wrongly fastened: 946 soldiers and sailors died. The tragedy was hushed up for fear of damaging morale at a crucial time. Possibly out of guilt, it continued to be kept a secret after the war until, forty years later, a valiant local man, Ken Small, doggedly dug out the lies and subterfuges and erected a memorial made out of a tank he raised from the sea-bed. It wasn't until November 1987 that an official memorial ceremony was held to commemorate those men.

Here I was, again dwelling on sad events, digging up dark secrets. So much for lightening my darkness. The next morning the rain had stopped so I decided to have another go. I am hugely affected by the weather and this time the sun was shining. As I crossed the fields to Dancing Ledge, I smelled the wild honeysuckle, heard and saw the larks hovering in glorious song, and in the distance was the sparkling sea. This was better. Enid Blyton loved the Isle of Purbeck. In *Five Have a Mystery to Solve*, Julian says, 'I somehow feel more English for having seen those Dorset fields surrounded by hedges basking in the sun.' I know what he means. Nothing can compare to England on a summer's day. It is a country of infinite variety: dramatic, gentle, rugged, curvaceous, spectacular, bleak, pretty, it constantly surprises and takes my breath away with its beauty.

Dancing Ledge looked stunning in the sun. Gazing down from the distance of the cliff, this time the pool glistened invitingly. I decided that I was too old to plunge into it. There were too many people watching to go naked, and no best friend to hold my hand. I could admire the view, but too much time had passed to be ecstatic. Tennyson said it all:

> *And the stately ships go on*
> *To their haven under the hill;*
> *But O for the touch of a vanished hand,*
> *And the sound of a voice that is still!*

> *Break, break, break*
> *At the foot of thy crags, O sea!*
> *But the tender grace of a day that is dead*
> *Will never come back to me.*

In 1945 it was all over. First the war in Europe. Then, after the world-changing horror of the atom bombs on Hiroshima and Nagasaki, the war with Japan. But the aftershock waves of the War continued. Service people returned home strangers to their wives and children, as did shattered men from POW camps. But we all rejoiced. Bonfires. The royal family and Churchill on the balcony of Buckingham Palace. Street parties. Jellies and junket, tinned fruit salad with evaporated milk for cream. A feast in the still-rationed times. But I don't remember the celebrations being as rapturous as one might expect. Perhaps everyone was exhausted and fearful of a future threatened by weapons of unimaginable power. I certainly was. Made old before my time, at the age of eleven I had enough experience of death and destruction to realise the implications. It was a threat that hung over my youth.

My generation are dying out. Soon there will be no one left who lived through that period. I wonder if Blair and Bush would be so gung ho if they had. A man from the Ministry of Defence was quoted as saying that terrorism in London is as bad as the Blitz, and as big a threat as World War Two. Oh no, it isn't, Sonny Jim.

Statistics sanitise suffering but those for World War Two are shocking. According to the Imperial War Museum about 55 million adults and children died between 1939 and 1945 and many more later from wounds, mental and physical, inflicted by the conflict. There were 30 million displaced persons, refugees wandering around Europe made homeless by bombs and being sent to the camps; 13 million children were abandoned. Of the 6,000,000 or perhaps more Jews slaughtered, 1,200,000 were children. In Britain 60,595 were killed as a result of the bombing, a miraculously small number, considering the size of the onslaught and if you compare it with 100,000 that died in one night in Dresden. It was a filthy terrible war.

It left the country bankrupt. A costly loan from the Americans, which we have only just finished paying off, helped us out. As did the spirit of the people. During the war, being neighbourly was a necessary ingredient of survival. The evacuees and the local kids eventually had to accept one another, and learn to tolerate their differences, or life would have been a constant battle. The grown-ups helped each other out in the certain knowledge that some day they in their turn would need assistance. The Blitz spirit was real; 'we can take it' was the bloody-minded stance; and humour, the secret weapon. Because everyone was suffering in one way or another, it was easy to imagine how others felt. Empathy led to sympathy.

It was, paradoxically, a kinder age. Despite the brutality and hatred that prevailed, such public expressions of spitefulness as *Big Brother* and the message boards on the web would have been unthinkable. In my working/lower-middle-class world it was not considered admirable to be cynical or rude. I remember my father being mortified when his sister accused him of being 'sarky', short for sarcastic, because of some glib remark he made. We and, I think, most children were taught a rigid sense of duty. He was very angry with me when one of my school reports said I was 'sometimes inconsiderate of others'. During

The rough patch in our beloved village in Provence where John and I used to sit together watching our neighbours playing boules.

Now alone, I took this rather arty photo of the Phwah bed covered in writing materials. Note the blue paint effect created by Joanna and me.

John cowering inside the sumptuous suite we had in Oman. He was much happier ministering to his wood stove at home in France (*right*). He didn't have to worry about his coiffeur there either.

At Joanna's magic wedding in the garden at Lucky. Ellie Jane, the bride, mother of same and Abigail. All well into the champagne.

Left: My mother was an exemplary grandmother – note Ellie Jane's immaculate white socks.

I am a less good influence on my own fabulous grandchildren.
Above: Molly Mae, Talia, Louis (hidden by Molly Mae's luxuriant hair) and Lola.
Left: Charlie, seen here 'introducing' his brother, Alfie, in *Hello* magazine mode.

Above: Jack, Lola and Charlie.
Right: My son-not-in-law may have been trying to tell me something when he offered me the role of mother-in-law from hell in his production of *The Anniversary*.

Some of the lovely cast of *Cabaret* on my balcony in the glow of a sunset.

Proud Madam Chancellor of Portsmouth University.

Louise adjusting my wig for *Cabaret*. My make-up place is not a thing of beauty. My dresser Debs tried to tidy it for the photo but it's still a mess.

Left: My mother was an exemplary grandmother – note Ellie Jane's immaculate white socks.

I am a less good influence on my own fabulous grandchildren.
Above: Molly Mae, Talia, Louis (hidden by Molly Mae's luxuriant hair) and Lola.
Left: Charlie, seen here 'introducing' his brother, Alfie, in *Hello* magazine mode.

Above: Jack, Lola and Charlie.
Right: My son-not-in-law may have been trying to tell me something when he offered me the role of mother-in-law from hell in his production of *The Anniversary*.

The House of Terror Museum in Budapest certainly terrified me.

Budapest is full of statues and memorials. This row of shabby shoes by the Danube first puzzled then disturbed me.

The statue of a man on a bridge turned out to be the noble Imre Nagy, executed in 1958. It is now used as a photo opportunity.

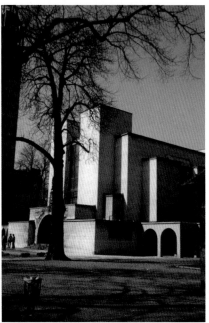

My new love affair with Modernism started with this church in Buda (*right*). It has the same clean lines as the one I love in Saignon (*above*).

In Statue Park, outside Budapest, are piled all the ex-heroes, including the massive Russian soldier removed from the Liberty memorial (*left*). The sinister wrapped figure (*below*) could be the toppled Stalin.

My sister Billie on her travels in Africa and Egypt with fellow ENSA artistes. Bobby Pett is on the right of Billie, clinging to the tree.

Courtesy of Billie Barbour

Left: Billie with her husband, Roy Barbour, performing the act that took them all around the world.

Above: At her eightieth birthday party in Antibes, teaching Jack a magic trick.

Courtesy of Billie Barbour

My luxury villa in Chiang Mai (*above, left*) with its outdoor jacuzzi and view of the rice fields, where a wedding party was processing past.

I fell in love with this elephant. After his blissful bath we set off on an idyllic trek.

Left: Grandma Hancock's birthplace: the superintendent's house behind the Pimlico sewage pumping station.

Below: Grandfather Hancock's branch of Thomas Cook's in Milan.

A more elegant later lifestyle. *Above*: My father, Enrico, with his Italian nanny.

Right: My mother, Ivy, Grandfather Hancock, Aunty Cis and Grandma Hancock, wearing an elongated version of her tippet.

Above: Possibly taken at the Blackgang Hotel on the Isle of Wight, where I was born. Standing are Grandfather Hancock, Aunty Cis and my debonair dad, with a restraining hand on Nanny Woodward's shoulder. My mother is seated in the middle, sandwiched between the warring grandmas.

The flamboyant, gutsy Madame Zurhorst.

The entry in a trade dictionary that showed she was one of the very few women traders in the City of London.

Dancing Ledge in Dorset. How did two nine-year-old girls climb down those cliffs in the dark?

Obst- und Gemüsehof zur Horst

My ancestral home in Germany turned out to be Cold Comfort Farm.

Karl Marx Allee, East Berlin's main boulevard, is
an impressive example of communist social housing.

Irina (*top, right*) loved it all, especially the nostalgic ballroom upstairs at the
Sophiensaele and the cheery, rough and ready café downstairs.

The Brandenburg Gate shook off its recent sad memories to welcome visitors
for the World Cup.

Joachim's talks brought Venice to life for me. The amazing mosaic floor of St Mark's Cathedral (*below*) pre-dated Bridget Riley.

Carpaccio's little white dog takes centre stage in two of his religious pictures.

These bronze horses inside St Mark's devastated me.

A bizarre picture by the Bellini brothers in the Brera, Milan, that made me chuckle.

Whereas this exquisite
Caravaggio made me cry
at its beauty.

It reminded me of my
Albert Starling with its
light and shade and
portrayal of careworn
people. Blasphemy,
I know.

Some of the lovely cast of *Cabaret* on my balcony in the glow of a sunset.

Proud Madam Chancellor of Portsmouth University.

Louise adjusting my wig for *Cabaret*. My make-up place is not a thing of beauty. My dresser Debs tried to tidy it for the photo but it's still a mess.

John, a bit fed up with my camera disturbing his peace, in France. Now the family enjoy the same spot. On this occasion Matthew, Jack and Ellie Jane.

Left: Lola has a quiet read whilst Banan, the village dog, sleeps behind her.

The family at Climping to celebrate my seventy-fifth birthday. *From left to right*: Lola, Charlie, me, Ellie Jane holding Louis, Joanna holding Alfie, Matthew, Jack and Matt. Alfie is giving me his 'who is this diddle-oh?' look. Louis seems to share his suspicion.

Alone, but happy, in front of the Duomo in Milan.

the war we had been expected to 'do our bit'; fourteen-year-old lads were employed as messenger boys, having to deliver dreadful telegrams to grief-stricken families. They would knock on the house either side to get support for the recipients of their dire news. There was compassion even in the young.

How did the war affect me personally? For the duration, a crucial five years of my childhood, I had no safe home, a lot of fear, no holidays, no toys, not much food, in fact none of the good things that my grandchildren have. My primary education was erratic, and at times, non-existent. I was lucky that, despite a sleepless night of air raids the night before my exam, Miss Markham, got me through my scholarship to grammar school. Here, a band of dedicated teachers channelled my wild, verging on disturbed, behaviour into enthusiastic learning. My father's exhortation at the end of the war, when the crimes of Nazi Germany were fully revealed, that it must never happen again and it was down to my generation to see that it didn't, contributed to my tiresome obsession for righting wrongs – my Messiah complex, as John called it.

I have a facial tic when nervous, I doodle flags, and I feel guilty if I have a bath deeper than five inches. I find it hard to give myself permission to be happy. I have had periods in my life when the fear that lurks beneath the surface breaks out and immobilises me. My first reaction to any situation is anxiety – fight or flee. I am wary where my children are bold but I am tough and street-wise and I can handle bullies. The dark side of life absorbs and sometimes overwhelms me. All these traits, which I trace back to my wartime childhood, were assuaged by my relationship with John. Despite its ups and downs, he was my rock-like Mr Giles. Now, without him, there has been danger of those demons returning. It is my current battle to see that they don't. I must remember that there were also cowslips, watercress and Dancing Ledge.

So, how long does a man live, finally?
And how much does he live while he lives?
We fret, and ask so many questions –
Then when it comes to us
The answer is so simple after all

A man lives as long as we carry him inside us,
For as long as we carry the harvest of his dreams,
For as long as we ourselves live,
Holding memories in common, a man lives.

From 'So Many Different Lengths of Time'
by Brian Patten

9

King's Cross · Pimlico · The City · Milan · Guernsey

HAVING CONSIDERED MY WARTIME childhood and the effect it might have had on my psyche, I was given an unexpected opportunity to delve even deeper into the past. I am constantly asking myself, when I set my sights too high, 'Who do you think you are?' so to appear in a TV programme of that name seemed apposite. The format of the show is investigating the subject's ancestry – but what if I turned out to be descended from Jack the Ripper? As they would be asked to appear on the programme too, I put this possibility to my family. My grandchildren didn't care so long as they could be on the telly. 'They'll try to make you cry,' Jeremy Paxman, a previous subject of the show, warned me but I was fairly sure the only danger would be of my forebears boring everyone to tears. Instinctively I guessed they would turn out to be urban, relentlessly working- to lower-middle-class and dull.

I didn't have much for Lee McNulty and the rest of the researchers to go on: the only close relatives I knew superficially were my two grandmothers. But nothing of their husbands, not even their names, and certainly no relatives further back than them. In desperation I showed them a striking old photo of a cartoonish lady with huge eyes that I had found in my mother's belongings after her death, and which her best friend Ruby deduced was maybe a relative she had heard talk of with the odd name Madame Zurhorst. Mary Cranitch, the director, said they would see if they could unearth anything in my story that might be of interest to the viewers. Waiting for their verdict I feared my place on the planet was going to prove so insignificant that I would be ignominiously cast aside, my lineage discredited. So I was relieved to hear that they had dug up in my story some previously uncovered areas of social history. There followed two of the most fascinating weeks of my life.

We started with another trip to my childhood world, the Carpenter's Arms public house in King's Cross, where I spent my earliest years living in the flat above the pub, whilst Dad and Mum and one of my grannies worked in the bars. Despite the gentrification of parts of King's Cross, the pub has the same tatty grandeur as it always had. The old spotted mirrors and antique light-fittings remain; it is still a spit-and-sawdust joint. Walls have been knocked down, so there is no longer a public, saloon, and ladies' bar – but the door marked private is still there, and behind it the stairs on which I used to sit and listen to my mother at the tinny piano, singing duets with my father. Even the cracked lino, which felt cold on my bottom through my pyjamas, is unchanged. One song in particular I still know by heart, which has an odd poignancy now.

We have been gay, going our way;
Life has been beautiful, we have been young,
After you've gone, life will go on
Like an old song we have sung

When I grow too old to dream,
I'll have you to remember;
When I grow too old to dream,
Your love will live in my heart.

When we visited with the crew, there were but three customers. One had been there since I was a child, perched on a barstool, concentrating very intensely on his drinking with scarcely a glance at us. The resident glazed drunk moved very slowly and carefully towards me and, nose to nose, mouthed, 'I know you.' In the corner was another old boy, supping barley wine, and watching over his glass, barking the odd irrelevant comment. The trains rattled under the building, shaking the glasses, but the fat, slightly dusty barmaid, clad in a voluminous black top over tight woollen black leggings, took no notice. How long it will be able to remain in this time warp without becoming a gastro pub I dread to think. Where will the locals go then? They are creatures left behind by a frantic world.

Our next trip was to Bexleyheath: much changed. Our house in Latham Road has acquired a garage and back extension on to the now through-lounge. The garden is very smart. Gone are the air-raid shelter and vegetable plot, to be replaced by lawn and flowerbeds. The owner said that, during the conversion, he had found remains of extensive bomb damage. Other than that, no traces of that dramatic era were to be found; although, not long after our visit, people were sent to a local school hall whilst an unexploded bomb was defused.

The director led me into discussing my two grannies, who had lived in our front room and shared our lives. One, Nanny Woodward, ' Louisa tickle an' squeeze 'er', was down-to-earth and helped take care of me as a child, whilst my mother worked, first in the pub and later in a shop. The other, Grandma Hancock, 'all fur coat and no knickers' was rather grand and condescending, and never lifted a finger to help, swanning around in a moth-eaten fur tippet, and unsuitably dressy clothes.

Starting on Grandma Hancock, we visited a place I had passed thousands of times when I lived in a nearby basement flat with my first husband, Alec Ross – the Pimlico pumping station. Resembling a charming Venetian palace, I had no idea that it was actually part of the London sewage system built following the three cholera epidemics in London in 1831, 1848 and 1853. The last one alone killed 20,000 people. The river was awash with raw sewage and the stink in the city was overpowering. Joseph William Bazalgette was charged with solving the situation and he came up with a plan to divert the waste from the Thames via new sewers, pumping it along to reservoirs and treatment centres outside London. The palace in Pimlico was one of the pumping stations. The whole place, inside and out, is a wonderful memorial to the Victorians' industrial vision; even for the dispensing of shit they built something truly beautiful.

My great-grandfather Benjamin Croft, an engineer who had served his apprenticeship in various dockyards, was appointed as the first superintendent of the pumping station when it opened in 1875. Behind the works was a small house where the Crofts lived and my grandmother Emma Easter was born. I had often seen it when the Gatwick Express pulls into Victoria and wondered what it was – this Victorian building now submerged under a complex of very expensive flats. I suspect that if Nanny Woodward had known of Grandma Hancock's childhood, there would have been some pretty crude jokes flying around, but the fastidious Emma Easter would have kept it quiet. She always insisted that she was 'used to better things', which I took with a pinch of salt as one of her fantasies, all of which got more elaborate as she sank into senile dementia. But the next stage of the filming had me rethinking my dismissal of her stories about knowing royalty and going to grand balls.

When she married my grandfather George Thomas Hancock, she took a step up socially. Not that his background was grand – no education that could be traced, his father a strange combination, according to the census, of station master and hosier – but George was about to join a very good company, Thomas Cook and Son, the travel agents. This the researchers discovered from his marriage certificate. Thomas Cook was a strict Baptist, dedicated to leading people away from the demon drink. To introduce them to a healthy lifestyle, he organised temperance train trips and teetotal excursions, at first in Britain and then venturing abroad. It was the beginning of popular tourism. Ironic, considering my aversion to holidays.

In 1885 when my grandfather joined the company in a lowly position in the office, it was considered a job with a great future for someone who worked hard. And work hard they did, from 8 to 6 o'clock in the winter and 9 to 9 in the summer. But it was a good firm to be with, promoting promising employees, regardless of education or pedigree. They had a Mutual Improvement Society, with debates, lectures and music, which I suspect my grandfather took full advantage of, judging by the skills he used later. Before long he ended up as branch manager in Italy.

So the next stop for filming was Milan, where my father was born. I was given a suite at the ornate Grand Hotel, all red plush and gold. Verdi had died in a suite here and Toscanini and Caruso were regular visitors. Another of Grandma Hancock's stories was that Enrico Caruso was Dad's godfather. Sitting in the front room in Bexleyheath it seemed unlikely – but then so was my father's name, Enrico.

The night we arrived, I was wandering around with the crew and Mary the director, when I commented that a little mink scarf in the window of one of the shops was an upmarket version of my dotty grandma's tippet. A lot of nudging took place, which was explained when filming the next day. Coincidentally the

very chic shop that the fur was in was previously the headquarters of Thomas Cook.

To be a branch manager, as the Cook's archivist explained,
was akin to being an ambassador in those days. It would
involve accompanying VIPs, including royalty, to the opera,
and on sightseeing expeditions to art galleries and the like. I
was shown the impressive apartment my grandparents lived in
overlooking the Duomo, where they would have entertained
regularly. Grandfather, and probably Grandma as the hostess,
would have been expected to speak Italian and, when he was
previously based in Nice, French. How and when they learnt
those languages, heaven knows. Could it be that he had an
actor's ability to learn lines and fill out with improvisation?
Whatever, he was obviously a bit of a performer.

These early days of Cook's tours are astonishing. There are
photos of people dressed up to the nines, camping in tents in the
desert, and in long dresses being yanked up the steps of the
Pyramids by native servants. The demands on the representa-
tives could be onerous, as Cook's insisted on nothing being
deemed impossible. Piers Brendon in his excellent book on the
subject describes one such challenge.

> G. M. Piccoli, who served in Cook's Rome office between 1905
> and 1951, was a model courier to royalty. When the Maharaja
> of Mysore demanded not only to meet the Pope but also to have
> his orchestra perform in front of his Holiness, Piccoli arranged
> it. He also shepherded the Maharaja through further European
> adventures, featuring a performing parrot, a banished relative
> and assorted chorus girls. Acting on the orders of the British
> Government when the war broke out, Piccoli at last got the
> Maharaja home, together with his sixty tonnes of baggage.

Through the archives we discovered that my grandfather
assisted in opening up the Italian lakes for tourists. Now, if

I had known that when we were pedaloing across Lake Como, I would have been very cocky with John.

So why, after all this grand living, was my grandmother penniless, living with us, sharing one small room with another old lady? Why did we discover that my grandfather ended up in rented rooms in Bournemouth, moving steadily down the social ladder, eventually dying in one room in a boarding house? He died of pernicious anaemia, often associated with heavy drinking, which gives me one clue to his downfall. That struck a chord: alcohol has played a large part in my life with both my husbands and my father having problems with it. Another possible reason for his poverty made me sorry but proud. He is recorded as campaigning for pensions for the employees of Cook's. Quite a bold thing to do in such a paternalistic organisation. The pensions were granted the year after he left, so despite a lifetime's service he was not deemed eligible.

He is buried in a churchyard in Bournemouth. When I contacted them it was suggested to me that he should be added to a tour they conducted of famous people's graves on the basis of being tenuously associated with John Thaw. I protested that Grandpa Hancock had claims to fame in his own right. Similar to John, he held his own in a glittering world, using his personality and self-taught skills. So, too, my grandma. When I watched her dancing with a lamppost in Latham Road, little did I guess that she really had tripped the light fantastic in elegant soirées in Nice, Genoa and Milan.

Then the programme turned to my Nanny Woodward. Her no-nonsense exterior concealed a tragic secret. Census records and birth and death registers revealed that she gave birth to twin girls. Daisy Octavia died at one month old of premature birth, attended by Nanny and her sister Emma. Violet Hettie died in an overcrowded boarding house in Greenwich when she was seventeen months old of whooping cough, which lasted for five weeks, culminating in pneumonia and convulsions. Little could then be done for babies with this dire illness. I had it as a child and remember the horror of trying to breathe whilst racked with the endless wheezing cough that the name implies. Watching a second baby die in such agony, without being able to alleviate her suffering, is one's worst nightmare. While we were filming my daughter Joanna was anxious about giving her baby son all his injections, and I reminded her of how blessed we are that so many childhood illnesses have been stamped out by the brilliance of medical science; and the courage of the people who subjected their children to the crude methods of early inoculation when the concept of giving your child a dose of the disease to prevent it was a new and challenging one. Yet, thanks to them, polio, measles, scarlet fever, and smallpox, which were dreaded diseases when I was a child, have all but disappeared.

I doubt whether even my mother, who was born some five years later, knew of this awful period of her parents' life. Nanny's husband, Albert, was a cutler journeyman, and along with my mother they moved around various rooming houses in Lewisham, Greenwich and Woolwich. I remember Nanny as a tough, taciturn, bustling little woman, who apparently pulled a good pint, and took no nonsense from tricky customers. She was also a milliner and dressmaker and always worked, a constant bone of contention with her lady-of-leisure roommate.

Nanny Woodward's birth certificate proved a major breakthrough in the mystery of the portrait – which it was decided was a photo of a painting – of the lady with the funny name. Although Nanny's mother's name was Louisa Octavia Zurhorst she was not the woman in the portrait. Digging deeper into the archives, one generation further back, unearthed her even more bizarrely named grandfather, Hamnett Pinkney Octavius Zurhorst, 1817–1903. He was married to a milliner.

Perhaps she was the lady in the portrait? But the subject of the picture didn't look like a woman who made hats for a living. It seemed even less likely when we discovered that Hamnett died a pauper in the Penn almshouses in Greenwich – he would never have been affluent enough to commission a picture of his wife, and then have an expensive photo taken of it. Kerry Taylor, the costume expert at Sotheby's, noted the huge sleeves, high waistline and frilly hat, all of which would be worn by a fashion-conscious woman between 1830 and 1835. Obviously a woman of wealth, but flashy. Pointing out how she is showing off her jewellery and posing with an open book, Kerry observed that our woman lacked the refinement and aplomb of an upper-class lady. More likely to be *nouveau riche*, possibly a wealthy merchant's wife. She shows signs of age, and to have a portrait painted when one is old suggests she is either vain or has only now made it from working-class poverty.

After much searching through the beautifully handwritten city archives it turned out that Hamnett's father Frederich was indeed a merchant. Before that, Frederich's father Hermann, my great-great-great-great-grandfather, had come from somewhere called Malgarten in Westphalia, a region of Germany. I had to stifle my reaction to this discovery.

At the beginning of the nineteenth century the City of London was buzzing. It was at the root of the spreading tentacles of the British Empire. And Frederich was right in there, wriggling his way to the top of his trade. It can't have been easy for him as a German. For instance, when he was admitted to the Guild of Scriveners in 1815 he had to enlist several friends to sign as to his probity 'by reason of his being the son of a foreigner'.

All merchant ships would congregate to unload and reload in the Pool of London by London Bridge next to the Custom House. The magnificent Long Room inside was described by Daniel

Defoe as the best meeting place in Europe. It was in fact the first trading floor, where Frederich would have operated. The noise must have been pretty deafening with everyone babbling in different languages. The oil dripping from the lamps, the stink of the river outside (which my great-grandfather Croft had not yet cleared up) as well as fish in nearby Billingsgate market, plus a coal-burning fire in the middle, cannot have made it a very pleasant place to be. In fact many people suffered from Long Room Fever. One important entry on the payroll was a cat, to deal with the rats.

The Long Room now is a much quieter place, with people working silently on computers. Their quest is still to trap smugglers, but they use the web for worldwide communication, and the traders they trap deal in drugs, pornography, guns, endangered species and children for the sex trade – less attractive commodites than the brandy, spices and tea of the old days.

There were several Zurhorsts in the trade dictionaries, relatives of Frederich, all of which we identified. One in particular puzzled me: 'A. J. Zurhorst. Ready-made linen warehouse. Equipment for East and West Indies.' I eventually realised it must be Ann Judith Zurhorst, Frederich's wife. It was one of several shots that had to be re-taken because of my expletives. It was unheard of for a woman to trade in her own right, unless she was a widow.

So here, at last, was the subject of my picture. What a character she turned out to be. We found evidence of at least thirteen children, not counting those that would have inevitably died. It was clear she had a child every year, as well as running her business, and helping her husband in his. We went to Idol Lane, one of those lovely backwaters in the City that survived the Blitz, where they lived for some time. An impressive home, with the stores on the ground floor, so yet again one of my ancestors had lived over the shop. With all these children, it must have been much easier to work and entertain in the same place, while keeping an eye on the kids. The names she gave her children seemed to tally with the rather flash image of the portrait. As well as Hamnett Pinkney, there was Augustus Darby, Cornelius Felix, Octavia Augusta and Alphonso Gustavus. Perhaps she was aware, as our researchers discovered, that the Zurhorsts could be traced back to Charlemagne.

After making, and certainly earning, a great deal of money Frederich and Ann Judith had moved to Guernsey. So off we went, too. Guernsey is a beautiful island. Buildings rather like Bath or Brighton, smart restaurants with a French flavour and flashy yachts in the harbour. It is now, as it was in my great-great-great-grandparents' day, a tax haven. Which is why the shrewd Zurhorsts were there. Having made their pile, they wanted to hang on to it. I imagine this is where she had her portrait painted and almost certainly so did Frederich, although there is no record of his. Doubtless she had it made into the fashionable new photographs, to give copies to her numerous offspring. She could never sit still long enough to be painted when working in London.

Not that she was idle in her supposed retirement. One delightful census entry puts her first, as head of the household, listed still as a trader, obviously not embracing the concept of retirement. Poor Frederich is last on the list but has earned the title of 'gentleman'. I suspect that dear feisty Ann Judith was never deemed a lady.

We finished filming at a tranquil graveyard in the Guernsey countryside. I was told to look at the gravestones. I guessed what I was going to find, and was resolute that I would be unmoved. I wasn't going to be caught out like Paxman. Why should I cry? I didn't know this woman. But over the two weeks, I had built up such a vivid picture of her that, when I found her grave, I dissolved. I felt ridiculous but she had really been alive to me as we pored over all the ancient records and discovered her existence. The cruelty of mortality overwhelmed me. This woman had been such a vibrant, active being, sur-rounded by a huge family and respected by business partners. Even in her so-called retirement, she was caring for a sickly grandchild, who was buried with her, as is another splendidly named son, Alfred Septimus, who died at thirty-two. All that love – all that life – and now she is completely forgotten. Several generations on, we had to dig and delve to prove her existence, and fill in the holes with our imagination. Re-create her. She had disappeared. Does it matter? I suppose not.

She had a good life by the look of things. Various Zurhorsts became traders in America, Rotterdam, Hamburg, Ireland, even St Petersburg and – who knows – some of her spirit may still be flickering in her descendants. Ambition, the work ethic, a desire to learn and improve oneself despite little education, a love of cities, adventurousness: I see all those traits in myself and my sister. I see her energy and love of children in my daughters. Maybe it was her inherited strength that helped my grandmother through her ordeal with her dying babies. Ann Judith had probably mourned several of her own.

On both sides of the family is a rootlessness and a curiosity about the world. Above all, the strange discovery for me was that all of them lived and worked by the Thames; since being an adult, I have never been able to settle far from the river, and now live on top of it, and doubt if I will ever leave it. Something deep inside me connects to its muddy old depths.

When we finished I was told that, not long after Ann Judith died, that bastard Frederich remarried a wealthy widow who lived near by. How could he? After all she did for him? Anyway, Frederich obviously regretted it because when he died in 1861, aged eighty, eleven years after Ann Judith, he was buried with his first wife. I didn't bother to ask what happened to the merry widow.

When I met Julian Clary to shoot the titles for *Who Do You Think You Are?* we compared notes on our programmes, and both confessed to being disconcerted by the German connection that they unearthed. Indoctrinated during the war to hate the Germans and all they stood for, was it possible that it had a more profound effect on my attitude than I was prepared to admit? I was shaken by my reaction. Was I – lovely *Guardian*-reading liberal that I am – a racist?

In a story written by Mark Twain in response to the Philippine–American war of 1899–1902, an ancient stranger enters a church and says to the congregation:

Beware lest when you have prayed for victory you have prayed for many unmentioned results which follow victory.

Then he says this bitterly ironic prayer:

O Lord our God, help us to tear their soldiers to bloody shreds with our shells; help us to lay waste their humble homes with a hurricane of fire; help us to wring the hearts of their unoffending widows with unavailing grief; help us to turn them out roofless with their little children to wander unfriended the wastes of their desolate land in rage and hunger and thirst . . . We ask it in the spirit of love of Him who is the source of love, and who is the ever faithful refuge and friend of all who are sore beset and seek his aid with humble and contrite hearts. Amen.

From 'The War Prayer' by Mark Twain

Westphalia · Berlin

PLENTY OF GERMANS HAD flown over my head, but I had only ever met one, face to face, in my life. Apart that is, from the pale, young captured soldiers we stared at like animals in a zoo, through the wire of their prison camp, in Wilmington, near my home in Bexleyheath.

In the fifties, I lived for several months in a big rooming house near Bromley when I was playing in the repertory company. Mrs Kaiser was my landlady. Orangey-gold crinkly hair, steady hazel eyes, and a nervous shyness. I did not question her about her previous life, but she told me once that she and her family had fled Germany before the war when they saw the brown shirts multiplying, and knew of children reporting their parents for criticism of the Führer. At least 70,000 others left Germany, 55,000 of them to Britain. They were mainly, like Mrs Kaiser, well educated and talented – doctors, musicians, writers, filmmakers – and Germany's loss was Britain's gain. I do not think Mrs Kaiser was Jewish, just appalled at what was happening in her country. So I didn't count her in my impression of the Germans. I sided with my parents, who, having experienced two world wars started by Germany, were convinced they were a dangerous nation.

Then, not long after I finished filming *Who Do You Think You Are?*, I was asked to play Fraulein Schneider in the musical of *Cabaret*. She is an Aryan German who falls in love with a Jew during the rise of Nazism in Berlin. My first fear was that I might not have the stamina or vocal agility to do a musical, so I ran through some of the numbers with the musical director, David Steadman, to see if I could still sing. That seemed OK, so now I had to decide if I could get inside the mind of this character, empathise with her dilemma. Judging from my reaction to my German roots, that might prove to be more difficult.

I have never been able to travel to Germany since the war. It wasn't a conscious moral stance or grand gesture, I just didn't want to go. I still didn't. But I knew I had to. Both to further pursue my search for the Zurhorsts, and to get a feel for Isherwood's Berlin if possible, as well as hopefully to rid myself of this phobia. I booked to go to Westphalia, the Zurhorst family home. The plane flew to somewhere called Munster. It didn't sound terribly inviting.

On the train from Munster to Bramsche I felt sick with fear. Irrational but real. There was an elderly couple sitting opposite me, and I found myself thinking that cliché: 'What did you do during the war?'

My arrival at Bramsche didn't fill me with *bonhomie*. A few people alighted with me and soon disappeared. I was totally alone, in a bleak little unmanned station. The travel agent who had booked my journey had been assured there would be taxis outside. I doubt if there had been such a thing, ever. A horse perhaps or a mule. I ventured up a deserted road, lugging my luggage, and encountered two taciturn civilians.

'Taxi?'

'Nein.'

That was the extent of their help. Eventually, I found a shop that reluctantly gave me a card with a taxi number on it. I sat down on my case and waited for it to arrive. Several people passed by and not one gave me so much as a nod. When after about an hour the taxi came, not a word was spoken on the journey through completely flat featureless countryside.

Malgarten Monastery, where I was to stay, looked lovely, if forbidding. To get to the door, I walked past a beautifully tended cemetery. A woman led me through echoing corridors to a room painted in warm orange ochre with fragments of ancient murals on one wall. Things were looking up. I unpacked and went to ask her if I could have something to eat. She had disappeared. It was like the *Mary Celeste*. I began to think all the inhabitants were in the graveyard.

I wandered around the monastery, hoping for even a friendly ghost who might know of a nearby café. Outside, the road showed no signs of life. In an empty room I found a telephone directory. No phone. Thank God for mobiles. Sure enough, there were several Zurhorsts all keeping up the peculiar name tradition. Rudiger, Bernuhet, Joachim, Helmut and – rather unfortunately – Ranke, Stank and Traute, who sounded like a German branch of Dyno-Rod. I tried ringing one of these numbers, only to be greeted by a torrent of German, a language I find difficult to take seriously after all the wartime Hitler imitations and Danny the dachshund in *Larry the Lamb*. So, I studied my map and decided that tomorrow I would just turn up, as a nice surprise, at the nearby farm marked on my map as 'Zur Horst'. If I didn't die of starvation in the night.

The next morning, hearing voices, I came upon a group of Lycra-clad cyclists stuffing themselves with breakfast. It dawned on me that this place was a hostel, where you provided your own food. I affected a wan and hungry look, but no one offered me so much as a Rice Krispie. In fact, no one spoke to me.

I slapped on some make-up, and a smart dress, and set off on foot in the boiling heat for my ancestral home. About a mile along the road, I found a broken sign marking the entrance to the Zurhorst Farm. After another trek down an endless drive-way, between flat ploughed land, I saw in the distance a dilapidated, low house with tumbledown farm buildings either side of a crumbling courtyard. Hot and sweaty and gasping for a drink, I made for what looked like a farm shop, where three women glared at me. A wiry wrinkled crone edged forward with the two others standing guard behind, ready to spring at me should I attack. I pointed at myself, smiling and nodding.

'Zurhorst.'

Instead of throwing her arms around me with delight as I had hoped, she narrowed her eyes and turned and snorted at her bodyguards. Thinking she had misunderstood – understand-able, turning up unannounced as I had – I showed her my copy of the family tree, tracing with my finger their names leading to mine. She was unimpressed. She was probably nothing to do with the family. Wordlessly, she led me into the dark interior of the house, and sat me in a small room full of tables, which I presumed was a sort of canteen. And left me alone. Once more, all contact with humanity was cut off.

After about half an hour, I wandered into the courtyard. A howling dog, covered in cuts and blood, limped up to me and I looked desperately around for help. Then I heard the banging and spluttering of an engine. Along the drive, an old jalopy jerkily approached. Out stepped a tiny tramp in a battered hat, with years of grime embedded in his face and hands.

He ignored the bleeding dog and stood awkwardly in front of me muttering, 'Joachim.'

He attempted a smile, but the deeply etched lines were not easily bent upwards. Still, he spoke a few words of English. I thought at least there might be a glass of water or a cup of coffee in it. But no chance. Joachim hobbled into a room stuffed with dark brown furniture, and showed me a beautifully painted family tree. There was my branch of the family starting with Hermann. I wanted to feel something profound but hunger, thirst and sweatiness precluded ancestral pride.

And that was it. My return to my roots; an episode from *Cold Comfort Farm*. Instead of a tearful welcome over a glass of champagne, my relations seemed to dislike my interruption of their work, eyeing with suspicion my smart outfit and make-up. And maybe my Englishness. There was no time for senti-mental chit-chat or tending to sick dogs. Their lives seemed to be harsh rural labour. A bit different from Frederich and Ann Judith, poncing around in tax exile on Guernsey, having their portraits painted. Thank goodness my branch of the family got the hell out of it, and sought their fortunes elsewhere.

On the trudge back, I passed a place that seemed to be a restaurant. At last. Of course, no one was around, but at least the door was open and I collapsed on to a chair inside. After a time a huge man of middle years, sporting an alarmingly unsuitable gel-spiked hairdo, appeared. He spoke halting Eng-lish and had a decidedly odd fixed grin. I now found myself in a performance of *Of Mice and Men*. After guzzling down a glass of water, I asked if I could have a meal. He looked astonished and did the usual Westphalian disappearing act. In the dis-tance, I heard a lot of angry shouting from a female voice.

'Meine Mutter,' he said apologetically as he returned.

I guessed it was she who had made him don an ill-fitting black jacket and bow tie. He ushered me, with great ceremony, into a huge dining room swagged with chintz and decorated with dust-coated plastic lilies. He bowed low and handed me a lengthy elaborate menu. I was the only customer.

The sauerkraut and weird sausage were pretty disgusting but as it was the only place to eat I had no option but to return the next night. I caught fleeting glances of the crimson-haired, heavily made-up fat mother who did all the cooking but she never emerged to greet me. I did wonder if the scenario would turn out to be a Westphalian *Psycho*. I was glad I wasn't staying there and using the shower.

I tentatively made friends with the gentle giant, whom I christened Lennie. He told me in a whisper that his mother would not have him in the kitchen with her, which made it difficult collecting the food, as he was the only waiter. I wondered why he had chosen this miserable life, and he told me that once he had worked all over the world on cruise ships.

I asked, 'Why did you give that up?'

He shrugged, casting a glance towards the kitchen, 'You have to settle down and have a family.'

I was glad he had a life of his own. 'So you're married? Where is your wife?'

There was a long pause.

'She left.'

I was nervous when he told me he had something special to show me. It turned out to be a framed letter received by his father in 1938. Proudly, he pointed out the Heil Hitler at the end. I couldn't understand the letter and didn't much want to so I was confused as to how I should react.

I said feebly, 'Oh, that's nice.'

Encouraged by my compliance he went on to tell me that during the war judges stayed at the hotel who presided over courts that were held in the monastery. I shuddered to think what those courts might have been. That night I did indeed discover a small cell, with a metal door, covered in bolts and locks, down the corridor from my room.

All told I did not feel I had come home. In fact I could not have felt more alien. Especially after an alarming encounter with some workmen doing demolition work in the grounds of the hostel. I went for a stroll and passed a cobbled path that they were laying.

I expressed admiration in sign language and thumbs up, 'Gut.'

'Sie sind Englisch?'

My German did not extend to explaining my ancestry so I just said, 'Ja, ich bin Englisch.'

They did not react.

When I returned from my walk, and attempted to cross their work area, one of the men drove a digger, very fast, straight at me. I should have jumped aside, but I could see it was no jolly jape, but meant to frighten me. And so it did, but I stood my ground. I felt belligerently British, and I was damned if I would run away. He skidded to a halt, just short of my body. I graciously bowed my head to him and the other two who were watching, smiled sweetly, and walked past muttering 'bloody Boche' through my teeth. All my latent racism raged through my head. Instead of thinking all people in the sticks of any country are, by my reckoning, a bit odd, I blamed the whole German race for this nutter's behaviour.

Not long after the war, in 1949, I hitchhiked through Holland to work for a voluntary organisation doing some reconstruction work near Apeldoorn, just across the border from Westphalia. Then our welcome was ecstatic. But in Holland we were the liberators. It dawned on me that in rural Germany I was still the enemy. In fact the British had only very recently left a nearby air-force camp, much to the regret of Lennie and his mother because the officers used to eat in their restaurant. But to most of the inhabitants I suppose we were an unwelcome occupying power. My northern friend from Solo was stationed there just after the war and remembers being spat on in the street: 'You bombed us.' The digger men probably hated me more than I hated the Germans. That gave me pause for thought.

That night, I heard music coming from one of the distant barns. There was a Mozart concert in progress. I sat on the steps outside, soothed by the beauty of the music. I reminded myself that Bach, Beethoven, Richard Strauss and Wagner were all German, and contributed greatly to my quality of life. Yet, as I stood in the street with my case next morning at 4 a.m., hoping that the taxi would turn up to start me on my journey to Berlin, I couldn't help remembering Ernest Bevin's comment to Sir Brian Robertson about the Germans:

'I tries 'ard, Brian, but I 'ates 'em'.

Welcome to Berlin. It was with a jaundiced eye I took in my first sight of the city during the drive from the airport. My antipathy to all things German wasn't helped by my Turkish taxi driver who, like others of his ilk, bent my ear with all that was wrong with the city and its inhabitants. He'd been there for thirty years and never had he felt more threatened. A unified Germany was a dangerous thing. Healthcare was non-existent. He could get no treatment for his bad back, rotting teeth and near blindness – as his driving demonstrated.

My arrival at the Brandenhof Hotel was the first pleasant event since landing in Germany; super luxury and affable staff. In my minimalist room, I recognised a lamp based on a Bauhaus design that gave me pleasure, if very little light. It reminded me of another area of German genius. The congenial hotel manager welcomed me with flowers and suggested a boat trip to get a first impression of Berlin as a whole.

It appeared to be a vast construction site. A mixture of decaying old buildings and sensational new modern design, incorporating solar panels and wind machines. This impression was reinforced when I wandered around on foot. I wanted to go on a guided tour but though I got myself to Zoo station I couldn't find the meeting place. The buildings all looked identical. I managed to get completely lost despite two guide-books and a map. Every bus or metro I took landed me in

Alexanderplatz, in the old eastern sector. When I decided to have a look at it, the main road was closed and the whole area flattened ready for reconstruction. I felt thoroughly disorientated. My map was hopelessly out of date.

Exhausted after a frustrating day, I spotted a sign advertising Thai massage back near the hotel. The tiny pretty girl looked confused and I apologised for not booking but asked if she could fit me in as a favour. She reluctantly led me into a perfumed candlelit small room and invited me to lie on the floor on a stained blanket. She gave me a gentle massage, and I thanked her very much and gave her a large tip for being so sweet. Whereupon she surprisingly kissed me fondly on the cheek. When I related this incident to the manager of the hotel, he roared with laughter and pointed out that the place was a brothel, and I was probably a kinder customer than the girl was used to. So I spent a sleepless night worrying about her and the sex trade.

The next day, with the help of the hotel staff, I was slightly more organised. On their advice, I attempted to buy a Willkommen ticket that allowed me to travel on anything, anywhere, but the man in the office at the dreaded Zoo station was so aggressive and uncooperative that I told him to stick his Willkommen up his Arsch and left.

Gradually mastering the transport system, I set about visiting one or two sights. But I still felt ill at ease. However, I was glad to see that, unlike in Budapest, it seems the Germans are confronting their past. Parties of schoolchildren were solemnly listening to talks by their teachers in several war museums. In front of one exhibit, which was a re-creation of a shop wrecked on Kristallnacht, a small group of youngsters sang a quiet little song that tore my heart.

In the jagged frightening Holocaust Memorial building, I was frozen with fear in the dark tower when the door clanked shut and the only light was a slit in the ceiling, through which I could hear the distant city sounds. A brilliantly conceived sensory experience, more telling than all the heartbreaking exhibits illustrating the suffering of the Jews during the Holocaust.

At the newly trendy Scheunenviertel area of Mitte, I found it hard to reconcile the juxtaposition of smart restaurants and coffee bars with the monuments and plaques telling stories of Jews herded out of these same buildings and marched along these now boutique-lined lanes. I even regarded as sinister the way Berliners, young and old, obeyed their green-man pedestrian-crossing signs whether there was approaching traffic or not. Deliberately, I crossed when I shouldn't, even if I risked being run over.

That night in the hotel, a pianist and saxophonist were playing smooth jazz in the bar. I downed several Ernest Hemingway cocktails and, as the other customers left, I was joined by the waiter. I was drunk and tactless enough to confide my misgivings. He was a wonderfully frank young man. He told me his parents and grandparents denied knowing what went on before and during the war, but like me he found it unlikely when it was so obvious. This drove a wedge between him and his family, because his generation were taught to face up to the war crimes. He went on to point out that the whole area around the hotel was completely destroyed by the Allies. His grandmother was raped repeatedly by the invading Russians. He explained that since the Wall came down Berlin was struggling with two different ideologies: people brought up under Communism and people brought up under the capitalist system were battling to accommodate one another. His total honesty should have cheered me up, but he reminded me of two other distressing aspects of Berlin – the occupation and the Wall.

I had to get out of this tragic place, the backdrop to continual horror. Far from, as I had hoped, having my prejudices dispelled, I was on the point of leaving with them intact and even confirmed. Then a friend of a friend contacted the hotel, saying there were a couple of women she wanted me to meet.

One, Irina, lived in East Berlin and was the daughter of a leading Communist; the other, Ilona, was a West Berlin film-maker intent on exposing Nazi war criminals. A fascinating mixed bag that was too good to miss.

I met Irina at Hackescher Markt. I told her she would know me by my blue hat, but I instinctively recognised her. The red-haired woman striding towards me stood out in the crowd. Not her neat, yet inexpensive, clothes, but her bright-eyed energy gave her an eye-catching allure. She was soon laughing a gutsy laugh at my tales of confusion, and, arm in arm, we went off to look around her world.

Where I had seen roadworks Irina saw rebirth. She was hopeful that the new construction would bring life back to the eastern sector but it was the restoration of the old buildings that most excited her. She expressed herself upset by the total condemnation of everything about the eastern way of life. It was not all Stasi nastiness. Even though she admitted that an organisation that boasted 90,000 full-time and 175,000 un-official people spying on friends and neighbours created fear. Now, the secret files are revealing details of past betrayals, and causing much pain. But it was not like that to begin with.

She was dismissive of the current fashion for Ostologie that sentimentalises the food and cars of the old GDR, trivialising their lives under Communism. When she took me to some of the craft workshops and party and union meeting places, she reminded me that it was the Communists and Social Demo-crats that presented the biggest opposition to the National Socialists during their rise to power. Their feuds with one another made them a less powerful opposition than they could have been.

To begin with I was wary of her positivity, as she had a

vested interest. Her father was Rudolf Herrnstadt, a leading Communist activist and journalist, editor of the party newspaper, *Neues Deutschland*. She was born in Russia of a Russian woman. Her father was actively involved in the creation of the GDR.

Irina took me to Karl-Marx-Allee, East Berlin's main boulevard, to show me an example of Communist town planning. Massive monumental blocks with two large towers incorporating flats, a hotel, shops and a cinema line a road that is eighty-nine metres across. At first glance I could see it was impressive, but I found it bleak and inhuman. For my taste, the road was too wide and the buildings too uniform. Dictator's architecture, meant to impress. Then with Irina's help I looked closer. She showed me where her father's newspaper office had been and described how he had been closely involved with the creation of Stalinallee as it was then called. Built by the workers themselves, with their involvement in the designs, it was an experiment in pleasant living space for them. No expense was spared in making it attractive. It reminded me of the attitude the Victorian English took towards the nobility of work, as in my grandfather's sewage works. The fountains and trees in the street, the parks behind for sports and the rooftop communal space were all designed to bring people together. The shops on the ground floor provided all their needs. One whole section was dedicated to children, with a toy and clothes shop, and day nursery, with small furniture especially for little ones. Never mind stories of them all being forced to be potty-trained by one year old, this was a charming place and a godsend for the mothers.

The buildings' exteriors are made of elegant stone and Meissen ceramic with, when you look closely, exquisite detail. It wasn't all show either. The interiors followed the Bauhaus principle of practical elegance. We visited some friends of Irina in one of the flats who have lived there since they first went up and they said it was, and still is, a happy place to live. Would that some of our sink estates had been built with such loving concern for their inhabitants. I rued my habit of making quick superficial judgements; on closer examination this was a lovely place. Fortunately, others are changing their opinions too and it looks as though this majestic area will be preserved from the mania of razing East Berlin to the ground.

The unity that this estate fostered worked against the state. It was here, encouraged by Irina's father, that a strike led to the uprising of 1953, which had to be quelled by Russian tanks, after which the iron hand of Russia gradually destroyed the early idealistic socialist vision. Irina's father was thrown out in the process, as were all the original visionaries. Nevertheless, the uprising started a change of attitude, later felt in Hungary and Czechoslovakia, that eventually led to the fall of the Communist satellite empire.

The grotesque Berlin Wall, built to keep the citizens of the GDR from leaving, was the uprising's more direct result. In one museum there is a film of the events shot simultaneously from either side as the Wall was thrown up in one day in 1961. In the west, incredulous citizens are standing on stepladders with binoculars, waving tearfully to their slowly disappearing compatriots. In the east, armed soldiers are keeping people at bay. One young woman ignores a soldier's request to leave. He returns a moment later looking more threatening, and she eventually walks away, head held high, but why was it that none of them fought harder against this monstrous assault on their freedom? Not even, apart from that girl, just shout their disapproval? Were they too intimidated and exhausted from years of dictatorship of one sort or another to do anything? When the time was right, of course, they did. The sheer weight of crowds and feeling dismantled the Wall stone by stone on that glorious day in 1989.

The highlight of my tour of the eastern sector was a visit to

Sophiensaele. This was the first headquarters of the German Communist party, and obviously a frequent haunt of the youthful Irina. At the top of some dark stairs is a magic ancient ballroom. Faded and peeling walls, tattered drapes, one expects phantom dancers to whirl around the floor. In fact, there was a live girl in a black leotard and tights, rehearsing a Pina Bausch-type dance. Silent and intense, she was oblivious to our presence. Rosa Luxemburg, murdered and thrown into the river for her left-wing views, had lectured here, but this girl was probably putting the enchanting room to a more suitable use. It is now an important performance space especially for modern dance. Much more fun.

Downstairs is a rumbustious family café. Tables round a dance floor, someone playing a piano, children leaping about, people gossiping and laughing. Irina was greeted warmly by everyone. The atmosphere was unlike anything I experienced in the more sophisticated West Berlin. It had a feeling of a past era; indeed, the clothes were reminiscent of the fifties and the people were obviously not wealthy. Nevertheless, it had a joyful atmosphere.

The Palast der Republik was another venue where Irina had a good time as a girl. It was the seat of government of the GDR, but as well as its political purpose it had a bowling alley, shops, a disco and bars. It was a fun palace and a meeting place. Now, after removing the asbestos, no one quite knows what to do with the remaining empty shell. It has fallen foul of the desire to eliminate all trace of the GDR, which Irina finds hurtful. So it remains a gaping ruin – in contrast to the Reichstag, the government centre of West Berlin, which has been gloriously restored with a spectacular dome by Sir Norman Foster, the British architect.

I so enjoyed my time with this vivacious woman, Irina. I love it when people make me rethink perceived opinions. Life in the GDR was not all bad. Its brand of Communision, like many ideologies, started out for the good of the people and then went horribly wrong, but it was not the fault of visionaries like her father. On the platform of the metro station we said our goodbyes and hugged one another. She stayed and waved as the train disappeared, a poignant figure. She lives alone with her memories, hurt and bewildered by the way it has all turned out, but full of hope for the future. She had shifted my obsession with the Nazis into consideration of what happened in Germany after they were defeated. What horrors had we, the Allies – Russian, British, American and French – inflicted that made that man with the digger hate me so much?

The occupiers could have behaved better. Rape, the usual weapon of war, was widespread. A black market thrived, in which, when all else was spent, one's body was the only currency and the occupying troops took full advantage of that. The contrast with their comparative comfort must have been hard to bear for the starving civilians.

The Russians feature large in the story of Berlin. They were the first of the Allies to enter the city at the end of the war. The fighting was bitter for twelve hours and many civilians died, often killed by their own soldiers. I was chilled to discover that Anhalt station, which I used several times, was deliberately flooded by the Germans to stop the Russians' progress underground. Hundreds of people sheltering there were drowned and more were killed by a shell that flattened their dead bodies to a wall. In twelve hours, there was an orgy of destruction. Even 200 animals in the zoo were wantonly killed.

The British took part in one shocking operation involving the Russians. It was decided that all people of Russian descent should go back to the USSR. Stalin regarded them as traitors, particularly his soldiers who were taken prisoner by the Allies, including his own son Yakof. He did not want them. Despite this the Allies sent back, often by force, two million people, many of whom were immediately killed or sent to die in gulags or committed suicide rather than return to a crueller death in Russia. Irina told me one tale of British soldiers forcing a troop of Cossacks over a bridge into a wood in the Soviet zone, where the sound of gunshots told of their fate. The Cossacks showed amazing courage, singing their beautiful litany and protecting their womenfolk as they went. Some of the British soldiers wept, and to their everlasting credit threatened mutiny until the process was eventually stopped. But the whole deportation was a shameful episode.

The carnage wrought on the Germans by the war was annihilating. In Hamburg alone, a firestorm ignited by our bombing caused more damage than in all the British cities put together. When Victor Gollancz went there he wrote to his wife, 'you know I went to Belsen on Tuesday? So I don't for a single second forget the other side of the picture. But these Germans are in an agony of suffering.' In Hanover, not far from the dreaded Bramsche, home of my path-laying friends, only 1 per cent of buildings were undamaged. This city of Berlin that I was wandering around, admiring its renaissance, was 70 per cent destroyed and the area around my plush hotel 95 per cent.

I took respite from searching archives and visiting museums in a concert in the glamorous Philharmonic Concert Hall. I watched Simon Rattle prancing around producing music for smart Berliners. After this, uplifted by the music, I strolled to Potsdamer Platz with its spectacular Sony and DaimlerChrysler buildings. In 1945 a German officer described it thus: 'The whole expanse of Potsdamer Platz is a waste of ruins. Masses of damaged vehicles, half smashed trailers of the ambulances with the wounded still in them. Dead people are everywhere, many of them appallingly cut up by tanks and trucks.' Later, people died here trying to cross the Wall, which went through the middle. Yet here was I, a tourist, enjoying the sights and sounds.

The worst statistic to contemplate is 53,000 orphaned children who struggled to exist in the wreckage of Berlin. I was struck with the thought that were I to pose my accusatory question to some old people, 'What did you do during the War?' their reply might well be: 'I was six and I starved and froze all by myself in the ruins that you created.' Or maybe the very old might have been one of the Trümmerfrauen who, dressed in their absent husbands' trousers and coats, struggled to clear the mountains of debris by hand.

There, on the actual site of such suffering, came a complete change in my thinking. All thoughts of 'serve them right, they started it' were blown away. All I could feel was pity and shame. And impotence at the insanity of war.

Next I met Ilona. Another redhead – a recurring theme in my German encounters – and a whirlwind of activity. A woman with a mission – and a dreadful driver. In her quest to show me the beauties of West Berlin, particularly Charlottenburg, where she lived, she ignored traffic lights, stopped dead if she saw something of interest, and took both hands off the wheel to gesticulate or emphasise a point. As a member of the Institute of Advanced Motorists, it is a wonder that I opened my eyes long enough to see anything. The most astonishing thing about our hair-raising tour was that never did any other drivers, forced to skid to a stop to avoid her erratic course, honk the horn or scream abuse. In London she would have been, in my opinion fairly justifiably, a victim of road rage. In Berlin, they took it in their stride. One hands-off-the-wheel moment was the site of a Jewish shop guarded by armed police. The passion it provoked led me to suggest we stop for a coffee and talk.

Ilona Ziok is a highly esteemed filmmaker on the Continent. Her father was an aristocrat who was a member of the anti-Nazi resistance. The subject of a lot of her work is Nazi war crimes. She mentioned several times that she takes risks with her films as there are people around, often in powerful positions, that are hiding guilty pasts and wish to silence her. Her next subject is a Jewish politician said to have committed suicide, but whom she suspects and wants to prove was murdered. She is having great difficulty raising funding.

Her film *Kurt Gerrons Karussell*, which I watched to help me with background colour for the musical I was soon to rehearse, was the study of a Jewish comedy actor and director who was sent to a concentration camp where he organised concert parties to entertain the prisoners. Some of the songs they wrote for the shows are gutting in their attempt to laugh at their situation. Satirical ditties about waiting for death. Eventually, Gerron was prevailed upon to direct a propaganda movie, showing how wonderfully the Jews were being treated in these holiday camps. He shows children frolicking and eating sandwiches when they were in fact starving. Nearly all these jolly Jews and Roma were shortly to be gassed. Ilona deals compassionately with the man's dilemma, even leaving open the possibility that he was a director who couldn't resist the opportunity to exercise his craft and make his work as good as possible. If the project was an attempt to save his life, he failed, for after the film was completed, he too was murdered.

Ilona lives in the very area where Christopher Isherwood stayed when he wrote his story of Sally Bowles, the English girl out of her depth in the decadent Berlin of the 1930s. The Nollendorfplatz, where my character Fraulein Schneider had her boarding house, is still a gay area, as it was when Isherwood, Spender and Auden got up to all sorts of larks there. I wandered around to get the flavour of the atmosphere. Ilona is not happy that, at night, when the club clientele's louche behaviour spills into the streets, there is trouble from neo-Nazi thugs. The rise of such gangs is exactly what her life's work is dedicated to avoiding. Never again should it be possible for someone to rise to power and say as Goebbels did in 1926: 'This city is a melting pot of everything that is evil – prostitution, drinking houses, cinemas, Marxists, Jews, strippers, Negroes dancing and all the offshoots of modern art.'

That would be funny, if it were not that a man with that sort of all-embracing hatred, who in England would be dismissed as a crackpot who writes to Radio Four from Tunbridge Wells, ended up actually carrying out the extermination of millions. As well as his wife after she, in her turn, had poisoned their six children.

I am glad that Goebbels and other perverted acolytes of the Führer ended up sharing a stinking bunker with the madman and his dead dog. It is a suitably squalid end. To hell with 'there is that of God in everyone'. I hope they were in an agony of terror and despair. I can feel no scrap of compassion for any of them. I am glad that they are completely erased from the earth, Hitler's burnt bones buried deep in an unknown place in Russia. Only one story of their deaths touches me. A vase of dead spring flowers was found in the room where Hitler and Eva Braun killed themselves. At the end that little vacuous creature tried to pretty up her tomb.

As Ilona pointed out, many of the criminals got away, some with the help of the Vatican. I admired her determination not to let the wounds heal over and be forgotten. I agree with her. She felt a responsibility to her father and I feel the burden of being one of a dying generation that lived through one of the worst events in history. As Ryszard Kapuscinski says,

We must act responsibly. To the degree to which we are able, we should oppose everything that could give rise to war, to crime, to catastrophe. Because we who lived through the war know how it begins, where it comes from. We know that it does not begin only with bombs and rockets, but with fanaticism and pride, stupidity and contempt, ignorance and hatred. It feeds on all that grows on that and from that. That is why, just as some of us fight the pollution of the air, we should fight the polluting of human affairs by ignorance and hatred.

Mind you, easier said than done.

There is evidence in the archives of many attempts before the war to alert the governments of London, Washington and Moscow to the dangers of National Socialism, but they were ignored. Inside Germany those men who attempted to assassinate Hitler were brave not least because, as military high-ups and honourable Germans, it must have been so difficult to disobey what was after all the government of the country, however contemptible. Most Germans didn't. Even when, it seems to me, it would have been impossible not to protest. If I had seen my Jewish schoolteacher being forced to scrub the pavement with a toothbrush, I like to think that, no matter what, I would have lifted him from his knees and taken him away. And I am sure others would have followed suit. Similarly, if persecution on the scale of Kristallnacht had happened in London surely there would have been a counter-offensive, as indeed there was in the East End when Mosley's fascists tried to march there? Hugh Carlton Greene, who was in Berlin in 1938, described how 'racial hatred and hysteria seems to have taken hold of otherwise decent people. I saw fashionably dressed women clapping their hands and screaming with glee, while respectable middle class mothers held up their babes to see the fun.'

Was Hitler so charismatic? Mesmeric? Even in the bunker, at the desperate end, this ranting maniac's orders were heeded, and surrender not allowed, so thousands more died unnecessarily, and Berlin was destroyed. Maybe we would be saved from such blind devotion by our British cynicism and our habit of mocking our leaders. It is a cross that has been borne by

Blair, Thatcher, even Churchill. And long may it continue. Imagine what we would have done to Hitler. Did, in fact. I can remember marching round the playground singing

> *Hitler, has only got one ball.*
> *Goering's got two but very small.*
> *Himmler's got something sim'lar,*
> *But poor old Goebbels has no balls at all.*

We must always satirise and joke about and send up those in authority. One of the best bits of news I've heard about Israel is that Mel Brooks' *The Producers* is playing there. I wish this consummate mocker of evil would tackle Osama bin Laden and his thugs.

In the Resistance Museum, on the site where an attempt to kill Hitler was planned and the would-be assassins shot, there is nevertheless much to cheer one. Stories of people that were prepared to die rather than surrender their self-respect. One in particular took my breath away. There is a photo of a laughing girl with a briefcase, fooling around with a group of youths in soldiers' uniforms, who is the spitting image of my best friend Brenda Barry – she of the Dancing Ledge idyll. She was a university student named Sophie Scholl, a member of the White Rose group that fought vigorously to make people see reason. Condemned to death for treason she said, 'Such a fine sunny day and I have to go. But what does my death matter, if through us thousands of people are awakened and stirred to activity?' This young rare creature was be-headed for distributing leaflets.

The fact that Berliners have survived at all is a tribute to human endurance. What must it have been like? Living in cellars or hovels made out of rubble. Starving. Freezing cold. Thirsty. Probably ashamed. People wandering around with no home, no future, defeated, reviled, terrified and maybe realising the enormity of what they had been party to. The denazification programme of the occupiers saw to that.

The Allies may have made mistakes but many tried to help. A director I worked with had been one of the first group into Belsen. He was eighteen and was shovelling corpses into a pit with a bulldozer and told not to put any food into the outstretched hands as it would kill the skeletal owners. These lads could spend only ten minutes at a time in the huts, full of dying rotting people and excrement, before they were vomiting at the stench and filth. Very young men saw horrors that people who do not experience war cannot imagine. But they did what they could.

Seeing the scale of the problem, the Allies were generous. I can remember, despite rationing continuing, our school sent food parcels to Germany. The English and Americans operated an airlift to feed cut-off Berliners when the Russians closed the food routes. And the Allies, especially the Americans, poured in aid. Whether for political reasons or not, it was sent to an enemy everyone despised. Surely to be admired.

Out of this chaos, Germany miraculously recovered. Unlike after the previous war, with the Treaty of Versailles, they did not use their poverty and destruction as an excuse to become resentful and belligerent. They are part of the European Union and that will ensure that there will never be another war with Germany.

Whilst I was in Berlin, they were preparing to host the football World Cup. Everywhere there were banners saying in English and German 'time to be friends'. A quality I found in both my new women friends was naïvety, a sort of innocence. A trait that can be disastrous or productive. It implies an ability to open yourself up, to expect the best. I was afraid the Germans' childlike plea to be friends would be rejected. Thankfully it wasn't. The younger generation, without all my wartime hang-ups, accepted the invitation. They danced in front of the screens by the Brandenburg Gate, oblivious of its past history. Families from all countries had fun together. The inspirational choice to use the Olympic Stadium, built as a propaganda weapon for Hitler and his crew, and turn it into a symbol of the new Berlin that welcomes strangers of any race and colour was a total success. I was so glad for Ilona and Irina that everyone loved their city.

I left by train from the beautiful new Lehrter Stadtbahnhof station. Actually I missed my train. It was a revelatory moment for me. The realisation that it didn't matter; I was on my own. Great. I had no responsibilities. No one would be angry, or have to be looked after. That was a relief. I could sit and wait for the next train. What the hell? Time to enjoy the fabulous view from this brand-new shiny station. This city that I blamed for causing a blight on my childhood had enlightened my old age. A city I have come to admire, and, yes, after a lifetime's alienation, feel affection for.

What good is sitting alone in your room?
Come hear the music play.
Life is a cabaret, old chum,
Come to the cabaret.

From *Cabaret* by Joe Masteroff,
lyrics by Fred Ebb

Manchester · London

I WAS GLAD TO get home. My visit to Germany had been pretty
traumatic one way and another. I felt better though. It was a
murky corner of my mind that had needed spring-cleaning. My
blind hatred of all things German had been swept away by the
people I met and the stories they had to tell and it was a relief.

I had to visit the City of London on business, and walking
through the streets on a summer's day lifted my spirits. Lovely
girls with swinging hair, baring their brown tummies to the
world in their croptops. Smart young businessmen, full of
energy. This area that, like Berlin, was flattened by bombs
and fire is full of life again, with modern buildings melding in
with the restored old remains. St Paul's is a symbol of survival
in the middle and nearby the Eye, the Millennium Bridge,
Somerset House fountains, Tate Modern and the ridiculous
Gherkin are glorious new fun. Berlin has more to recover from,
and has had less time to do it, but it is getting there.

I went up to Manchester to record a radio play, and there,
too, they have rallied since the IRA bomb in 1996. The
opportunity was seized to rejuvenate and modernise the city

into becoming one of the most vibrant in England. Some of the venerable old Victorian warehouses have been converted into glamorous flats and restaurants. I was, however, appalled that the hotel I stayed in was adapted from the historic Free Trade Hall. A crucible of political reform and later home of the Hallé Orchestra, it also housed some significant modern music artistes. It was here that Bob Dylan used an electric guitar, and someone shouted 'Judas' from the audience, implying he had betrayed his folk roots. Now, it's a tacky bar, full of men in tasteless leisurewear, on office freebies, swilling their beer under red plastic mock chandeliers.

I don't think I have ever approached a part with such commitment as I did in the musical *Cabaret*. Rufus Norris, our brilliant young director, was given more or less *carte blanche* to reinterpret the show. It was clear from the first rehearsal that anyone expecting anything like the fabulous Liza Minnelli film version was in for a big shock. Numbers were cut, and the order changed, and even some of the book rewritten. All great pieces of work can constantly be reinvented. Anna Maxwell Martin was far more like the original Sally Bowles in Christopher Isherwood's story on which the show is based. She was English for a start.

In approaching my character, Fraulein Schneider, who runs the boarding house in which a lot of the action takes place, the main objective was to cut away any twee sentimentality in the part, and make her the grimly pragmatic woman who provides perhaps the most realistic storyline in the show.

Actors usually speculate, as part of their study of a part, on the life of their character before and after the space of time depicted on the stage. I am convinced that Fraulein Schneider would have used her wits to survive the war, and would certainly have been one of the rubble women clearing up her neighbourhood ready to start business again. A Brechtian character. She would never be happy after her rejection of Herr

Schultz, particularly as he almost certainly ended up being gassed and incinerated in an oven.

The number when Fraulein Schneider confronts the naïve young American man, Chris, with her decision to reject the love of her Jewish friend got to me every night, particularly as Rufus had me come out of the scene and confront the audience with the question I personally had been agonising over: 'What would you do?'

Whether it was my absolute involvement in the subject matter, or one of the benefits of age, it was the first show in which I suffered little or no nerves. All of my professional career I have been dogged by stage fright. Crippling, vomiting, paralysing fear. It has been a considerable drawback never to be at my best, indeed frequently to be very bad on the night when the critics are appraising the show. Most people are scared on first nights but, once they get on stage, forget their fear and often give their best performance, fuelled by adrenalin. My fear always continued until the curtain call, which I felt ashamed to take. I would spend the whole first night telling myself I was rubbish. So I was.

I have tried everything to overcome it. I still go cold when I remember the first night of the revue I did with Kenneth Williams, *One Over the Eight*, when I dosed myself with a combination of beta-blockers, supposedly to slow my heart rate and subdue the accompanying panic, and amphetamines, to give me energy. In the opening chorus my mouth and throat were parchment dry, my tongue sticking to the roof of my mouth. Before the next number, I took a slug of brandy, and I began to froth at the mouth. Not the best performance of my career. I was barely noticed, although I was the leading woman: a terrible missed opportunity to break into the big time. Or, as Kenny put it, 'An early promise not fulfilled.'

Eventually, late in my career, I discovered hypnotherapy, and it transformed my work. In *Cabaret*, although I still needed a booster session with Ursula James my hypnotherapist, the first night was a doddle. The confidence I had acquired on my travels probably helped. The wider perspective.

When I was young, it all mattered so much. I wanted to be a star. I wanted everyone to love and admire me. But I never really thought I was clever/beautiful/classy enough to succeed. It took me a long time to acknowledge my ability. To try new things, and not be frightened to fail. No one likes criticism. Only the other day, I checked the Amazon critiques of my last book to give my confidence a boost, because they are so complimentary, only to discover some nutter from Lincoln had added a diatribe of condemnation. He was barely literate and boasted that he couldn't be bothered to read most of the book, but for a while I was gutted. The difference was, it was only for a very little while. No lying in bed, staring at the ceiling for days on end crippled with self-denigration. Life is too short. Particularly when you are over seventy.

The *Cabaret* company were particularly nice. Most actors are, but in this group we became very close, maybe because we all had to lay our emotions bare. The choreography of Javier De Frutos was demanding and dramatic and he required the ensemble to be naked in some sequences, leading up to a final searing image of people stripping as they entered the lethal death-camp showers. The curtain always came down to shocked silence, before the audience erupted into cheers. Nudity is not something actors or dancers like undertaking, and it was approached with sensitivity in rehearsal. When the company stripped off for the first time, I was full of admiration for their chutzpah. Very soon all the inhibitions went and it became quite normal. The ensemble and principals were good friends, which is not always the case; when you have been acquainted with people's willies on a nightly basis, there is little room for the usual niceties.

All my working life I have been puritanical about conserving my energy for the show. Protecting my voice and keeping fit during the day, in preparation for the quite considerable physical and mental effort required for eight shows a week. I feel a great sense of responsibility to the audience, who have paid a lot of money and maybe come a long way to see us. Strangely, on this show, when you would have thought I needed, at my age, to conserve my energy to sing and dance, I took to going out a lot. We discovered that many of us in the cast were alone for Valentine's night. All these beautiful gay and hetero lads and lasses spent so much time rehearsing and doing class, as well as working unsociable hours, that they found it difficult to meet partners; alas, the theatre is not the high life the outside world imagines. Still, as we were raucously dining, we eyed a morose couple in the corner, and decided we were having a much better time, particularly when I went downstairs and caught the man locked in a passionate embrace with a very young lady who was drinking in the bar below.

Despite my hectic and hugely enjoyable social life, I never missed a performance, which made me regret a lifetime of misplaced self-discipline. I was beginning to make something positive out of my absence of responsibility. Instead of regretting having no husband or kids to rush home for, I was using my new-found freedom to enjoy myself.

One night, during the performance, rushing to tell a piece of juicy gossip to our stage manager in the prompt corner, I stumbled on an unfamiliar step in the wings. My already dodgy knee gave way, and I crashed to the ground, breaking my finger and pulling a piece of scenery on my head. I managed to finish the show, and was then carted off to A&E in the nearby hospital by my very handsome director and stage director. Unfortunately, it was New Year's Day and the place was full of wounded drunks. After over two hours' wait, during which I filled in numerous forms, I was interrogated by a young trainee doctor, who was also considerably the worse for wear. After wearily examining my lumpy head and dangling finger, he produced two more forms for me to fill in to get a head scan and finger X-ray.

'And how long will that take?'

'Another couple of hours.'

'Sorry, I'm off.'

Whipping out another form, 'Well, you'll have to fill in this. '

Then he said rather leerily, 'And will these two young men be with you tonight?'

Chance would be a fine thing.

Having signed my form exonerating him of any responsibility for my subsequent death, I agreed to bind my finger to the next one and not let myself go into a coma, though he was nonplussed as to how I should distinguish between that and going to sleep. I played the rest of the run and, indeed, will live the rest of my life, with a crooked finger, as a result of my amateur bone-setting. A rather sadder consequence is that I can no longer wear my wedding ring. It has to go on a chain round my neck. In a way, this is symbolic. Forced upon me, but maybe timely. I was no longer married, but that marriage is still close to my heart.

The subject matter of the show did not allow for too much of the usual high-jinks that keep you sane in a long repetitive run. But we had the odd giggle. One night a piece of scenery flew in too soon, narrowly avoiding killing the dancers. The following night the audience must have thought it another bit of sexual deviance that two of the cabaret nudes were sporting builders' hard hats.

I had a line in my opening number: 'When I had a man my figure was boyish and flat.' One day I aberrantly sang 'When I *was* a man my figure was boyish and flat.' It convulsed the cast, but the audience took the idea of Fraulein Schneider being a transsexual in their stride, along with all the other sexual ambiguities going on in the show. Or indeed in Soho.

As I wandered around Soho on a Saturday night, looking for a taxi, I wondered at the queues outside clubs that provide a world I wot not of and have left it too late to explore. I have a touching school sewing book belonging to my Aunty Ruby from 1921 that amuses me. It is full of meticulous examples of stitches with names like faggoting and whipping. If I ran one of these Soho clubs, I'd call it The Sampler. Except that only old gits would know what that was. Nobody does dressmaking or mending these days. If socks get a hole in, then we throw them away. How the world has changed. Most people would say for the better. On Christmas Day 2006 I was not so sure.

I spent Christmas Day at Kids Company, where we served lunch to about 800 kids who had nowhere better to go. Families broken by division, prison, violence, drugs and alcohol result in bewildered, deserted youngsters – the feral children, as the press has disgracefully christened them. I had a wonderful time with them all, full of love and cuddles, fiercely protected from any potential trouble by Karen, a beautiful, streetwise girl who has become a friend.

I struck up a similar relationship with Sandra, a sixteen-year-old from the area in Manchester where John too roamed the streets as a child. Although I have sometimes harassed her with unwelcome advice, we two have formed a bond. Her upbringing has been the polar opposite of mine. It has been difficult for me, with my obsessive Protestant work ethic, to get my head round Sandra's lifestyle. I took her to the newly sparkling canal area for lunch. Suggesting we look at the menus of all the cafés before we chose where to eat, she flounced about a bit, telling me to decide. She didn't care. So good had been her act up until that day, I had not realised she can barely read.

When I gently prodded this out of her, she flew at me. 'What do you think it's like? Can't read where the fuckin' bus is going or text or use a computer.'

She furiously admitted that all the text messages and emails she had sent me had been dictated to a friend at the hostel where she lives.

It turned out she had approached a college about literacy classes but they had offered her special tuition 'with a load of spassies', her charming word for people who were in the same difficulties as herself. She was inordinately worried that that would lessen the respect of her friends. I insisted that she must persevere if she wants to get a job or training, even suggesting she get some work, however menial, to give her something to do other than drifting around the streets and getting into trouble.

'If I get a job they'll cut my assistance. It'll all go on housing and eatin' and fings.'

'Yes, that's what a job is for.'

'That's stupid, I'd rather sell drugs. Then I'm free.'

'But what about all the kids you are harming like you've been harmed?'

Shrug. 'That's the way it is, in't it?'

'Where do you think the money comes from for your assistance?'

'The fucking government.'

'No, me, my taxes. That I pay from my wages.'

Shrug. 'That's your fault, you're stupid.'

I was also considered stupid that I didn't leave the café without paying, whilst the waiter wasn't looking. As I settled the bill I could see her outside having a quick drag of a spliff and talking aggressively on her mobile. When I challenged her about the gun I overhead her discussing, she said she needed it to protect herself.

A lot of her chat is bravado to impress. Her desire for respect is real, but she only knows how to earn it by the values of the street. The old ethics of work, achieving success in your career, creating and supporting a family – a big laugh, that – serving society, don't enter her thinking. Why would they? She has never been exposed to them.

She was pushed from pillar to post as a child, through various care homes and hostels, so that she never settled at any school long enough to learn the basics of education. 'They didn't like me because I was trouble.'

She beat up her mum because her mum beat her, and had allowed Sandra's father to do the same to them both. He sexually abused Sandra as a child, as did his friends. Her various siblings, by different fathers, don't keep in touch with her, because of her violence. One sister is now in prison and Sandra was thrilled that she had been in touch to ask her to send a blanket to her. 'Maybe she'll be nice to me now.'

Running out of things to suggest that might help or motivate her I asked, 'If I could give you anything in the world, what would you like?'

'To die.'

Someone with no aspirations, other than to hang around the streets doing nothing much, who would, not surprisingly, prefer death – which she has made several attempts to achieve – is well nigh impossible to help. Certainly not by an overworked, ill-equipped social service that works to the bureaucratic rules. It is useless to lock Sandra away in one of the youth prisons in which children have been further brutalised. Several have been injured and two died as a result of legalised rough handling, one tactic of which is euphemistically called nose restraint. Which actually means punching in the face. This is just normal adult behaviour in Sandra's world, and she wouldn't turn a hair, let alone suddenly become a well-behaved member of the society they represent.

After childhoods of abuse, it is no wonder that children like her react so violently to supposed threats and sabotage every attempt to help them. Yet still the likes of Pat Stewart, with her On the Streets initiative in Manchester, and the saintly Camila Batmanghelidjh, founder of Kids Company, persevere. It is only at places like these that no one ever gives up on them, however impossible they are. And neither will I. Sandra will give an impish, vulnerable smile, after the turmoil of her life has provoked a frantic outburst, and I melt with love for her.

As my daughters had been with their in-laws for Christmas, we spent New Year together. John had an obsession with cameras. We always accused him of taking very boring photos and complained bitterly when he insisted on wielding his video camera at family events. Abigail had secretly found his old films and had them converted to a DVD for each of us. It took me a long time to pluck up the courage to watch mine. It filled me with remorse. Firstly, a lot of it was filmed when he was on his own, presumably not to annoy us. Although it was always in fun, I was bitterly sorry for all the mocking. He seemed to be having a lovely time doing the recording. There was sound on the camera, and so he is chuntering away doing a running commentary. In one sequence the whole family, including his father, can be seen having a whale of a time through the doorway into the next room, whilst he quietly chats to his baby grandson in a pram.

He was usually rather awkward with the grandchildren, but here he is loving and sweet. 'Hello, little Jackie. How are you?'

Raspberry from Jack.

'Oh, I see. Fair enough.'

Then he wanders around his 'estate' as he called the garden. Focusing on one drooping rose he says, 'Here's a rose I planted. Doesn't look too happy. Come on, little mudger. Perk up.'

Panning across the house, his voice is full of pride. 'There – beautiful, I tell you.'

Not being a country girl, I never had quite the passion for our house in Wiltshire as him.

Two days before he died there he said, 'Do you like it here now, kid – a bit?'

To my deep regret I said, 'I love anywhere with you.'

Which if, as I now suspect, he knew he was dying, must have been heartbreaking for him. Why didn't I tell him that I loved it? How amazing it was, that he had achieved this wondrous place? After the slum he grew up in. How grateful I was, and how comforted I would always be by this home we had created? But I was in agony. I knew he was about to die and thought he didn't. Or if he did, he seemed not to want to discuss it. But did he? Maybe I got it wrong? Perhaps he was desperate to talk, and I prevented him. 'Oh, that way madness lies; let me shun that.' All the words unsaid, the appreciation not voiced, the overwhelming love not expressed. Too bloody late now.

Regret is a pernicious emotion. And a waste of time. Just don't do it again. Which is why I shower my grandchildren, and Karen and Sandra, and any child who needs it, with paeans of praise, to the point of embarrassing gush. Unconditional love is not easy all the time. But grandchildren are there in short bursts and I can last those out without being mean as mothers sometimes have to be.

My other regret danger area is the anniversary of John's death, which falls on the day before my birthday. In 2007 it was part of an extraordinary week of sunlight and shadows. It started by me winning a prize. When it comes to awards I am the eternal runner-up. I have been in the final four for numerous BAFTAs and SWETs and Oliviers over the years but I am always the bridesmaid. This year, nominated for *Cabaret*, I went along to the Olivier awards ceremony out of duty to the show, ready to do my good-loser act – a little shrug of the shoulders, a moue of regret and then vigorous, happy applause for the worthy winner – and lo and behold, I won. What is more, the year before I had already won a prize for my book. Suddenly I care less, and it all happens.

I remember Thora Hird telling me that if I hung on till I passed seventy, I would get given awards for surviving and managing to struggle up on to the stage to receive them. Whatever the reason I was thrilled. I had a great night. Award ceremonies, I discovered, are much more enjoyable if you win.

I was at one of these functions when I was herded into a queue to pose for the press in front of the sponsor's logo. Alan Bennett was standing there on his own looking bewildered. Anxious for him, despite not knowing him very well, I grabbed his arm and said, 'Stick with me.' The result was a terrible photo in the *Evening Standard* of a frightened cringing man with Cruella de Vil. I wrote apologising for my presumption and had this letter back which sums up modern ideas of celebrity with Bennett's customary wit and gentleness:

Dear Sheila

No need to apologise, as I never saw the picture and was just thankful to have someone to accompany me past that terrible rank of photographers. The only photo I saw was of me and somebody (name unknown) who was a girlfriend (or a former girlfriend) of someone who was in (or used to be in) Westlife. Such is fame!

The *Cabaret* company and friends, the night following the ceremony, showered me with flowers and cards. I felt very special. Then embarrassed. For my birthday was the same week and they had to do it all again. It was a good excuse for some parties and I relished every minute of them. On the anniversary of John's death, I did not allow more than one quick thought of how much more wonderful it would have been if he had been there with that look of pride I loved so much. I was pleased for me. That would have to do.

The same week, my dear friends Richard and Annie Briers celebrated their golden wedding. It was a sweetly nostalgic event. They held it at Julie's, one of the first trendy restaurants in London. In the sixties and seventies it was a haunt for people working in the theatre and films. A friend of ours, Barry Krost, who is now in Hollywood, would hold a salon during Sunday lunch, around a huge round table. In winter there was a roaring fire. All the papers were provided, and we devoured the latest critiques, Tynan being our most feared and revered protagonist. We were also very political, from all sides of the spectrum, some quite nutty, but passionate. As we began to have children, they too were brought along. I remember bundling my daughter and Alan Bates's son into my car, and driving around the block to get them to sleep, in between the roast beef and treacle tart.

Now, here we all were, older and greyer, celebrating Richard and Annie's fifty years together. Some, like handsome brilliant Alan, were dead. It was a bittersweet occasion. Remembering when I was young and lusty and full of plans for the future, and how we would change the world. I didn't have to assume a dining character here, they knew me too well as myself. The Briers girls, Lucy and Katy, made charming speeches in praise of their parents that ruined my mascara.

When John was alive I lost the habit of friendship. We only needed each other. Without him, I had insidiously become demanding of my daughters. Why didn't they ring? Why no visits? I might be lying dead at the bottom of the stairs with a broken neck and no one would know. Or care. I spent Christmas alone. How neglected am I? After all I've done and do for them. The worst thing about being alone is how obsessions escalate, especially at four o'clock in the morning. With no calming 'no, wait a minute, wait a minute', small irritations erupt into volcanoes.

A crisis was reached when one of my daughters didn't buy me a birthday present or card. Actually she was away and got caught in a cyclone and was sick as a dog, having just discovered that she was pregnant with Louis – but that was no excuse! When I confronted her, a blazing row ensued in the course of which certain truths dawned on me. The starkest of these was that I had no God-given right to demand love from anyone. Or company. Or respect.

As the show came to an end, I made a resolution to enjoy my friends more, and lean on my family less. I had started going out after the show with friends. And enjoyed it. I stopped waiting to find out if my daughters wanted to see me on my Sunday off, and arranged lunch out with one mate and tea with another. It was good. I can't gossip with my daughters as I can with my friends. Botox and hip replacements hold no interest for them.

We have such rigid expectations of family relationships. Most are based on sentimental misconceptions. My forty-year-old daughter's wail of 'I want a mother' broke my heart. What she wanted was the all-loving, placid, selfless supportive mum of the tabloids and storybooks. Or indeed my own darling dedicated mother. Not the cantankerous, moody, working, unreliable reality. But, and here is the breakthrough – this is who I am. My friends see other sides of me. Dammit, there are other sides to me. But they are not a lot of use if you want an archetypal mother. Nor am I fair to want storybook daughters who care for their ageing mum like the woman on the Solo tour. They have lives to lead. They are all leading them productively and well and I am deeply proud of them. During my journey of the last few years they have struggled to help me but it was a road I had to travel alone. They are always there if I really need them, but they are not responsible for my entertainment. So, as I heard every night in *Cabaret*, 'What good is sitting alone in your room?' I need to 'come hear the music play'. It takes a gigantic effort. But it can be done, as I had begun to prove. As soon as I stopped whining and demanding, our relationship became much better for everyone. Not the stereotype in women's magazines, but richer and more realistic. Breaking free of the supposed duties of a mother/daughter relationship, we moved on to something more relaxed and enjoyable. Being together was no longer an obligation – it was a delight.

To mark this step forward, I gave a big party on the day of the Boat Race, which passes my house. When writing the invitations I was aware of how many new names had been added to my guest list since John's death.

At one point during the party, my daughter whispered, 'Who *are* all these people?'

And I was able to say, 'My friends.'

Things were very definitely changing in my life. The last year had given me confidence. I was feeling quite grown-up. About bloody time.

Look thy last on all things lovely,
Every hour. Let no night
Seal thy sense in deathly slumber
Till to delight
Thou have paid thy utmost blessing;
Since that all things thou wouldst praise
Beauty took from those who loved them
In other days.

From 'Fare Well' by Walter de la Mare

12

Venice · Fontenay Abbey · Milan

I DECIDED TO GO to Venice. I had crossed a few bridges in coping with life on my own, mostly by branching out into new experiences. I was living in a new house in London, had new friends, had a new more profound relationship with my daughters, and had visited new places. I had endeavoured to move on from my life with John, eschewing nostalgia. Fear of looking back on our lives together was beginning to limit my horizons. Examining my wartime childhood had been bene-ficial. I now needed to venture to a place where in the past I had been supremely happy with John. It was a risk.

No one was around to come with me and I figured I would need some company on my first visit without him, so I enlisted for a tour with a lecturer on the Genius of Renaissance Venice. I thought sharing a common interest might help me overcome my groupitis.

It started well. The approach by sea to Venice was, as always, so gobsmackingly beautiful that there was no room for any other reaction but awe. My fellow tour members seemed friendly and the hotel, on one of the smaller canals, was a fifteenth-century merchant's house. No palace, but up-market enough to have its own ornate well, fed by the guttering on the roof, and a grand stone staircase to the upper level.

The first gulp of memory was the square near the hotel, which I recognised as a place where John and I had watched two white-masked figures in flowing peacock-blue and green robes, dancing a stately, impromptu silent gavotte, away from the exuberance of the main carnival. It mesmerised us, and I recalled it now with pleasure not pain. So far, so good.

St Mark's Square was the next challenge, and here again, sitting on my own in the sun, sipping a coffee, listening to the music, and reading my study books for the tour, I smiled as I watched people feeding the thousands of pigeons, remembering John's snarled 'rats on wings'.

It is not as perfect as it seems, this exquisite city, built on stilts in the sea. It is proud of being a republic, although of course government involved only the patrician class, led by some decidedly dodgy doges. The palace is pink and shiny and beautifully proportioned, yet it houses a soundproof torture chamber. St Mark's Basilica next door is a complex oriental/Gothic/you-name-it-they've-got-it-type building in which there are untold treasures, many of which were pinched from other countries. Even their patron saint was stolen when they decided that such a grand city needed someone more impressive than poor old St Theodore and his rather odd crocodile, who were banished to a very tall pillar in the Piazzetta, where no one can see them. In fact it may not even be St Mark in the sarcophagus that everyone venerates, or indeed anyone at all, but never mind, it is a sumptuous cathedral. I was going to look on all things lovely and enjoy them for John.

Our tour started in earnest the next day. The lecturer, Joachim, was German, tall and rangy, with the vague air of a university don until he started talking about his subject when he became focused and brilliant. Not just because he was extremely erudite and he knew Venice well, having lived there for several years, but because he was in no way blasé or jaded about its beauty. In fact on several occasions he was moved to tears by sights he had talked about many times. I liked him for that.

There were several of his groupies on the journey. They repeatedly go on his tours and hang on his every word. Venice is such a cornucopia of delights that it is easy to miss the detail. My appreciation was made more profound with the guidance of his knowledge. Most of my fellow travellers were much better informed than I, so, once more, I had to bite my tongue, lest I bored them with my naïve questions.

The rebel in me sometimes wanted to challenge the accepted view of what was a masterpiece. I don't like following the party line (that's why I could never go into politics). In the Scuola di San Rocco I dutifully gasped at the decoration on the walls and ceiling by Tintoretto that took him twenty years to complete, but they made my neck ache and I preferred the *trompe-l'œil* wood carving that Francesco Pianta had done on a side wall. I loved the pair of spectacles on the mock bookshelf and the wicked caricature of a bug-eyed Tintoretto, which I hope made him laugh.

I became intrigued by the lives of these genii that lived and worked in Venice. I speculated on the personalities of the men behind the masterpieces. With all the *scuolas* and churches vying with one another to get the most fashionable artist or sculptor to do up their building, was there rivalry? Tintoretto may once have worked for Titian. Was Titian pleased at his pupil's success? Or a bit miffed to see the younger man getting jobs that he might have done? What did Gentile Bellini, no mean painter himself, feel about his brother Giovanni getting the lion's share of the praise? Or did he recognise his superior talent? Did they all get fed up with being used as upmarket interior decorators? For several of the days we were there, the weather was freezing and the buildings felt icy. How wretched was it to clamber up scaffolding and lie on your back painting a ceiling in a cold echoing church? Did they wear gloves on their frozen hands, as they covered the stone walls with radiant colour?

The Frari was like a fridge when we shuffled past all the huge and, frankly, pretty ugly monuments, skilfully carved but so overpowering. Joachim helped by pointing out brilliant details, like a stone wave effect or a perfect depiction of a manuscript, but the overall impression depressed me. Then, there in a separate chapel, is the Giovanni Bellini triptych of the Madonna, before which even his brother must have piped a tear. It is quite simply perfect. How did he achieve that three-dimensional effect? The frolicking cherubs playing music and having the time of their lives are a delight. Angels often add a bit of fun to the most reverent pictures. I noticed one cherub showing his bum to the viewer in the corner of a very sombre Titian.

Once I got on this track, I kept looking for tiny details that suggested the artist was bored with having to do religious subjects. Imagine if some of those superb talents had been born later, free to do what they liked, instead of endless Madonnas. Madonnas, what is more, that fit the mythical pattern of piety and white skin, acceptable to the leaders of the church, but hardly realistic.

My yardstick for depictions of Mary is in a small stone retable in the choir of Fontenay Abbey in France. It is a nativity scene, a carving of Mary lying flat on her stomach, absolutely knackered, and beside her is Joseph, or maybe a shepherd, sitting leaning forward on a stick, equally exhausted. Behind them is the Messiah lying in a box, with a comic cow's face looking at him, hopefully solicitously, but it could be, based on my experience with cows, about to bite baby Jesus. How history would have been changed if Jesus had been eaten by a cow. And you can bet your life Mary would have been blamed, and a lot of artists and church builders would have been out of a job. It is a tiny carving and easy to miss because there is a spectacular tile floor in front of it, but it is worth turning your back on that to see what it would really have been like in that smelly stable with a demanding new-born baby. And, let's face it, there aren't many portrayals of the Virgin Mary that make you laugh. You come away from the abbey thinking that perhaps those Cistercian monks actually liked Mary, which is more than you can say for many of the cold, religious statues and pictures of her you find in Venice.

The artists did their best to bring the same old subjects to new life. Veronese, commissioned to do yet another *Last Supper*, went to town with a much more jolly meal than usual. He was summoned by the Inquisition to explain why the picture contained 'buffoons, drunkards, Germans, dwarves, and similar vulgarities'. (The poor Germans were being got at even then.) Unabashed, he simply changed the name to *Feast in the House of Levi*, to which, presumably, Jesus just happened to drop in. Carpaccio, told to do the *Miracle of the Relic of the True Cross at the Rialto Bridge*, poked the subject matter into a corner and gave centre stage to a little white dog in a gondola.

Carpaccio, who before this visit was just raw meat to me, has become my all-time favourite Italian artist. He is the Stanley Spencer of Venice. You can visit and revisit his St Ursula series in the Accademia and see a new, funny or touching detail every time. I suppose it is a reflection of my ordinariness that I find him a relief from all the grandeur, verging on pomposity, in Venice. Carpaccio's paintings in the humble Scuola di San Giorgio are charming: accessible and human and full of life. There is the little white dog from the gondola popping up again in a picture of St Jerome in his study. The holy man is gazing out of the window, thinking lofty thoughts, while the little dog, again centre stage, is looking at him thinking, 'Oh come on. Get on with it. When are you going to take me for a walk?'

In Palladio's classic San Giorgio Maggiore, we had a moment to treasure. A choir was rehearsing for a concert. One of the monks sang a haunting medieval canto that sounded like a Jewish lament. Listening to it, in this magical building, with the door open to reveal the lagoon and Venice glistening in the sea beyond, had Joachim and me quite out of control.

To recover we all went to the best cake shop in the world, near Santa Margherita, bought a feast and went back to the hotel to scoff it. A very grumpy German man in the lounge started huffing and puffing at the noise we were making. High on cakes and transcendence I blurted out, 'For God's sake don't mention the war.' I was mortified that after my visit to Germany, and in front of Joachim, I could revert to my old knee-jerked prejudice. Me and the Inquisition. Joachim laughed it off, obviously used to cheap jokes.

He had another special delight for us. He got permission to visit St Mark's Basilica after it was closed to the public. Usually it is so crowded, it is impossible to see anything properly. Especially the floor, which is a miracle in mosaic, some of it incredibly modern in design, looking like a Bridget Riley painting. As we stood awestruck, the church was gradually illuminated, so that the mosaics sparkled. Talk about bling. Even Sandra would have been struck dumb. We felt privileged to absorb the splendour in silence, without the chatter and pushing and shoving of hundreds of people. Then we were invited to go up to the balcony, on which the originals of the famous horses are kept, those on the exterior of the church being replicas. For some reason for me, who am not greatly fond of real horses, the sight of them was devastating.

It was not because they are so real. Or that one of their faces is wild with desperation to get out of their dark prison, his veins standing up on his neck, eyes staring into the distance. Another is looking down in resigned despair at its fate. They are incredibly lifelike. I imagined what hell it is for them, these horses who have travelled the world, to be condemned to stay trapped inside, gawped at by uncaring humans. They have been to Greece, Rome, Constantinople, Paris, Rome, even to London, and until fairly recently stood outside the Basilica, looking down on St Mark's Square. Their feet are pawing the ground ready for flight. Mad, I know, but I too felt the panic I saw in their bronze eyes. My feelings were wide open, ravished by too much beauty. Suddenly I was overwhelmed by sorrow, remembering John hadn't seen them. We had been exhausted by sightseeing and decided we'd seen the replicas so that was enough, we couldn't walk another inch. So he didn't see these amazing creatures. And never would. I couldn't bear it.

Just when I think I am balanced and coping, out of the blue, grief wallops me in the gut. I was perfectly all right as I climbed the stairs, then in a trice my composure disintegrated. The next day I pleaded illness. In a way I was ill. A sickness of the soul. I lay in bed, listening to the sounds of Venice outside, bells, footsteps, voices, life, but I wanted none of it.

Knowing the pattern, I forced myself out of bed the following evening, and went for a walk. Big mistake. I found myself outside a restaurant we had visited together. I went in. It was completely different. Whereas it had been a little local café, it was now in some guidebooks, so full of tourists. Too late to withdraw, I choked down a plate of spaghetti.

Inevitably someone approached. 'I know I'm intruding but would you sign this? We loved your husband. We were so upset when he died. We felt we knew him. We miss him terribly.'

Nice people, but I wanted to shout: 'You didn't know him at all. You miss Inspector Morse, not the funny irreverent guy who sat with me at this table, where I'm trying not to scream as I smile politely. Yes, I am as lonely as I look. *I* miss him agonisingly. He hurt, frightened, dismayed but never bored me. In this café he romanced me and made me roar with laughter.

We took a gondola back to the hotel and it was bliss. I ache for him and the fun and the love and the held hands.'

But of course I actually said, 'Thank you, that's very kind.' And walked back to the hotel in the dark, weeping.

I had a letter from an Anne M. Bartlett, a woman who had read *The Two of Us*. In it she said, 'Someone should campaign for the right to weep. It is all very well to cycle home from wherever, with tears flowing freely, being dried by the wind, but how acceptable would it be if I had been a resident in a retirement home? Would the staff have decided I was depressed and asked the doctor for medication? How many elderly people are deprived of the right to relive their memories, with tears for past errors, or past delights, because the staff think they are deeply unhappy? And from the first medication would come confusion and loss of memory.'

She is right. There is nothing wrong with tears, be they of pleasure or pain. It will always be like this. I'll be all right, and then without warning I'll be engulfed by waves of grief. That's OK. The world is full of wonders but also tragedy. It has to be endured, even – strange choice of word this – relished. Anguish is the limit of human experience and it stretches the emotional muscles, just as do uncontrollable laughter and rapture. A corseted contented life is not for me. I must not push away memories of John just because they might make me cry, because that way I will lose the joy as well as the pain.

Next day, of course, I was fine. The sun shone and I opened my eyes again to the world around me. And it was good to see.

Venice is a nice place for dogs, with no cars to menace them and lots of pigeons to chase. I bet Carpaccio's little white, fluffy fellow had a good time when he had wrenched Jerome away from his contemplation and his lion. Why do the locals always stand up in boats, including the gondoliers, and passengers in the *traghetto*s ? Where *are* all the locals? I saw one old lady being pushed in a wheelchair, by a butler, in white gloves. Her face was like a medieval painting, with its patrician sternness and beaky nose. Her make-up was a white mask with crimson lips. She wore a purple turban and an ancient voluminous mink coat and her long thin fingers were covered in huge rings. A Venetian Edith Sitwell. She stared ahead of her, trying to not see the vulgar backpackers and inelegant tour parties. A relic of a bygone age.

Whilst we were admiring the exquisite marbles outside the Scuola San Marco, some kids were using them as a goal, walloping a football at them. I couldn't join the general disapproval as I was pleased to see that, to these children, it was not a museum but their home, where all the walls just happened to be beautiful.

Venice's 270,000 remaining residents are gradually leaving, swamped by the floods and me and the fifteen million other tourists a year. La Serenissima belies its name by becoming chaotic, packed with jostling crowds, mangy pigeons, and noisy motor boats. There is graffiti on ancient walls, dog shit on the cobbled stones, and the usual detritus of tourism everywhere. The jewellery shops and smart boutiques are being replaced by tacky souvenir shops. The gondoliers sing camp songs to giggling passengers, instead of being the superbly graceful, superior beings they once were. Carnival is no longer a mystical rite where beautiful handmade masks allowed anonymous rich and poor, aristocracy and servants, to dance and get up to all sorts of things together but is now a show, provided for the public, and a bit tawdry.

I have a plan. How wonderful it would be if the bridge joining Venice to the mainland were blown up. Then everyone would have to approach by boat. But only little ones with no engine. I would ban all the motor boats that are eroding the buildings and certainly forbid the gigantic cruise ships to come anywhere near its hallowed shores. Anyway, no one should be allowed to visit Venice for a few hours just to tick it off on a world cruise. At least a week should be obligatory. How can you possibly get any idea of its wonders in less? It would take the city back into the gentler times that suit its character. In this ecologically aware age, it could set such an example and preserve Venice from further decay in the process. Venice would become a place for people who are prepared to make a big effort to get there and truly appreciate and respect it. If you drop a crisp bag in St Mark's Square you will be thrown into the lagoon. It must go back to being a Canaletto painting. If you can't swim or row or sail, and don't know anyone who can, hard luck, you just can't go. Because it is on an island, and the bridge has gone. There are no trains and the exhaust fumes from cars stay on the mainland. How lovely that would be. I must start rowing practice at the gym.

The group had a farewell dinner on our last night. We had had an enlightening holiday. They were entertaining people: a reluctant complaining man, doing the trip under sufferance, with a lively intelligent wife, who surely must have wanted to wallop him; several couples hugely enjoying the release of retirement, gleefully spending their kids' inheritance. Some made new friends during the trip.

One woman remained remote. She was immaculate, middle-aged and rather attractive, apart from being a bit twitchy. She was besotted with Joachim, having been on several of his tours. She listened devotedly and was teacher's pet, knowing all the answers and asking clever questions. She became beautiful when she smiled, if Joachim paid her a compliment. I suspect she was cripplingly shy, for she always went off on her own in free times, and shied away like a frightened horse if I tried to talk to her. On the last night she looked terribly down, and I wondered to what sort of life she was returning.

I too was a bit of a loner in the free time, what with mini nervous breakdowns and curiosity about things not on the regulation routes. But I did spend some time with an admirable woman. When I enquired about the patch over her eye, she explained she had just had a massive operation. Something to do with platinum being injected into her brain to seal up an aneurysm. She had been told she must not travel any more. The only possibility of changing that verdict was to have this operation, which stood a very good chance of killing her. Without hesitation, she chose the life-threatening course, so appalled was she at the thought of being grounded. Her credo was that after a lifetime of marriage, career, children and widowhood, you visited Asia and the Far East in your seventies, Europe in your eighties, and toured England in your nineties. She would rather die than not proceed with that agenda. This was the first trip after her operation, and she was as energetic as anyone, even though her head 'didn't like the flight much', hence the eye patch.

And yet, despite liking the group very much, I didn't strike up a special friendship. I need a particular type of mate for travelling. They have to like wandering off down back alleys, particularly in Venice where some of the most potent sights are the crumbling echoing canals that featured in Nicolas Roeg's classic *Don't Look Now*, one of John's favourite films. My companion has to be a guide and history book freak, prepared to stand in front of buildings reading out information, or sit in cafés studying. They have to be ready to trudge around looking for cafés that have only locals in, so that we can have an authentic, if sometimes foul, meal. They have to be able to emote without inhibition at glorious sights, and dismiss as overrated rubbish some of the objects lauded by the *cognoscenti*. Sitting people-watching in cafés and earwigging conversations is also a must.

I have one friend, Julie Legrand, who ticks all those boxes but if she is not available I would rather go on my own with curiosity as my powerful driving force. Joachim told me about a splendid Bellini to be found in the Brera Art Gallery in Milan.

The train from Venice went straight there. Why not? Take the train – before I blow up the bridge – and pursue my new passion for pictures.

It felt very Grand Tour to be visiting a city for its art. It was also an opportunity to revisit my father's birthplace, this time without the film crew.

I love trains. Not only do you get a feeling for the landscape but you also meet some interesting characters. On this trip, it was a study of Europe meets the United States of America. Already settled into their seats when I arrived were a southern belle and her husband. She was a rather large Blanche DuBois, with long red-gold curls in a style that hadn't changed since childhood, framing a very lined, yet pretty, face. She stuffed herself with pastries, delicately wiping the corner of her mouth with her little finger before bunging in another cream-filled mouthful. Every now and then, with a flirtatious giggle, she popped a morsel into her equally fat husband's mouth, brushing the crumbs from his new Gucci leather jacket with fastidious care. If he looked about to drop off to sleep and, heavens to Betsy, dare to snore, she would nudge him quite viciously with her elbow.

When some beggars got on the train, she got into a terrible state. 'Why don't they stop these folk coming on? I guess they haven't been attacked like us.' Presumably meaning the Twin Towers.

The Italians in the compartment looked on with detached bemusement. There was one man who could not have been more of a contrast to the open, baby-faced American man. Italian men's faces seem so morose in repose, eyes staring into the middle distance, world-weary. Once they start talking, their whole demeanour changes and they become animated, gesturing and shrugging, seeming always to be in a state of high excitement. My father must have picked up these characteristics growing up in Milan, for he embarrassed me as a child by being so unlike all other Englishmen. So showy-offy I thought then. Now I cherish the memory of his difference.

There was a furniture fair taking place in Milan. It is now the centre of up-market exhibitions of design, be it cars, décor or fashion. It is not as beautiful as Florence or Rome, having been devastated during the war, but it is now the epitome of modern chic. My eyes boggled at the goodies in the elegant shops.

All the hotels were full of these furniture folk from around the world, so I was booked into one that my excellent travel agent Sejal Patel didn't know anything about. It wasn't great. Although it probably will be, when all the drills and banging of renovation have finished. The first room I was allocated had a hideous smell of drains, so I asked to be moved. Whilst they sorted it out, I was directed towards a bar to await the preparation of the new room. I sat in a corner and watched.

Loitering in the bar were two obviously not-very-high-class tarts, with a shifty-looking guy that I gathered was their pimp. They did not appear to be unhappy, so I was entertained watching them primping themselves, ready, I imagined, for some clients. The edgy man was on a mobile a lot, glaring at his watch. After a while, in came a geeky-looking young man in an anorak, carrying a suitcase. The girls' jaws dropped as he approached them and practically dislocated when he opened the suitcase and started to try to sell them some paperback books. The pimp was not best pleased, but the girls were hysterical with laughter, and actually bought a few. The young man closed his case, shook hands with them all, and left. I have no idea what it was about. Had he inadvertently cold-called a couple of prostitutes? Or was it a very clever sales technique to book an assignment with them, knowing they would, nine times out of ten, find it funny and buy some of his wares? Whatever, he, and later they, left the hotel in high spirits.

The next little playlet was more of a tragedy than a comedy. Into the bar, empty apart from me tucked in a corner, burst three men and a woman. If I had been directing, I would have told them to be more subtle and get the wardrobe department to rethink their costumes. Everything about them shrieked villains. One was the double of Alfred Molina but that actor would never have worn a sharp, slightly tight, but beautifully tailored pinstripe suit, garish silk tie, over-polished, lace-up leather shoes, and lots of gold jewellery, with a huge diamond ring on his little finger and oily slicked-back hair. I had not seen Brilliantine used since the fifties, and would have told Alfred it was over-the-top. His first action was to bring out a plug, disconnect a table lamp, and put his mobile on recharge. Then, he scooped up nuts from the counter titbits and poured them into his mouth, which he continued to do with the olives and cheese biscuits, until the counter was cleared. He seemed to suffer from St Vitus's Dance for he was never still for a moment, his black eyes, too, darting in all directions. Of course he didn't notice me, as I am old. The resultant invisibility can be an advantage sometimes. I could become a private detective or a spy.

Another man, similarly attired, whom I assumed to be his brother as they looked alike, was much more still. In fact, eerily so, panther-like in movement, and eyes steely and steady. They reminded me of the Kray twins, with whom we had an uneasy relationship at Theatre Workshop in Stratford East, because it was on their manor, and Joan Littlewood thought they were 'amusing clowns'.

The third man was much older, almost definitely their father, grey-haired, with a deeply furrowed, peasant face, incongruously dressed by the wardrobe department in an immaculate if more subdued suit, except for the brocade waistcoat.

With them, but ignored, was a willowy blonde in black trousers decorated with studs and a white leather jacket with a lavish fur trim, which seemed a new acquisition from the way she tenderly stroked it with bejewelled hands. She was drugged out of her mind, judging by the pinpoint pupils in her vacant eyes. Alfred pointed at a seat and she sank into it and gulped from the glass he thrust at her.

The three men, having ordered champagne, spread themselves around a table, where they carefully rearranged the chairs, leaving one vacant. They conferred intensely. Father at one point barking at Alfred to sit down and listen. Glances were cast at the door and their huge watches. It was a dramatic build-up for an important new member of the cast to enter. Expecting a Marlon Brando type I hardly noticed the little character actor who came into the bar; surely nothing to do with my plot. He was a frightened weasel of a man, wearing a cheap faux-suede jacket, slacks and loafers. My villains all rose as he came in and engulfed him in bear hugs and kisses on the cheeks. Champagne was poured and proffered, and titbits replenished by a terrified barman, and pushed towards the new arrival, as he cowered in the vacant chair. There was much laughter and backslapping from the family which the blonde was struggling to take in, but when she unsteadily approached to join the party, she was roughly returned to her chair by Alfred.

Eventually the peasant Godfather waved his sons away and focused on the Weasel, sitting uncomfortably close, talking head to head. The two sons eyed the scene from a distance. It went on for about half an hour with the Weasel making occasional squeaks, only to be talked down by Daddy Villain.

Alfred suddenly saw me in the corner, scribbling in my notebook. My cover was blown. He strode over, stood towering above me, and offered me some champagne. It was quite a clever bit of acting to make such a generous gesture seem like a threat. I was quite good too, snapping into the same character who had defied the earthmover in Germany, and graciously but firmly declining with a polite smile, eyes looking into his. The scene might have developed unpleasantly, had not Dad summoned him back to the table in the nick of time. I was judged harmless and left to sit in my corner.

Alfred produced a flashy gold fountain pen, the other son some papers from a briefcase, and all loomed over the Weasel whilst he signed the documents in three places. Any pretence at interest in the Weasel instantly disappeared and, without delay, they packed up the documents, guzzled the dregs of champagne, unplugged the mobile, grabbed the blonde, and left. The Weasel, alone, sank into his seat, with his head in his hands, weeping. God alone knows what he had signed away. His land, his home, his daughter? I was tempted to try to comfort him but my Italian would not have been adequate. I did try a sympathetic smile as he stumbled out of the bar, but he didn't notice. I fear his storyline would not have had a happy ending. I asked the staff about it but they said they had not seen anything. I told them of my suspicions that they were criminals of some sort, and they laughed it off evasively. The next morning one of the desk clerks took me aside and told me that when they paid their bill, which they were reluctant to do, their signature proved them to be members of one of the Mafia families from Naples. No one recognised the Weasel.

The next day I sat with a coffee near Grandfather Hancock's gracious flat in the Galleria Vittorio Emanuele, wondering if Grandma Hancock had once done the same with some of her husband's rich clients. My dad maybe played in the arcade with a top. A civilised fantasy, slightly undermined by a well-dressed man loudly singing the entire Frank Sinatra repertoire into an imaginary hand-held mike. He was not asking for money, but immersed in his own world, seemingly quite mad. In a respectable way. A total nutter whom no one seemed to notice but me. Maybe only invisible people can see others like them.

I was ready for my quest to see the Bellini. On my way through the Brera I was stopped in my tracks by another picture, *Supper at Emmaus* by Caravaggio. The three men and one woman, suspiciously regarding a weary Christ, are wrinkled and weather-beaten. The woman in particular has a face drawn by hardship and it will take a lot to convince her of this son-of-God stuff. The lighting of the scene is magical. Many years ago, John and I bought a picture of an old man and woman at a table, listening to the sound of a rocket outside, summoning the lifeboat to a wreck. It is by a Victorian artist who rejoices in the name of Albert Starling. It is probably the only good picture he ever painted. I managed to buy a landscape by him on eBay and that was rubbish. Irreverent as this may be, the Caravaggio brought him to mind. The same light and shade, the same care-worn figures, the same meagre food on the table. I guard my Starling as carefully as I would a Caravaggio, because I believe that Albert, whoever he was, achieved something wonderful with that one creation. Though I would probably insure my Caravaggio for more than my Starling.

The Bellinis were well worth the trip. My favourite was painted by both the brothers, Gentile and Giovanni. The great Giovanni finished it after his brother died. What a hard task that must have been. It is huge. It is called *St Mark Preaching in Alexandria*, and is an extraordinary hotchpotch. It seems to be set in St Mark's Square, with a version of the Basilica sitting amongst various mosques and obelisks and towers, as well as the odd camel and giraffe. St Mark is standing on a rostrum that looks like a portable canal bridge. And he is, for some reason, wearing a pink frock and a blue stole borrowed from the Virgin Mary. There are some ladies with flowerpots on their heads, completely covered with white sheets, and some men in huge turbans made from the same material. Standing in rows are the mystified members of the *scuola* that commissioned the picture, one of whom is turning his head to whisper to the man next to him, 'Who *are* all these weirdos?' Was it Giovanni who put in those touches to cheer himself up after his brother's death? Perish the thought. I was chortling to myself when an American guide glared at me as he solemnly lectured his group of students about the rich iconographical details.

Stuff that. I am a novice and enjoy the pictures on my own terms. I do intend to learn more, because there is no doubt that knowledge can enrich my pleasure. But I am moved deeply to laughter or tears only if I feel a connection with the artist, albeit imagined. I found the same when I started working on Shakespeare. I love the fact that the Bard was also an actor in the company. Writing to a deadline. Every now and then in his plays there is a long speech, or an incongruous comic scene at a tragic moment. When I worked with the Royal Shakespeare Company these were endlessly analysed by the actors and directors in a scholarly fashion. I always felt they were just the result of some irritable actor moaning, 'D'you realise I haven't said anything for two pages?' or 'All this mayhem is going on and on, couldn't we have a funny bit here? Or a song? Maybe someone could exit pursued by a bear? That'd be good for a laugh.'

How lucky I am. I already have Shakespeare and music. Since John's death I have started to enjoy poetry and modernism and travel, and now Joachim has introduced me to art. A bit late in the day, but what a wonderful gift for my old age.

Now that death
seems not so far away,
I whisper to myself
how much I want to hold
the knowledge in my heart and head
that life itself can be enough –
its beauty and its awesomeness
as well as deepest tragedy

I do not want the need
to seek an offer, or a promise
of something else to come,
to help me face my end.
Such promises don't strengthen
me, they feel so false,
a prop, I want to do without.

From 'Whispering to Myself' by
Joan Woodward

13

London

OUT OF THE BLUE came news of a very special work of art. My publisher, Bloomsbury, received an email from someone in America who had seen a picture in the press of me holding the sepia photo of the portrait of my ancestor Madame Ann Judith Zurhorst to publicise *Who Do You Think You Are?* Astonishingly, she, Linda Carter, has the original oil painting. The image was attached to the email. There, in glorious Technicolor, was Ann Judith, my great-great-great-grandmother. No starchy old girl posing discreetly, but the vivid, funny, flamboyant character we had conjured up, in satins, silks and diamonds: a feast of red and turquoise and frothy white lace. The signature, after some delving at Sotheby's, turned out to be a J. R. Wildman, operating from 1823 to 1839. It is a wonderful picture. I venture to suggest that, like Albert Starling, this artist considered minor by our present-day dealers, produced much more lively portraits than some of his famous contemporaries. Or maybe, like Albert, he just pulled off one splendid work inspired by a potent subject.

I have seldom wanted to possess anything more than that picture. The owners in Florida, descendants of Ann Judith's son, Charles Zurhorst, who emigrated to the United States from Guernsey, are equally attached to their distant relative. But I will go out there and see them in Key West and get a copy made, as well as researching the artist and the history of the picture. How did it get there? Where was it painted? What a fascinating prospect. How much fun Ann Judith has inadvertently bequeathed to future generations. Such an ebullient creature was bound to leave something behind. Some powerful vibrations.

What do I mean by that? I cannot embrace any of the simplistic versions of an afterlife. They seem so mundane. Pearly gates, old friends and lovers waiting (God forbid all of them should be there), a very overcrowded heaven. But one look at John's 'crowd of stars' in Provence convinces me that there are dimensions we have not yet explored. The cosmology faculty at Portsmouth are investigating whole other universes. There are parts of the brain and its function that are still a mystery, so anything is possible. Only a closed mind would deny that. Beyond our present comprehension. Inexplicable to current science.

My gentle youngest daughter Joanna, having found the love of her life, Matt, wanted to hold the wedding ceremony in our garden in the country: a risky decision, with the English weather. A few weeks before the celebration, I was driving across London in torrential rain, thinking what a disaster it could be, when a bus went by with a huge picture of John advertising some *Sweeney* DVDs. Almost instantly the rain stopped. I phoned, laughing, to tell Joanna I was sure it would be all right.

My faith was shaken when, on the morning of the wedding day, it was filthy weather. Then, an hour before the ceremony started, contrary to weather forecasts, the clouds cleared and it was a glorious English summer's day. I was feeling sad that

John was not there to see his beloved daughter and all of us rejoicing in his beautiful garden. Then, as Matt and Jo said their vows to one another, the perfectly still air was ruffled by a sudden breeze that drifted though the trees, rustling the leaves, and wafting Jo's veil. It lasted for only about a minute but everyone was spellbound by its strangeness.

There are many vivid dreams, lost articles recovered, and decisions made that I could put down to being answers to pleas of 'Come on, John, where is it/what shall I do?' But I know that is irrational. To bank on an afterlife seems self-deluding in order to find comfort. No harm in that, mind.

One of the hardest things about growing old is the loss of one's friends. As John Gielgud said whilst attending yet another funeral, 'It's hardly worth going home.' With each death, a chapter of your life is closed. In the space of a few months, George Melly has disappeared and with him my youthful visits to dingy jazz clubs to thrill at his shocking hedonism. Then Dick Vosburgh, gag writer to the stars, who was one of the few people who believed in my talent when we were fellow students at RADA, even writing material for me when I performed in his student revues, where we earned a much-needed crust. Howard Goorney, one of the first idealist Communists I knew of, scourge of Equity, our union, mainstay of Joan Littlewood's company, and later husband to one of my friends Stella Riley; an admirable man. Dame Cicely Saunders died in her own hospice. I could not share her religious beliefs, but she influenced me profoundly, not least in how I dealt with the death of my first husband, Alec Ross. I am still involved with the work of St Christopher's Hospice, which is why I do not have the horror of death that grips some people.

I have now seen many people die, both those close to me and patients in the hospice. The process of dying can, if necessary, be soothed by modern palliative care. Which should be available to all but is not. I was made to ponder long and hard about assisted suicide when I recently played a woman dying of a cruel disease who chooses to go to Switzerland to kill herself. It was a soliloquy for television by Hugo Blick, which brilliantly got inside the mind of someone who calmly prefers to die rather than suffer any more. Playing a woman forced to go through such a gruelling and slighty sleazy process to achieve her choice caused me to question the illegality of her action in this country that made that ordeal necessary. Yet I know from my work at St Christopher's that with skilled nursing those last weeks or even days can be a very productive period of one's life. Tying up loose ends, not least in relationships. Sometimes having the time to discover new skills. I have on my wall a superb painting by a young man who had never held a brush before, done while he was dying in St Christopher's.

This book appears to be a lot about overcoming fear. Which is a bit how, when I look back on the pattern of my life, it has been shaped. A series of obstacles and challenges that frightened me. The glorious discovery is that it is up to me how I deal with them. Life can throw what it likes at me, but it can't govern how I react to it. I can choose to survive or go under. Down to me. So how do I anticipate the biggie – death?

From what I have observed, it doesn't seem too bad. There comes a time when people go in on themselves and concentrate on the process of leaving. It seems possible to decide to die or hang on a bit longer, unless of course it is sudden and un-expected, which, although most people think it preferable, is actually much harder for those left behind. One woman in the hospice kept going for months, against all odds, until her first grandchild was born. She died a week after he arrived.

I can understand why she wanted to see the baby. My family took me away for a wonderful weekend break to celebrate my seventy-fifth birthday. I revelled in the love I felt for them and received in return and my pride that, despite dodgy parenting, they had turned out to be fine young women and had chosen, after a few previous disasters, splendid partners. As I watched my grandchildren leaping around I was warmed by the thought that their vibrant life force will still be reverberating long after I am gone. They must learn to shoulder the responsibilities I will be offloading. They have to take over changing the world. I will let them discover for themselves, after I have gone, that it is an impossible task. They will fervently agree with politicians saying 'This must never happen again', and ignore their Nana when she snarls 'Oh really'. They seem like fighters to me. There are bits of me, my mum and dad and even wonderful Ann Judith swirling around in their gene pool – let's hope it's the good bits. They will be my afterlife, my reincarnation. And that's good enough for me.

I like going to sleep when I am tired, so if death is like that, I shall enjoy it. I would like to postpone it for as long as possible, because I love living, but my curiosity makes me really want to know what happens after I have breathed my last on earth. I wager there's nothing. If there is something I may lose my bet but it will be a nice surprise – I hope. If there's nothing, I will never know, because I will be nothing, nowhere. Which is a shame but can't be helped. For now, I will tidy up my affairs, so I am not a nuisance after my death, and forget about it for the time being.

Funerals, nowadays, are often celebrations of people's lives, rather than a gloomy meditation on grief. It can get a bit irritating, with jokey pop songs accompanying the disappearance of the coffin, but it is usually uplifting. When my dear friend Sheila Gish died a difficult death, all the horror was dispelled when her coffin entered the church. Her daughters had painted it all over with vividly coloured flowers and the congregation cheered and clapped as it was borne in, in the same way that in life an audience would have greeted this glamorous brilliant actor.

When another friend, Stella Moray, died in 2006, I and two

friends, Helen Cotterill and Faith Brook, went to lunch at Peter Jones, overlooking the Royal Court Theatre, where we had started our forty-year friendship. We put a photo of Stella in front of an empty chair, and got very tipsy, contemplating which old muttering crone would be the last one sitting at a table with three photos. When I explained our mirth to the waiter he was taken aback. It seems that to some people death should not be laughed at. But I think everything should. It helps.

After Stella's death we were given a CD she had made years before, probably as an example of her work for auditions. It was wonderful. She had had a good career, delighting audiences at the old-time musical theatre The Players, performing in West End musicals, entertaining the troops during the war, but she had never achieved great stardom. The CD was a revelation. She should have been huge. I was astonished by the power yet subtlety of her singing voice. It is grossly unfair that she did not receive more recognition and in her old age had to worry about money. Yet she was a happy woman. Always delighted at other people's success. Generous in her praise. Enriching the lives of her friends with her bawdy humour and kindness. There was no sign that she felt overlooked. I wonder if J. R. Wildman was as sanguine about his allotted rung on the ladder of fame.

How many people can honestly say that they have lived a fulfilled life? I am in a panic about what I want to be able to do before I die. Most of my achievements are mediocre. I find it difficult to be satisfied with that. John thought he was 'just a telly actor'. He had not done many films, or played Hamlet or Lear, so he didn't count. He could not accept that what he had achieved, moving on from a dreadfully deprived childhood to world-wide audience affection, was worth anything. One of life's hardest tests, when you are old, is to accept what you are and where you have got to, and be content with that.

Now, I have to be content with being on my own, without a

partner to share my life. I can't pretend it is what I would choose. I am envious of those friends with a good relationship to keep them company on the last lap. I have, to the delight of my friends and family, been on a very few dates, but it hasn't worked for me. John is a hard act to follow. Not because he was wonderful – he wasn't always – but we had reached a stage, after many battles, of a profound, yet not boring, peace. That takes time and energy, and I am running out of both. I just can't be bothered.

I went to a few gatherings to put myself about a bit and I hated it. There is always deafening music and babbling voices, so I can't hear a word that anyone is saying. The nadir was reached when I accepted an invitation that came from the *Financial Times* to a party to be held at the Victoria and Albert Museum. It sounded interesting. Although I could not imagine why I had been asked. I wondered even more when I got there.

I dolled myself up and forced myself through the huge doors. Inside, were hundreds of men in suits and a very few women, doing what I believe is called networking. Loudly. Undaunted, I walked though the seething crowd, attempting to catch someone's eye. Not a hope. Not a drink or a titbit came my way. After circling the room, without a soul talking to me, or even smiling, I walked out of the doors again.

Outside, stretched on the pavement was a vagrant. He struggled to sit up, slowly got me into focus and smiled blearily. 'How nice to see you, Miss Hancock. May I introduce my friend?'

His friend was just visible inside a filthy sleeping bag, and all he could manage was a grunt and a proffered grimy hand. Which I shook. I politely declined the swig from the can proffered by the gentleman. For that he was. We had a little chat, my new friend admired my car, and waved as I drove off. So not an altogether wasted evening. I met some nice people.

I went to Sandi Toksvig's celebration of her civil partnership with Debbie. It was a joyous occasion. Sandi's children – who are some of the loveliest, most grounded children I know – were having a ball. I asked another guest, a well-known writer, how she managed to be so prolific. She fondly referred to her companion, explaining she organised all the everyday things for her. She was the archetypal wife.

Two women living together can be a very successful union. I have known many such relationships, not necessarily lesbian, that seemed happy. After the First World War, the huge death toll of men left thousands of women with no hope of marriage and a life of solitude ahead of them. Some of the teachers at my grammar school were just such victims and had formed partnerships with fellow teachers. My father's sister too lived with a woman all her life; they took care of one another until the end. My aunt was disfigured by smallpox as a girl and presumably no man wanted her but her companion loved and fiercely protected her. Whilst I was doing *Cabaret*, two of my gay friends came backstage to see me. One, who is a musician, has suffered a stroke and finds speech difficult. His lifelong partner, who is a retired nurse, watched him anxiously. At one point, when his friend was struggling to shape a word, he finished the sentence for him, stopped, and cried, 'Oh, I am so sorry dear, I mustn't talk for you.' It was a demonstration of such gentle understanding that I defy anyone to question the validity of same-sex love.

However, in the absence of the love of a good man or woman, I do worship my car. Motors have always been my passion. After my Lambretta in the sixties, I graduated to a pea-green convertible Morris 1000, then a cream MG, then a beautiful white Morgan. When my children were young, I had to have boring old estate cars, but as soon as they were off my hands, I started on Jaguar sports cars. I still have one. I maintain it is more environmentally friendly than some old banger, but of course it is disgraceful. I have tried to assuage my guilt by running my hot water and electricity on solar energy, for the environmental lobby is getting to me. I pray that science will come up with something that makes a beautiful vehicle acceptable again. I cherish my car. Mind you, I recently visited a car show where the *Top Gear* gang were doing a display. It was not pretty. Jeremy Clarkson, with his belly hanging over sagging jeans, making adolescent jokes about being a petrolhead. I realised I looked equally absurd. A 75-year-old woman in a supercharged sports car. But I'll be defiant a little bit longer. Then I'll join the green people who drive those ugly electric snails. Or even ride a bike, jumping the lights, running people over on pavements, and being as sanctimonious as they. Or get that elephant.

When I am driving my powerful, purring beautiful car, I do not feel in the least bit old. Getting out of it is harder these days, but I suppose that is to be expected. I creak more now, and if I don't take regular exercise I seize up completely. But then I have never felt particularly well. Some bit of me has ached all my life. The only time I feel really fit is for about two minutes, under the shower, after a swim. When I went to a party at Buckingham Palace to mark the Queen's eightieth year, I marvelled at her stamina. She had to attend numerous parades and public appearances to celebrate her birthday, and when I commented on this she said, 'Yes, it has gone on a bit.' How her pretty little feet must ache at the end of the day. Mine kill me if I walk up to the shops, never mind trudging round talking to thousands of gaping subjects.

According to Psalm 90 my time is up. I have had my 'three score years and ten' plus a bonus of five. But there is a get-out clause: I can make it to four score 'by reason of strength'. Which is why I can be regularly found lying backwards on a big blue ball, levering two weights over my head. Standing above me is my personal trainer, a vision of masculine physical perfection, and a necessary incentive, as I loathe exercise.

I'm shaken when my age catches up with me, as they say. When I visit the John Lewis store, I park my car in the garage under Cavendish Square, because the young men in the basement love my Jaguar and wash it beautifully. Then I climb the three flights of stairs up to the street. The last incline has become my personal Everest. For fifty-odd years I have skipped up easily, but now I arrive red-faced and panting into the sympathetic arms of the *Big Issue* and *Evening Standard* vendors. I steel myself for the five floors of John Lewis. Take the lift? Never. The woman who has just moved, not into a bungalow, as befits her status, but to a three-storey house? We are talking wartime childhood here, 'we will never surrender' and all that.

The stark truth is that, within sight of the finishing post, I am actually enjoying the race more than I have ever done. Because time is short, I have never been so desperate to relish every minute. I do not intend to waste any time being old and grey, and full of sleep, and nodding by the fire. In recent years, my husband and many dear friends, some younger than I, have had life wrested from them. In deference to them, I will value mine.

My northern friend from the Solo holiday phoned me the other day with a shocking story. His son is serving in Iraq. They were attacked and three of his friends, only fifty yards away from him, were killed; another lost a leg; another, an eye. He came home in a plane with three corpses and two men whose lives are ruined. It is not like World War Two when everyone shared the horror, and the servicemen were heroes. These men come back to indifference towards an unpopular battle. His father was appalled by his son's dead eyes, contemplating the mutilated world. It never ends, the pity of war.

After all my agonising in Germany and Budapest, I am not really much closer to understanding the horrors of World War Two. It is still a darkness in my mind that cannot be obliterated, however much light I shine on it. I find no answer to the question 'why did it happen?', except the disturbing one, that cruelty is part of our nature. So is bigotry. I can only try to suppress it in myself, by reason. By confronting it. That is what the bravest individuals I have come across have done. They challenged the status quo, and tried to heal the hurt. They are the people that vindicate the human race and I am grateful to them. Ken Small and his tank, Imre Nagy, Sophie Scholl, the young soldiers coping with the nightmare of the concentration camps, even my grandfather and his small battle with Thomas Cook.

I still relish a battle or two. Preferably on behalf of someone else. I have engaged in much navel-gazing over the years – too much. I find other people much more interesting now. As an actor I have been looking in mirrors, tarting myself up for shows, for sixty-odd years, so my face is of no more interest to me. I much prefer gazing at Sandra's brown skin and lustrous wicked eyes. When you are old, you have a wealth of experience that can be shared to help others avoid pitfalls. Because we, in England, as opposed to the Continent, tend to separate the generations, much is wasted. The vitality and freshness of youth for the old, and the wisdom of maturity for the young.

I received a thrilling opportunity to bridge this gap. In 2005 I was awarded an honorary degree by Portsmouth University. Why? You might well ask. As did I. Well, I was born on the nearby Isle of Wight. I appeared in many a season in the Shanklin Repertory Company, and on Sandown Pier I was in a concert party with Cyril Fletcher. I have toured to Portsmouth in various Agatha Christies. Not really credentials for a Doctor of Letters. Working-class women of my generation did not have the educational opportunities that are available today, so I wasn't going to look a gift horse in the mouth: I donned my purple gown and fetching beret and was as proud as punch that they should be so kind. Then in 2007 they went further. They paid me the enormous honour of inviting me to be their

Chancellor. I was delighted. What could be more wonderful in my seventies than to be involved in the futures of thousands of young people?

Although I used to covet the posh period residences of the staff at Oxford University when we visited in John's Morsing days, I am thrilled to be involved with one of the new universities. I have the use of a lovely flat overlooking my birthplace and the exciting redevelopment of Portsmouth with its iconic Spinnaker Tower. The university is growing and changing all the the time. Portsmouth is not complacent like some of the ancient colleges. Nothing is set rigidly in tradition: we are not hidebound by history. There is important research going on – not least into brain tumours, which as I know from my grandchild's experience is still a grey area – but the students are all-important. The young people who come to us are from every part of society, and indeed the world. At my first day of welcoming new students and their parents, some were the first generation of their family to attend university, and they were thrilled, as I was for them. Having left formal education aged fifteen, I feel a bit of a fraud, but I am so grateful for this chance to explore a whole new world that I missed out on when I was young.

I am frequently asked, usually by taxi drivers, 'Not thinking of retiring then, Sheila?' No, I have never enjoyed my work more, especially the companionship. The humiliations seem amusing now. There is no chance of getting above myself. Even after sixty-odd years in the business, I still have to audition for parts and be gracious when twelve-year-old directors, who have never heard of me or bothered to find out that I have been schlepping about working since before they were born, ask, 'What have you done?' I sometimes answer faux-naïvely, 'You mean today?' I keep meaning to pack it in. Then, along comes a part that simply has to be played.

I met a traveller from an antique land
Who said: 'Two vast and trunkless legs of stone
Stand in the desert . . . Near them, on the sand,
Half sunk, a shattered visage lies, whose frown
And wrinkled lip and sneer of cold command,
Tell that its sculptor well those passions read
Which yet survive, stamped on these lifeless things,
The hand that mocked them and the heart that fed;
And on the pedestal these words appear:
'My name is Ozymandias, King of Kings:
Look on my works, ye Mighty and despair!'
Nothing beside remains. Round the decay
Of that colossal wreck, boundless and bare,
The lone and level sands stretch far away.

From 'Ozymandias' by Percy Bysshe Shelley

14

Budapest

I WAS OFFERED THE part of the mother of a German Nazi concentration-camp commandant in the film of the book *The Boy in the Striped Pyjamas*. Directed by Mark Herman, who was responsible for one of my favourite films, *Brassed Off*, it was a gift from heaven. On top of that, it was to be filmed in Budapest. It was Budapest and its Terror Museum that had set me off on a winding road through my childhood and the events around it. Whereas I had made my personal peace with Germany, I never really felt at ease in the same way with Budapest.

There is no better way of really getting to know a place than to work there. With the film company, we had translators and, anyway, performers world-wide have a common language and modus operandi. It was shocking to discover that many of the extras were respected actors, desperate for work. Which is why they were so wonderful. In the ballroom scene in which I appeared, I watched enthralled as they all created individual characters and scenarios for themselves, rather than just waltzing mindlessly. When I had to walk through the room as a woman defying the growing threat of the SS, they needed no direction as to how they should react. They knew only too well and used their real-life experience. Some recoiled nervously, others furtively expressed agreement, just as they knew happened. Our producer, David Heyman, made a speech of admiration and gratitude at the end of the day's filming and several had tears in their eyes.

When I first arrived on set I was miffed to discover our English make-up supervisor had offloaded me on to a homely-looking Hungarian woman. I was very grumpy until I realised how much better off I was. If I were a star I would insist on having Anya for every job I do. Her English boss produced an ill-fitting, badly dressed wig on the day before I started work. When I arrived the next morning full of nerves – for the way I look is crucial to the building of a character – there, on the wig block, was exactly what I had asked for, but had been told was impossible. My lovely Anya had taken it home and worked on it in her own time. She was an artist. She had healing hands, so that at 5.30 a.m. having my make-up applied was like the most wonderful soothing massage. She fussed over me and made sure I looked right for every shot. I discovered she had to travel all over Europe to earn enough to live on and was pathetically grateful for the work being generated by the English and American companies now taking advantage of the benefits of Hungary becoming part of Europe.

Knowing how our Hungarian colleagues were were struggling to make a living made it uncomfortable to be wallowing in the luxury of my hotel, one of the many that have been developed for the potential tourist influx. The hotel had its own spa, where I indulged in Turkish baths, one night sharing the quite small steam room with a stark-naked Lufthansa pilot. We had a lovely chat culminating in, when he left, him shaking my hand and actually clicking his bare heels Germanically with the inevitable effect on his dangling parts.

One night in the restaurant I watched, as is my wont, a smarmy American man smoothly chatting up a very young Chinese girl. He oozed confidence and *savoir-faire*, until she went to the ladies', when he, without realising an old biddy was watching him, fell apart. Fingers tapping the table, then shakily lighting a fag, scared eyes darting about sightlessly. Could he satisfy her if he got her to bed? What would his wife/mother think? Should he just disappear? Then, as she sauntered back, he changed instantly from a gibbering wreck into his previous seductively smirking man-about-town. It occurred to me that perhaps everyone is acting a role. And maybe even the most confident are actually scared stiff.

I was invited to lunch in a restaurant in the old ghetto area where, in 1944, Eichmann had sealed 200,000 Jews into 2,000 houses before they were taken off to be slaughtered. The restaurant was an elegant revamp of an old crypt-like building. The trendy young waiter, who unusually spoke English, could not tell me its history. It clearly didn't interest him.

Now the ghetto is the up-and-coming fashionable place to be in Budapest. All the magnificent courtyards that lie between the alleys are being converted into chic flats. Old Jewish markets are becoming fashionable boutiques, galleries and performance spaces. That is where I would want to live. If I could deal with the ghosts.

Not just the Jews died here but apparently there are the bones of German and Russian soldiers buried in a hurry in the courtyards when they were killed during the fighting at the end of the war. The Jewish community erected a plaque commemorating the Russian liberation, only to take it down when they suffered under Stalin. Later, in recognition of the fact that, whatever happened after, the Russians did free them from the evils of Nazism, and sacrificed their lives in the process, the plaque went back up again. So it still goes on, this swinging from lauding to vilifying, and taking out each switch of allegiance on their beleaguered statues and memorials, in the effort to update their history.

Whilst I was there, János Kádár's burial place was desecrated. His skull was stolen and Fascist slogans scrawled on his tomb. Kádár was the Communist leader of Hungary from 1956 to 1988. He did some good and a lot of bad things, including being involved in Imre Nagy's trial and death. Nagy too was a Communist but his statue is still intact, standing on his bridge over nothing, looking towards Parliament, with lots of giggly people having their photos taken alongside it, wondering who he is.

As in East Berlin, anyone associated with the Russians or Communism is being razed from Hungarian history. One memento of the Soviet era, an obelisk that, like the Jewish plaque, commemorates the Russians who died in the Liberation, has survived only because it is protected by a pact with Russia and lots of barbed wire. Typically, it in its turn was erected on top of a previous memorial, which was a mound created out of earth from the territories lost in the Treaty of Trianon in 1920.

I was told that all unwanted statues had been dumped in a field some distance outside Budapest. This I had to see. It seemed appropriate to make the trip to look at these socialist ex-heroes on May Day when I had some time off from filming. The hotel doorman was disapproving of my visit. As a small boy he was made to go to May Day rallies in Heroes' Square that took place in front of a statue of Stalin. I promised to take a photo of it, if it was there, abandoned and disgraced.

When I visited the park it was in the process of being turned into a proper outdoor museum, some people having decided that, whatever they represent, some of the sculptures were worth preserving. The first thing you see after a long drive from the city is a huge red brick wall, set into which, flanking a gate, are, on one side, an impressive statue of Lenin and, on the other, standing together looking studious, Marx and Engels.

Budapest

Inside the wall the grandeur falls away for the ticket booth and shop are housed in a scruffy shed. However, I received the warmest welcome of anywhere in Budapest from the woman selling the tickets. She cheerily took my money as if it were a village fête, apologising that everything was in a bit of a mess but it would be very impressive when it was finished. I was rather sorry about this as I would have preferred the drama of seeing these icons of the past tipped into a field in a heap. Instead of which, they were now being placed round grass and flowerbeds in a pleasing pattern.

Some of the sculptures were phenomenally ugly. Vast, challenging, meant to intimidate. The socialist-realist monuments were worthy but on the whole rather nasty – all those healthy-looking idealised workers. Every now and then, though, something touched my heart: a depiction of grief in the martyrs' memorial; a group of children belonging to one of those twisted youth movements that dictatorships force on the innocent – a far cry from the twit-twooing Brownies. Even a lovely memorial to the people who fought in the Spanish Civil War had been jettisoned.

What was upsetting about these abandoned relics, hidden away from the city, was that, like Irina's father in Berlin, all these commemorated figures were of people dedicated to and often prepared to die for their beliefs, which they thought were for the good of the people. Statue Park is a lesson in misplaced loyalty; in the danger of putting your faith in groups with rigid ideologies. The causes are different now but we are still threatened by devotion to an ideal.

There are many stories of true heroism there that are now regarded as shameful. I asked the woman on the gate about one beautiful tablet and she showed me a booklet with a devastating picture of a group of handsome young men being killed in front of the Communist headquarters when they tried to defend it against what they saw as a Fascist uprising in 1956. The translation of the inscription read, 'These loyal to the people and the party will be forever remembered, who laid down their heroic lives on October 30th in 1956 in the defence of the power of the people.'

How wrong can you be on all counts? Yet they were young and passionate. Ready to die for what we now regard as a misguided vision. The irony is that I had already seen a memorial in the square by Parliament to some other equally brave young people who fought against them and also died in 1956 but who are remembered with honour. When I visited the marble tribute to them, some present-day youngsters were leaning on it, embracing, oblivious I am sure to what it was, as well as to the bullet holes still scarring the nearby walls. Just as I had sat unheeding on the walls that were all that remained of a once-great nation in Puglia. *Sic transit gloria.*

As well as the imposing one at the gate, there is another much smaller iron statue of Lenin inside. This one is more appealing and has a touching history. It was given by Khrushchev to the workers in the Csepel Iron and Metal Works in 1958. Ominously, it went rusty and began to disintegrate. The workers secretly recast and replaced it. When they heard it was going to be toppled in 1990 they hid it in some cellars. It is a strange *Bridge over the River Kwai* sort of story, where the pride in their work superseded their desire to be free of oppression. Recently they entrusted the statue to the park to be looked after.

I found the Russian soldier removed from the Liberation statue on Gellert Hill. Those Soviets certainly wanted everyone to know they were there – it is terrifyingly enormous. But I searched in vain for the doorman's statue of Stalin. I could find only a pair of sawn-off boots – Shelley's 'two vast and trunkless legs of stone' – that I believe were all that remained of his statue after it was mutilated by the crowd. There was another thing, firmly wrapped in sacking, perhaps too vile to be seen, that could have been Stalin, of which 'nothing beside remains'.

The Hungarian actors in the film solved a mystery for me. They told me where to find two other previous villains who, having left their country in disgust, were now restored to favour. The graves of Bartók and his student George Solti are very close to one another in Farkasréti cemetery. There was a nice little pussycat sitting on Bartók's grave, and on Solti's was a small bouquet with the message 'Little George has just been born'. Probably a grandchild. Which made their rather forbidding tombstones more endearing.

I was sitting in the hotel restaurant after my visit to Statue Park, congratulating myself on my progress since last visiting Budapest. I felt a bond with Budapest now. It is a city struggling to reinvent itself, which is, in a way, what I have been trying to do. We are both a bit weary and battle-scarred by the sad crazy march of time but we are making changes. Having met some of the people that live and work there I felt I understood the Hungarians better, just as meeting Irina and Ilona had overcome my racist attitudes to Germany. I was rather pleased with myself.

As I perused the menu, I noticed a Japanese couple near by. He was meticulously lining up his cutlery and snapping orders to the waiter, inscrutable and cold. Instinctively, I bristled. Then I caught my reaction. Oh God, do I have to visit Japan now?

If suddenly you do not exist,
if suddenly you no longer live,
I shall live on.

. . .

No, forgive me.
If you no longer live,
if you, beloved, my love,
if you
have died,
all the leaves will fall in my breast,
it will rain on my soul night and day
the snow will burn my heart,
I shall walk with frost and fire and death and snow,
my feet will want to walk to where you are sleeping,
but
I shall stay alive,
because above all things you wanted me
indomitable,
and, my love, because you know that I am not
    only a man
but all mankind.

From 'The Dead Woman' by Pablo Neruda

15

Provence

SOMEONE WAS INTERESTED IN buying the house in France. When I went to meet the prospective buyer, my eldest daughter Ellie Jane, her partner Matthew, and their two children Lola and Jack, were holidaying there.

The house was bursting with life. All my daughters are brilliant homemakers. The Lacanche was banging away cooking delicious meals; a table-tennis table had been erected under the shade of the remaining lime tree, which was flourishing since the felling of its partner. The children were roaming in the cherry orchard, collecting flowers or playing boules or sitting quietly reading. It was a complete change to their highly organised London social activities. They seemed to be enjoying the primitive life. We went for a long walk, with Ellie Jane dictating the route, rather erratically, from a map, causing Matthew to be fairly tetchy. I was intrigued to see her taking over my bossy organising role and Matthew morphing into John being grumpy about it. I enjoyed taking a back seat. At one point, Ellie Jane made us all stop and take in a magnificent scene of purple lavender and indigo-blue mountains, shouting,

'I love it here. It's the most beautiful place on earth.' Doubt began to stir about my drastic decision to leave.

When we went to the local lido, I was aware that my appreciation of it had been enriched by my travels. I looked at it afresh. I had not realised it is a fabulous example of modernist social architecture. Built in concrete in 1964, it has all the smooth curves and ship-like decks and railings of the genre. The diving board is like a lightning strike. Even the benches are a study in simplicity and practicality, using concrete and blue and white tiles. As I swam in its massive competition-sized pool, I feasted my eyes on this newly realised delight.

The house took on a different mood with the family filling it with life and laughter. It was a joyous few days.

Then they left.

It was a mark of my adaptation to being alone that I was not bereft. It was the day of the farmers' market in Apt. Unlike the huge Saturday market, there are just a few stalls, with goat's cheese, lavender products, seasonal fruit and vegetables and local wine. I have become acquainted with the stallholders over the years and they greet me warmly, some with a handshake, some even with the standard three kisses on alternate cheeks. I am sure these tactile connections between everyone, parent and child, young and old, girl and boy, help the mutual respect that is a feature of their behaviour. It is very inclusive. It certainly cheers me up. As well as the old-world courtesy, mainly among the older inhabitants, of greeting one and all when you enter a shop. 'Bonjour, monsieur/madame.' Not so customary in Tesco.

Just as John was Monsieur Um Er in the *pâtisserie*, I am probably known as the Lady in the Blue Hat. I have a jaunty cotton number to shade my wrinkles from the sun, which is much commented on. Total strangers, mainly men, say, 'Quel joli chapeau.' It doesn't happen on Hammersmith Broadway.

In France I am a bit of a character. Nothing to do with the

telly, for they do not know about that, but a lot to do with their friendliness. That I am noticed at all has to do with the regard paid to older women. We are not invisible there. The pace of life allows you to spend the time of day with people. No wonder they are rejecting the attempts to cut their holidays and lengthen their working hours. They do not want to relinquish their leisure and family time to pursue what they call the Anglo-Saxon obsession with work.

Pottering around Apt on my own, I was aware how much more acute my observation has become after my travels. That afternoon, after the family's departure, I sat for about an hour in a café, watching an old-fashioned barber in a tiny shop opposite, turning out every client with identical haircuts and moustaches, created by comb, scissors and a cut-throat razor, held in a triangle, with little finger delicately cocked. Maybe it was just nostalgia for time spent sitting on the bath, watching my dad shave, but the scene had a balletic grace that I found absorbing.

My favourite café has a few hard-drinking men sitting on stools at the bar, looking like characters from a school-book in the forties. Le Père de Toto, round and jolly in a beret and *bleus*, and the tall gaunt guy with a moustache that Toulouse-Lautrec often featured in his pictures are still there, their faces weather-beaten and cheerful, or doleful when they discuss politics. Butch men enjoying their pastis still greet each other with three kisses and lots of hugging, and I am welcome to join them but can't keep up the pace. Today, we have a few jokes, then I sit in a corner with my coffee and *Guardian* and *La Provence*.

The local paper is full of a new find, during demolition work, of three beautiful Roman statues. It seems Apt is an even more important Roman city than previously thought, with a huge amphitheatre seating 6,000 under the medieval cobblestones. It certainly feels as though it has been there a long time. The whole Vaucluse is steeped in history. It has been inhabited for a million years, from Neolithic discoveries through Celts, Greeks, Romans, and wars of religion. Probably the omnipresent Habsburgs have had their oar in, too, if I investigate. But I haven't time. For, of course, I am leaving.

To have a last look around, I went for a drive, trying to see it as if for the first time, as I did with Germany, Thailand, et al.

Following the Roman thread, I discovered a bridge has been built next to the Pont Julien, to divert cars from its ancient road. I have driven over the original bridge many times and never really looked at its wonders. It is a miracle of engineering, the top of the central span of three arches seeming so thin, yet it has withstood 2,000 years of to-ing and fro-ing. It was said that the Millennium Bridge in London went wrong because the crowds somehow marched in step, causing it to wobble. What price the legions crossing Pont Julien? They knew a thing or two about building, those Romans. I got out of my car, and sat by the dried-up riverbank, gazing at it for a long while, re-creating its story in my head. I had plenty of time. No one was expecting me.

Then I drove to a favourite haunt of John's and mine, the Abbaye de Sénanque. It was at its most beautiful, with lavender blooming purple against its austere simple white walls. I decided to sit in on one of the services. Quaker meetings for worship have no music, so every now and then I need a dose of choral singing. Nowhere is it more potent than at Sénanque. The Cistercian Order have lived there on and off since 1148. They lead a life of prayer and work on the land, with minimal use of words, so as 'to retain all day that atmosphere in which God can be found'. It seems to agree with them, for their tombstones show they live to a great old age. I once lost my way after a service, and came across the monks having a bit of a laugh together. I was glad it wasn't all prayer and silence.

The monks glide into the small chapel, bare of ornament but

for a vase of flowers and the lit host. I covet their white gowns with black-lined hoods, that flow and drape as elegantly as any couture garment. The two-thirty prayers are sung, unaccompanied, in harmony of a minor key. They are the saddest sound in the world. I believe these afternoon prayers are a meditation on the death of Christ, so maybe other services are more jolly.

It suited my mood that day. I was overwhelmed with sorrow at the thought of leaving. The truth is, I love it in Provence. Not because of memories of John. The place itself, and the way of life. I have a sense of belonging. London is exciting and beautiful and I need it to stimulate and thrill me. My allegiance to my native country, warts and all, knows no bounds, but, as I have discovered, my roots are more complicated than I thought, and I do genuinely welcome the fact that I am a European. As I sat in the chapel, the chattering in my brain stilled by the calm, one thought emerged: this is madness.

How can I leave? Everything has changed since I made that first decision. Shifted. Even the *hameau* has moved on. The quince tree, for the first time, now that it can see the sun after the removal of the lime tree, is full of delicate blossom. At long last, work is being done on the dying cherry orchard, trees felled or pruned, the whole place being brought back to life.

Christiane and Roget have left. The vineyard has been bought by a wealthy Swedish businessman who, as a child, rode on a tractor and has dreamed of working on the land ever since. Everyone thought he would come a cropper when faced with the reality, but he is out, every day, all day, in the searing sun, happily tending his vines, and now produces a very good wine. A young single mother has moved into another of the houses and entertains us with her romances. She has a lovely child, and a soppy dog, both of whom visit me regularly. The dog, Banan, cannot believe I allow him indoors. The only original inhabitants left are André and Denis. I still can't understand a word they say, but we have known each other for eighteen years now, and the affection between us old-timers is real. I was worried for them when two young, gay Parisiens bought the remaining house. The contrast in their lifestyles could not have been greater, but they have managed an awkward friendship.

The Parisiens have perked us up no end. Their house has been revamped with designer style. They collect modern art and fine wines, and entertain smart people from Paris. Their terrace is a-twinkle with candles and fairy lights in the trees, and they cook delicious alfresco dinners, with discussions lasting long into the starlit night.

They suggested I improve my own shabby house. Not to alter its rustic character, but just to make it more comfortable. An electric heater for when I can't face lighting the wood stove, and a proper bathroom. One day over coffee Patrick asked me why I didn't I replace my tatty old sunshade for something more stylish. It is unwieldy and not very attractive but I demurred because John had persuaded the prop men to bring it all the way from Verona, where it was used in a scene in *Morse*. It felt disloyal to discard it. After Patrick left, I was sitting in its shade, finishing my coffee. It was a perfectly still, boiling-hot day. Suddenly a violent gust of wind came from nowhere, tossing the parasol out of its stand, and whirled it down the garden, where it ended up as a shattered heap of wood and canvas. No one else in the *hameau* had experienced any wind at all. As with Jo's wedding, I know there is a rational explanation, nature plays strange tricks, but I took it as a message. John always used to get irritated by my reluctance to spend money. Anyway, it decided me; I bought a new parasol and took the house off the market.

To have the gift of being alive and knowing it, seems such an astonishment, that it would be churlish to spend one's time being miserable because one knows it's got to end sometime.

From *Eternity's Sunrise* by Marion Milner

Saignon

I AM SITTING OUTSIDE Chez Christine in the morning sun. My bowl of *chocolat* is cooling whilst I eat my warm almond croissant straight from the oven. With my writing, acting, grandmother and university duties, I am busier than I have ever been, so it is good for a while to have nothing to do. To just be. The past is past, the future is limited. But, I am here now. Feeling good. I used to be fearful. There was a lot to lose. Now I've already lost a lot of it, I am less afraid. I survived, and I will again.

Some people dread old age but I am having a ball. At my age, I can get away with anything. At worst, I will be labelled eccentric or senile. I can leave when I'm bored, boo when I hate something, love whom I choose, be outrageous, self-centred and downright silly. I do sometimes feel lonely, but increasingly, loneliness has become a valued solitude. On my own, I will laugh, cry a lot, be thrilled, be desolate, have fun and take risks. My last lap is going to be hair-raisingly exciting.

The doors of the church are open. The choir is rehearsing 'Ave Maria'. It is not going well. It is too high for the soprano and her voice keeps cracking. They don't seem concerned, judging by the laughter. People pass and shout a greeting to me. Or just smile and nod.

In the notebook I found by the bed after John's death, he had written, when he was in France taking a respite from treatment for cancer: 'We went to Saignon for morning coffee and it was lovely up there. Sitting there with Sheila outside the church was very healing I know. I am full of love for my wonderful, wonderful wife. What would I do without her? Don't ask! I am a very very lucky man.'

How blessed am I to have experienced such love. How could I want to put it out of my mind? Not go to the place where John had felt so happy? To bask in its glow? I am a very, very lucky woman.

Sometimes things don't go, after all,
from bad to worse. Some years, muscadel
faces down frost; green thrives; the crops don't fail,
Sometimes a man aims high, and all goes well.

A people sometimes will step back from war,
elect an honest man; decide they care
enough, that they can't leave some stranger poor.
Some men become what they were born for.

Sometimes our best intentions do not go
amiss; sometimes we do as we meant to.
The sun will sometimes melt a field of sorrow
that seemed hard frozen: may it happen for you.

COPYRIGHT ACKNOWLEDGEMENTS

I am indebted to the following books for background information on World War Two: *The Third Reich* by Michael Burleigh (Pan Books, 2001), *In the Ruins of the Reich* by Douglas Botting (Methuen, 2005) and *The Children's War* by Juliet Gardiner (Imperial War Museum/ Portrait, 2005). I am also grateful for help received from the staff at the archives of the Imperial War Museum in London, the Hungarian National Museum in Budapest and the German Resistance Memorial Centre, Berlin.

Copyright Acknowledgements

Other

Extract from *Resident Alien: Quentin Crisp Explains it All* by Tim Fountain, published by Nick Hern Books Ltd (www.nickhern books.co.uk). Reproduced with permission.

Extract from *The Change* by Germaine Greer. Copyright © Germaine Greer. Reproduced by permission of Aitken Alexander Associates.

Extract from BUSZ PO POLSKU by Ryszard Kapuscinski. © Copyright 1962, 1990 by Ryszard Kapuscinski.

Extract from *Moon Tiger* by Penelope Lively (André Deutsch 1987, Penguin Books 1988, 2006). © Copyright Penelope Lively, 1987.

Extract from *Eternity's Sunrise* by Marion Milner. Reproduced by permission of Paterson Marsh Ltd on behalf of the Estate of Marion Milner.

Extract from *The Bell Jar* by Sylvia Plath reprinted by permission of Faber and Faber Ltd / The Sylvia Plath Estate.

The author and publishers gratefully acknowledge permission to quote from the private letters of Anne Bartlett and Alan Bennett.

Photographs

All photographs, unless otherwise stated, are from the author's private collection and are used with permission.

For the following photographs within the plate section the publishers would like to credit:
p.2   *Bottom*: Cliff Kent
p.3   *Bottom right*: Matthew Byam Shaw

p.4 House of Terror Museum courtesy of the Terror Haza, Budapest

p.6 Photographs courtesy of Billie Barbour

p.10 Dancing Ledge © John Allen, 1998–2006; www.imagesof dorset.org.uk

p.12 *Right*: *Saint Augustine in His Study* by Vittore Carpaccio (*c.* 1460–1526) in the Scuola di San Giorgio degli Schiavoni, Venice. Photo: SCALA, Florence
Left: *The Miracle of the Holy Cross on the Rialto Bridge / Healing of a Madman* (detail, gondoliers) by Vittore Carpaccio (*c.* 1460–1526) in the Accademia, Venice. Photo: SCALA, Florence, courtesy of the Ministero Beni e Att. Culturali
Bottom: Bronze horses from the Basilica de San Marco, Venice. Photo: San Marco, Venice, Italy/The Bridgeman Art Library

p.13 *Top*: *St Mark Preaching in Alexandria, Egypt*, 1504–07 (oil on panel) by Bellini, Gentile (1430/35–1507) & Giovanni (1425/30–1516). Photo: Pinacoteca di Brera, Milan, Italy / Giraudon / The Bridgeman Art Library
Middle: *Supper in Emmaus* by Michelangelo Merisi da Caravaggio (1573–1610), held in the Pinacoteca di Brera, Milan. Photo: SCALA, Florence, courtesy of the Ministero Beni e Att. Culturali

p.14 *Right*: © The University of Portsmouth
Bottom: © Mary McCartney, Camera Press, London

p.16 © Sven Arnstein / Stay Still / Photoshot

A NOTE ON THE TYPE

The text of this book is set in Linotype Sabon, named after the
type founder, Jacques Sabon. It was designed by Jan Tschichold
and jointly developed by Linotype, Monotype and Stempel, in
response to a need for a typeface to be available in identical
form for mechanical hot-metal composition and hand
composition using foundry type.

Tschichold based his design for Sabon roman
on a font engraved by Garamond, and Sabon italic on
a font by Granjon. It was first used in 1966 and
has proved an enduring modern classic.